THE FINNISH

COOKBOOK

Also by Beatrice Ojakangas

GOURMET COOKING for TWO

THE FINNISH
COOKBOOK

BY BEATRICE A. OJAKANGAS

International Cookbook Series
General Editor: Charlotte Adams

ROWN PUBLISHERS, INC., NEW YORK

ACKNOWLEDGMENTS

No project such as this can ever be done alone. There are many who deserve a special "thank you."

First of all, a grateful thanks to my husband, who spared the time to endure the role of guinea pig and sounding board while he toiled for his Ph.D. And to my children, who have at times been baffled by an odd array of "taste panel" meals, stacks of interesting piles of notes labeled DON'T TOUCH, and who have, for their young ages, been amazingly understanding.

A hearty thanks goes also to our relatives and friends in Finland, many of whom enthusiastically donned their aprons, opened their kitchens, and demonstrated their own regional specialties. "Thank you" too, goes to the Finnish Marttaliitto and to the farmwives' organizations that were so generous in offering information, especially on the specialty foods and historical backgrounds of many of the Finnish foods.

While in California, my fellow editors at *Sunset Magazine* were most inspiring, encouraging, and helpful. Without their uninhibited enthusiasm I might still have just a pile of recipes and notes.

And to all who have helped me along the way I'd like to say *tuhat kiitokset*—"a thousand thanks."

Library of Congress Catalog Card Number: 64-23811
ISBN: 0-517-501112

Printed in the U.S.A.

20   19   18   17

CONTENTS

To
All Finns and
Friends of Finns

Introduction

THE FINLAND WE MET

It was my grandparents who originally stimulated my interest in Finnish foods. I could recall such names as *laatikko, piirakkaa, kropsu,* and *klapsak-kaa,* but my parents could give only vague descriptions of dishes that Grandma had prepared as her mother had prepared them in Finland. I became very curious. I tried to find the recipes in American cookbooks, but of course they weren't there. Grandma (or *Mummu,* as we called her) made these foods without recipes, and in my unthinking days before she passed away, I let these treasures go with her. However, I did gain from her the ability to speak and read Finnish, and this has turned out to be the key to the collecting of these recipes.

My husband is also of pure Finnish ancestry, and his grandmother added another curious word to my Finnish food vocabulary: *lapskoda.* But she, too, died before I had enough sense to question her and get her recipes.

Later, relatives in Finland sent me two Finnish cookbooks. I searched them and found many interestingly different dishes, but still not the things our grandmothers had prepared.

In 1960–61 my husband received a Fulbright grant, and we had the good fortune to live in Finland for a whole year. Further good fortune led us to relatives we had not known existed, and they were eager to prepare, serve, and give me the recipes for dishes that are truly and typically Finnish. Yes, even the dishes our grandmothers had prepared!

In our travels we crisscrossed Finland from east to west and from the south to northern Lapland. We stayed in the homes of friends, relatives, and strangers, and in hotels and campgrounds. We spent Christmas, as well as Easter and Midsummer Day, visiting in the countryside. We not only got acquainted with the people and their everyday foods, we also celebrated the traditional festival days with relatives and friends with whom we felt very much at .home.

The Finnish women who shared their recipes with me were also eager to get some American recipes. So we exchanged recipes, and now apple pie, American style, is being made in many parts of Finland.

In general we found that food in Finland has its own character, although in the first-class restaurants there is much international and general Scandinavian influence. Many traditional Finnish dishes, such as molded or jellied veal, various butter cakes and cookies, sweet yeast breads, and fruit soups, are similar to those in Scandinavian cuisine, because the ingredients available are almost the same throughout these countries.

It takes a discerning eye to tell the *voileipäpöytä* of Finland from the *smörgåsbord* of Sweden. But in Finland this buffet table usually holds a greater variety of fish dishes, particularly fresh-water fish, and special filled pastries, which are traditional in Karelia (Eastern Finland).

The similarities between the foods of Western Finland and Sweden are easily explained by the physical proximity of these two areas. The similarities are noticeable in both modern and certain traditional foods.

The foods of Eastern Finland have many similarities to those of Russia, but, interestingly, only in very old and traditional dishes. The filled pasties and pastries, the Easter *pasha* (*pashka* in Russia), and even the bread—the sour rye loaves that are thick and round, in contrast to the thin, hard, sour rye loaves of Western Finland—are similar to those of Russia.

But Finland has very many interesting traditional dishes of her very own, many of them strictly regional. Karelia, in Eastern Finland has an especially rich tradition of various pastries, filled savory pasties, and foods made of sour milk which are not at all common in Western Finnish cuisine. Savo, a province in east-central Finland, is famous for fish dishes such as the traditional *kalakukko* (fish baked in a crust), for Eastern and Central Finland has more than 50,000 lakes. In the Western provinces—Pohjanmaa, Satakunta, Uusimaa and Varsinais Suomi—the traditional dishes center around dairy foods, whole-grain cereals, and salt-water fish (most often Baltic herring).

THE PEOPLE AND THEIR COUNTRY

Before our visit, we thought of Finland as a tiny country. Actually, it is larger than Great Britain, and as big as Minnesota and Iowa together, although its population is only four and one-half million.

Finland lies between the same parallels of latitude as Alaska and has one-third of its area north of the Arctic Circle, but the ocean currents keep the southern part of the country surprisingly warm. It is the land of the midnight sun in the summer, and is in almost complete darkness during part of the winter. Pines, granite, and water fill the landscape throughout the country. Finland is one of the countries standing literally between East and West, for she shares a border with Russia on the east, Norway on the north, and Sweden on the west. Even on the national emblem, the Finnish lion is facing west, waving a Western-type straight sword and stepping on a curved Eastern scimitar.

The Finnish culture is almost completely free of adulteration from other countries because Finland has had almost no immigrants in recent history. (The people tend to emigrate southward rather than northward.) This means the Finns are of quite pure national stock; most family trees can be traced back fairly easily in the records within a single community. For example, we traced three of our eight "roots" to the beginning of the 1700's through the church records of the communities.

The country is divided into 15 provinces. Before the winter war in 1939–40, Karelia in Eastern Finland extended halfway to Leningrad from the present Finnish-Russian border and included the northern and western shores of Lake Ladoga, a large lake now completely within Russia. Many of the traditional Karelian foods included in this collection have their origin in this area.

Today Finland is a bustling, energetic land. New churches, apartment houses, and office buildings are being built everywhere. And creative designers and artists are turning out some of the world's most beautiful porcelain, glassware, textiles, and buildings.

THE FINNISH PERSONALITY

As we became acquainted with the Finnish people, we became increasingly aware of the differences in the customs, food, and even the personalities of the people from different provinces.

There are classic stories depicting the slow and very quiet nature of the people from Häme:

> Once two Hämeläinen brothers were on their way into the woods for a week of logging. One brother pointed at some tracks in the snow and said, "Jänis" [rabbit].
> Upon passing the same spot on their return a week later, the other brother replied, "Kyllä" [yes].

Then there are the laughing, effervescent Karelian, the rather stiff, bashful, yet dignified individual from Pohjanmaa, and the quick-witted personality from Savo, with his tall tales and stretched short ones.

The speech of the people too varies tremendously from one area to another. A few dialects are so different that Finns from different regions often cannot understand each other!

Because of these differences, it is somewhat difficult to describe the typical

■🍥■🍥■🍥■🍥■🍥■🍥■🍥■🍥■🍥■🍥■🍥■🍥■🍥■🍥■🍥■

Finnish character. But we can safely say the Finns are a nation of rugged individualists when it comes to likes and dislikes, work and achievement. They are quiet, meditative people who are proud to be Finns, proud of their freedom, and very aware of their fathers, brothers, and sons who fought and too often died for this freedom. They are personally proud of Marshal Mannerheim, the Father of their Country, who led them to their independence and in their wars to preserve it. Independence Day in Finland is a solemn, commemorative day.

There is a very important characteristic of all Finns that is best described by the word *sisu*. Finnish-to-English dictionaries define it as "enduring energy" or "to possess guts," but it is more than that. It is a never-say-die individualism that Finns seem to be born with; they have the physical energy and mental endurance to stick to a job until it is done, and done well. It is the reason why Finns (e.g., Paavo Nurmi) seem to excel in individual sports rather than team sports, and it is why Finns are known for being good workers.

Although *sisu* might make the Finn appear tough and hard-shelled, he is really extremely sensitive. Finns have a feeling and concern for their fellow man, whoever he may be. Even though the long wars with Russia have laid heavy burdens on them as individuals and as a nation, they don't hold a grudge against the Russian people. They will often speak of a Russian as a *raukka*, meaning sympathetically a "poor dear fellow." They seem to realize that it is the system ruling the man that is the dreaded thing. A touching poem "Meeting in the Wood," by a war poet, describes a Finnish soldier as he fills his gun and thinks, as he kills a Russian soldier, of how the Russian will be missed somewhere by someone.

Before the winter war with Russia, President Pääsikivi went to Moscow to see if a peaceful settlement could be worked out. At the railroad station in Helsinki, a large crowd had gathered to see the President off on his mission. A farewell program had been planned, but before it was completed, the whole crowd of Finns spontaneously began singing, "A Mighty Fortress Is Our God" . . . for somehow, it was the real thing.

If you are interested in following through, you might check the history books to see against what great odds the Finns fought their war and remained independent. (A short reading list of books about Finland is included at the end of this book.)

THE FINNISH LANGUAGE

The Finnish language is an interesting one. The following conversation illustrates the alliteration that is possible, a device often used in Finnish poems:

"*Kokoa kokoon koko koko.*" ("Gather together the whole lot.")

"*Koko koko?*" ("The whole lot?")

"*Koko koko.*" ("Yes, the whole lot.")

Words, even the common, everyday ones, can be very long. A sign on a door in Helsinki reads:

APTEEKKITAVARAINTARKASTUSLABORATORIO

which means "Pharmaceutical Inspection Laboratory." A popular Finnish party game consists of trying to think up the longest possible word. Even in the newspapers, a word will often take up two lines on a column!

Finnish is also an unusually expressive language. Depending on the words used, one can talk very harshly, using abrasive *k*'s, *s*'s, and rolled *r*'s. Or, using words such as *laulaa* (to sing), you can talk very soothingly, almost melodically.

The language is also descriptive, as can be shown by translating the meaning of some of the months of the year: February is *Helmikuu*, meaning literally "pearl moon," the month of the year when the countryside is covered with a glistening, pearl-like whiteness. April is *Toukukuu*, or "sowing moon," June is *Kesäkuu*, or "summer moon," July is *Heinäkuu*, or "hay moon," August is *Elokuu*, or "harvest moon," and September is *Syyskuu*, or "autumn moon." During October, appropriately called *Lokakuu*, or "mud moon," there is a lot of rain, and since the country roads are mostly un-paved, it is not unusual to find Finns standing next to their bogged-down vehicles, rolling their *r*'s. November is *Marraskuu*, or "death moon"; except for the evergreens, all countryside greenery and color has vanished, the days get shorter and darken, and the Finns become more quiet and solemn. December is *Joulukuu*, or "Christmas moon."

Finnish bears no resemblance to the Latin, Germanic, or Slavic languages of Europe. However, it does have similarities to Hungarian, Estonian, and the Lappic tongues. The language has been traced back to central Russia, between the Volga River and the Ural Mountains, the homeland of the Finno-Ugric family of languages. It is interesting that Finland is the only country of this language group still in the free world.

The Finns know that their language is different and difficult, so much so that Bishop Michael Agricola, the Lutheran reformer who established the written language four hundred years ago, felt it necessary to declare that God heard and understood even the Finnish tongue! That the language has survived at all is rather amazing, for the country was ruled by Sweden for six hundred years and by Russia for one hundred years; it was not until the mid-1800's that Finnish became the official language of state.   Although Finland has two official languages, Finnish and Swedish, only 8 percent of the population is Swedo-Finn, and most of this group live in the southern and western part of the country. All students must learn both languages in school; in addition, they may later elect to learn English or German too and commonly both. The twenty-five hundred Lapps, however, speak Lapp, and in most cases, Finnish, too.

WAR REFUGEES

One of the least known, yet most amazing facts about Finland, is the way she handled refugees from Karelia during the war. When the Russian armies moved into Karelia in 1939 and again in 1944, all the Karelians evacuated their homes, leaving behind their treasures and their beloved homeland. The 420,000 Karelians (not one of them chose to remain behind), making up 10 percent of Finland's total population, were displaced from 12 percent of Finnish soil. They were welcomed into the homes of the other Finns and lived there until their resettlement could be worked out. The move was smooth and almost without difficulties and was accomplished without a single refugee or relocation camp. Later, all the Karelians were given homes to replace the ones they lost.

The main problem that arose under this the home-sharing plan had to do with differences in bread-baking habits. Whereas Karelians had been used to baking bread almost every day, the Western Finns baked it only twice a year, dried it, and ate it hard. The Karelians said they couldn't chew it; the western Finns said it was good for the teeth. So the Karelian wives, cooking in Western Finnish kitchens, baked often, and the Western Finnish housewives complained that they baked so often the brick ovens were cracking.

Also, the displacement of this 10 percent of the population brought about a great imbalance of wealth. Something had to be done to compensate the Karelians for their property losses. To do this, it was decided that the rest of the Finnish people, who had suffered less, give both money and property—jewelry, gold, anything of value in proportion to their total wealth. Our great-aunt happened to mention one day that when she was first married, she had had gold rings like those I wore, but she had given them to the Karelian fund.

It was not an easy life for any Finn at that time, but the people who shared their wealth did so gladly. The Karelians, on the other hand, received their compensation humbly and adjusted well to their new environment. But they did not forget their beloved Karelia. One Karelian lady we met said she still dreams of her old home almost every night. And the Karelians today say that they cannot blame Russia for wanting Karelia—it was just so beautiful!

FINNISH INTEREST IN AMERICA

The Finns are proud of the part Finnish settlers played in America. There were as many Finns as there were Dutch along the Hudson, or English in the Bay Colony; the colony of "Swedes" in Delaware was composed largely of Finns, for Finland at that time was part of the Swedish empire; it was mainly Finns who cleared the forest for the future site of Philadelphia; and it was the "Swede" Finns who taught the English settlers how to make log cabins by laying the logs horizontally, rather than upright, in stockade fashion.

John Morton, one of the signers of the Declaration of Independence, was of Finnish descent. Finns were among those who forged westward into the country which looked more like home to them than the peaceful valley along the Delaware River, for they were accustomed to the strenuous work of the forests.

And of course, tens of thousands of Finns came to America around 1900 and settled in Minnesota, Wisconsin, and Michigan. Here they helped to clear the land and lay the foundations for future cities, towns, and highways.

THE SAUNA—THE FINNISH BATH

No introduction to Finland would be complete without a mention of the sauna. It is as much a part of Finland as the people. Just as many stories are told in the sauna as are told about it. Though the days of the "co-ed" sauna are gone forever, it is not unusual to have sauna parties, or for committees to adjourn their meetings to the sauna, or for a group of old friends to relax and exchange *juttuja* (stories) in the sauna.

The classic sauna is a small log cabin, usually located on a lake shore.

It consists of at least two rooms: a dressing room and a heated bathing room. The dressing room is usually equipped with nothing more than benches along the wall and hooks for one's clothes. In one corner of the heated room—the sauna proper—stands a stove topped with loose rocks. Three or four different levels of benches line the opposite walls.

To "take a sauna," you undress, climb up onto one of the benches, and sit there, basking in the heat, occasionally switching yourself with dampened birch boughs. Some people enjoy taking *löyly*—the steam created by throwing water on the heated rocks; others may take only a very short löyly or none at all. While you absorb the heat of the sauna you become more and more relaxed.

A sauna properly taken will bring you to the point where your mind becomes blank—you almost sleep while remaining awake. It is indescribably soothing and very relaxing. The bathing-and-steam ritual is followed by a cooling-off period then by re-entry into the heated room; then there follows a soap-and-water scrubbing, a cold splash of water, a cold shower, or a jump in the lake. The hardiest souls in winter top off their sauna with a roll in the snow, or climb through a hole in the ice and dunk themselves in the water below. The shock of this cold treatment after the heat of the sauna, is not as great as it sounds.

Saturday night is sauna night, as are the evenings before such holidays as Christmas, New Year's Day, and Midsummer Day. Visitors are always offered a sauna on these days. Guests who have traveled any distance are offered a sauna regardless of what day of the week it is. The welcoming sauna followed by sauna coffee is one of the fondest memories we have of Finland.

The sauna has always played an important part in the lives of Finns. Our grandparents and all the generations before them were born in the sauna, for it was a clean and sterile place. Athletes take sauna to relax after a strenuous event. During the war, the Finnish soldiers couldn't go without their sauna, even on the battlefield. A six-hour rest period was time enough for a two-hundred-man battalion to build a sauna and take their baths. Some say that when the Finns advanced into Russia, they built a sauna at each resting point, and left a soldier behind to man it so that the sauna would be hot when they retreated.

Even the Finnish settlers in America first built saunas on their homesteads, and then lived in them while they built their houses.

■⊘ఏ■⊘ఏ■⊘ఏ■⊘ఏ■⊘ఏ■⊘ఏ■⊘ఏ■⊘ఏ■⊘ఏ■⊘ఏ■⊘ఏ■⊘ఏ■

A TYPICAL FINNISH FARMHOUSE

It was a thrill to step into the farmhouse that my husband's grandmother had left as a teen-ager in the late 1800's. It is a two-story wooden structure, of perfect rectangular shape except for the sheltered porch. The house is still in use and the present head of the family, Heikki, is Grandma's nephew. Typical of all the farmhouses in Western Finland, it is painted red, with white window frames. We stepped into an entrance hall, called the *porstua,* which has a wooden floor, scrubbed white, with long, colorful, hand-woven rugs forming paths to three different doors. We entered the door to the right, which opened into the living room—kitchen, called the *tupa.* On the left is a large wood stove on which all the cooking is done. Behind it is the brick oven which is also built into the framework of the house. It is so large that a hundred loaves of bread can be baked at a time. The loaves are placed in the oven on the heated bricks with a long-handled wooden device that has a large flat disk on one end.

Poles on which the flat round sour rye bread loaves with a hole in the center are hung to dry extend across the ceiling of the tupa. Also in the tupa are a wood box, wooden cupboards, a painted massive wooden table similar in style to our picnic tables and having long, well-worn, painted wooden benches on each side, a large grandfather clock with its graceful hourglass curves, and a rocking chair with its typical very long, curved rockers. In the winter a loom is also in the tupa. Finnish women love to spend their long winter hours weaving linens and tapestries, mostly for their own use.

The tupa has another doorway which leads to other rooms. These are usually bedrooms, and in the larger farmhouses there is a guest parlor that is not used unless there are visitors in the house.

In the corner of each room other than the tupa there is a tall round brick heater that reaches to the ceiling. In the winter, the small fireboxes of these heaters are fired for several hours until the bricks are hot; when the fire is out, the dampers are closed and the bricks keep the room warm for about two days.

Throughout the house, the floors are covered with hand-woven runners, the walls are bedecked with tapestries—*ryijy* rugs and other hangings—all strikingly handsome handiwork of the women of the house. Every bit of linen used in the house was woven at home from home-grown flax, including the tablecloths, towels, draperies, bedspreads, and even some articles of cloth-ing. The love of weaving is most characteristic of the western Finnish farmwives. This house, the one that Grandma lived in before she emigrated to the United States, is typical of the average western Finnish farmhouse.

HOW A CITY FINN AND A COUNTRY FINN SPEND THE DAY

Living patterns and eating habits of the Finns today fall into two general groups, urban and rural. Our neighbors in Helsinki, Pekka and Raija and their two small daughters, Suvi Marja and Maarit, compose a typical urban family. Pekka works in an office six days a week from eight thirty to five o'clock each day. He has a month's vacation in the summer, which he usually spends with his family at their summer cabin on a lake.

When Pekka has his morning coffee before going to work, he usually has a couple of open-faced sandwiches, too. Sometime between eleven o'clock and one he has a dish of *puuroa* (cooked cereal such as oatmeal, rice, or farina). Later on Pekka and his associates have coffee and perhaps another open-faced sandwich. Sometimes he has lunch with his business associates, in which case the meal includes the appetizer tray called the *voileipäpöytä*, with its pickled fish, cold cuts, cheeses, and breads, followed by an entree of fish or meat and potatoes, milk, and a simple dessert. He may drink *kalja* (a beerlike beverage), or pilsner with little or no alcoholic content, or *olut* (a beer available in varying degrees of alcoholic content). Coffee is not served with the meal.

Meanwhile, Raija will feed the children puuroa, and she too, will have a bowlful with a glass of milk. One of Raija's favorite casseroles for the evening meal is *maksalaatikko* (a liver-rice casserole), and she serves it with preserved lingonberries and sliced pickled beets and cucumbers.

Pekka often works late in the evening, but the children are not put to bed until he is home. Then, so that they can have some time together, Pekka and Raija often stay up late. We sometimes had coffee with them at eleven or twelve o'clock at night.

Raija's day is a busy one. She cares for an apartment with two bedrooms, a living room, bathroom, kitchen, and outdoor balcony. The baby, Maarit, sleeps in her buggy on the balcony four to five hours a day regardless of the weather. (Finnish mothers are told by their doctors to keep their children outside at least four hours a day. This is a real chore when the weather is blustery, rainy, or when there is a lot of work to do!) While the baby is sleeping, Raija must do her daily shopping (the tiny grocery stores are in neighboring apartment buildings at street level) and tend to Suvi Marja as she plays outside in the sandbox or snow.

Saturday is especially busy because it is the day when the weekly house-cleaning has to be done. The rugs must be taken outside and beaten, the bedclothes aired, the floors washed. Once a month all the mattresses are taken outside to be beaten and aired. Twice a year the closets and clothing must be cleaned and aired out. Raija, like most good Finnish housewives, does all this religiously.

The living pattern and eating habits are slightly different in the country. Let us return to the farm, the one my husband's grandmother left when she came to the United States. Heikki, Grandma's nephew, is the master of the farm and Maija is his wife. One son, Manne, is married and now lives in the city of Oulu. Another son, Mauri, is in agricultural school; the oldest daughter, Liina, works in a bank in a neighboring village and shares an apartment with girl friends. Marina, who has finished school, and Keijo, the youngest boy, are at home.

Like most farm families, they arise between five and six in the morning. Maija first starts the fire in the kitchen stove and puts the coffee water on to heat. When the coffee is made, Heikki, still a little sleepy-eyed, enters the tupa. Marina, who followed her mother into the tupa, has already sliced thick pieces of *pulla* (a braided yeast coffee-bread), piled them on a plate, and set it on the table. Heikki also likes to dunk *korppua* (dried hard toast or rusks) in his coffee.

Morning coffee drunk, the women then tend to the barn chores—in Finland it is the women's duty to take care of the livestock, feed the cows, and milk them—and the men head for the fields, or they may go into the woods and take up where they left off the day before in harvesting their own stand of timber.

After milking, the women prepare *aamiainen* (breakfast) which is usually served around 10:00 or 11:00 A.M. On the typical menu are boiled potatoes, pork gravy, fish or meat, a basket of sour rye bread, a dish of butter, and a special homemade cheese: *leipäjuusto*. Dessert is a bowlful of creamed rice, oatmeal, or farina, or in the summertime, fresh wild berries such as raspberries, strawberries, or cloudberries (a yellow raspberry that grows in arctic swampland).

When there are guests for a meal or for coffee, Maija, according to custom, will not sit at the table. Heikki eats with the guests.

After aamiainen, the men will *levähtää* (rest) for a little while. In the summer they may lie down under the shade of the birch trees that encircle

■✑■✑■✑■✑■✑■✑■✑■✑■✑■✑■✑■✑■✑■✑■

the house. The women clean up the dishes, put the food away, and tend to routine housework. Between 1:00 and 2:00 P.M. is coffeetime, and again, the men come into the house from their work.

The women milk the cows around 4:00 P.M., and after that they prepare the evening meal. Later in the evening, coffee is served, quite casually, whenever anybody wants it. When there are guests, the coffee table is set with pulla, pound cake, and a variety of butter cookies.

Heikki and Maija are active in civic and community groups, Heikki with the creamery co-operative, politics, and the horse-breeding society (he has an outstanding team of horses that have won many prizes in competitions), and Maija with the Maatalous Naiset (a farmwives' organization). Heikki and Maija often hold meetings in their home.

Saturday is a busy day on the farm as well as in the city. It is the day when the women scrub the wooden floors until they are white, get every room meticulously clean, and place fresh evergreen branches outside the door so people can clean their feet before entering the house. They bake on Saturday too, pulla, as well as other coffee-table items. If there is still some of the coffee bread left from the previous baking, they slice it and dry it in the oven to make korppua. Once or twice a month they make reikäleipä (sour rye bread with a hole in the center). The practice of baking only twice a year is not as common today as it was in the past.

The women bake as early in the day as possible so that they have time for the afternoon chores, the most important being the scrubbing, preparation, and heating of the sauna.

Then, of course, on Saturday evening there is the grand climax to the week's bustle—a relaxing sauna.

Although a full description of Finland and Finnish people would fill volumes, I hope that this glance into Finnish life will spark an interest to learn more about this vigorous northern country.

USING THIS BOOK

The recipes in this collection have been tested with ingredients available in the United States. All measurements are level. All cooking temperatures indicated are Fahrenheit, and all baking is done in a preheated oven. Certain ingredients, such as different types of flours, are available only in health-food stores; for these, satisfactory substitutions are given. Rye flour, however, is generally available in supermarkets.

■◌◌■◌◌■◌◌■◌◌■◌◌■◌◌■◌◌■◌◌■◌◌■◌◌■◌◌■◌◌■◌◌■◌◌■

You may wish to supplement special dishes with Finnish products that are available in the United States. Some are found in fine food stores, and some in supermarkets. "Finn Crisp" is a crispbread flavored with caraway that is available in both fine food stores and supermarkets. When it was first imported into the United States it was so hard that there were actually legal claims made against it (for teeth allegedly broken when biting into it). Today it is softer and easier to bite into. Another variety with a floury coating is available, and though it is a dry bread, it is very soft.

Smoked reindeer meat is imported, but the supply does not nearly meet the gourmet demand. Lingonberry preserves, certain Finnish cheeses, and a type of candy called Marmalaad have found their way onto the American market. Incidentally, many regard Finnish-made Emmenthal cheese as superior to the Swiss original, and think that Aura cheese compares with the best Roqueforts in Europe. Finnish Tilsitter, available in fine food stores, is excellent. Cloudberries now appear on the world market as a preserve. The flavor of cloudberries is reminiscent of fresh, slightly green apricots, but is not tart. When the rich, heavy, natural syrup of this berry is combined with sugar in the right proportion, it can be stored without even being cooked. The Finns make fine, rare liqueurs from cloudberries and another arctic berry, *mesimarja*.

1. Breads

Breads deserve the first place in this collection of recipes, for they are the mainstay of the Finnish diet. A meal without bread is not a meal, according to Finns, and because vegetables and fruits are less abundant than grains in this far-northern country, interesting varieties of rye breads have developed.

The breads of long ago were made of only flour and water, but today other flavoring ingredients such as caraway and fennel seeds are added to bread dough to suit individual tastes and special occasions. Rye and barley are the two grains that ripen during the short growing season in Finland; this explains their extensive use. Different varieties of breads, developed in different areas of Finland, come from the use of different proportions of rye and barley flours, different liquids, and different degrees of sourness and leavening action.

Sour rye bread is the favorite of the Finns. The "souring process" that creates the flavor characteristic of this bread stems back to the days when yeast, as we know it today, was not available for leavening the bread. Then the dough was left to ferment, thus creating the gas which soured the dough and made it rise. The Finns love the flavor of sour rye bread so much that it is the thing they crave most when they are homesick in a foreign country.

In Western Finland, round thin dark sour rye loaves with a hole in the center are traditional. In the past, these loaves were strung up on poles that extended across the ceiling of the tupa. They were then allowed to dry and were stored in the *aitta* (a separate little wooden shed, away from the house). Bread was baked twice a year: in the spring, to prepare for the long days of summer work ahead, and in the fall, immediately after the harvest, to stock up for the long, dark winter. Memories of the fall baking create a bit of nostalgia among Finns, for in the fall, the fresh grain was the choicest and the bread the best. Freshly baked sour rye bread made with freshly harvested grain is one of the choicest things a Finnish hostess can offer her guests.

Sour rye bread was also a staple in Karelia (Eastern Finland), but there it was shaped into thick round loaves and baked at least twice a week instead of twice a year. The Karelian homemaker set the bread dough the day before the baking and baked it early in the morning, for it was a great treat to have fresh bread for *aamiainen*. Karelians complain bitterly when they must eat the hard bread of Western Finland.

Wheat flour was almost unknown in Finland until after the 1900's. It was, and still is, imported, and has been reserved mainly for fancy baking and holiday breads.

In the recipes that follow, wheat flour (white flour) is added to the bread in place of part of the rye flour because it makes the dough easier to handle. For the same reason, Finnish cooks today use part wheat flour in making these old and traditional breads. When a recipe calls for "potato water," use the water in which you cooked peeled potatoes. The reserved liquid can be stored in a jar in the refrigerator until it is needed.

HINTS ABOUT BREADMAKING

It is important, when baking bread, not to kill the yeast by too high temperatures nor to retard the yeast growth by too low temperatures. Always dissolve yeast in *warm* (not hot) water if you are using active dry, granular yeast, and in *lukewarm* water if you are using compressed yeast. ("Active dry yeast" is specified in the recipes in this book; however, compressed yeast can be substituted for it, ounce for ounce, if you prefer.)

Never add too much flour at a time. It is difficult to give the exact amount of flour necessary for a bread recipe because it varies with temperature, humidity, and even with the way you handle the dough. If you "dump" flour into the liquid all at once it will be very difficult for you to get a smooth mixture, and you may add too much flour, making the dough too stiff. It is better to start with too little flour than too much. So add flour gradually.

Make bread the "lazy" way. The more "rest" periods you give the batter and the dough, the easier the dough will be to handle when you are kneading it. Interruptions are actually good for the dough! During each rest period some absorption will take place, and the yeast will be working. The resultant dough will be springy and "lively."

After the dough is shaped into loaves, do not let it rise too high (overproof). If it does, punch down and reshape it and let it rise again.

■଼ଔ■଼ଔ■଼ଔ■଼ଔ■଼ଔ■଼ଔ■଼ଔ■଼ଔ■଼ଔ■଼ଔ■଼ଔ■଼ଔ■଼ଔ■

SOUR RYE BREAD   Ruisleipä

This is the loaf that most Finns call "bread." When I asked Finnish cooks
I met to name the foods most typical of Finland, they invariably said "*ruis-
leipä*." It is most truly the staff of life in their country, for if all the foods
that are imported were to be suddenly taken away, the Finnish people would
still be able to nourish themselves with rye bread.

This recipe is baked in two different ways: in the Western Finnish flat
round loaf having a hole in the center, and in the Eastern Finnish thick
round soft loaf. Traditionally, in Western Finland, hundreds of loaves of
bread were made in one baking (especially in the past); Eastern Finnish
housewives baked more often but made fewer loaves at a time.

The souring process in this bread serves only to produce an authentic
flavor. The recipe is equally successful without the sour-bread starter. When
making the bread for the first time, allow 3 to 4 days to develop a good
sour flavor.

½ cup Sour-Bread Starter (recipe below)	1 package active dry yeast
2 cups warm water or potato water	¼ cup warm water
3½ cups rye flour	2 teaspoons salt
	3–3½ cups sifted white flour

Turn the sour-bread starter into a large mixing bowl and stir in the 2
cups water or potato water slowly until well blended. Blend in 1 cup of
the rye flour and stir well. Cover lightly and let stand in a warm place
(about 85°) for 20 to 40 hours, depending on the degree of sourness desired.

Dissolve the yeast in the ¼ cup warm water, then stir into the soured
mixture. Add the salt and very gradually beat in the remaining rye flour.
Add the white flour, a little at a time, beating well after each addition.
When a stiff dough is formed, let it rest in the bowl for 10 to 15 minutes,
then turn out onto a floured board and knead until smooth. Place the dough
in a lightly greased bowl turning to grease the top, cover, and let rise in
a warm place until doubled in bulk (about 1 to 1½ hours). Turn the dough
out onto a lightly floured board and divide it into 2 parts after reserving
about ½ cup of the dough. (This should be stored in a covered container in
the refrigerator for your next baking.)

To make Eastern-Finnish-style loaves, shape each of the 2 pieces of
dough into a ball, and place on a lightly greased baking sheet. Cover
lightly and let rise until almost doubled (about 30 minutes) before baking.

For Western-Finnish flat loaves, shape the dough into 2 balls, as above, but flatten them by patting to about 1-inch thickness, keeping the shape round, until the dough measures 8 to 10 inches in diameter. With the fingers, make a hole in the center of each loaf and stretch it to about 2 inches in diameter. Dust the top of the loaf lightly with rye flour.

Place the loaves on a greased baking sheet and prick all over with a fork. Cover lightly and let rise in a warm place until puffy and smooth, but not doubled in bulk (about 30 minutes). Bake in a moderately hot oven (375°) for about 45 minutes or until the loaves are very lightly browned. Makes 2 loaves.

SOUR-BREAD STARTER

About 2 days before you plan to make sour rye bread, prepare this starter. Mix ½ cup milk (at room temperature but not scalded) with ½ cup rye flour. Let stand, uncovered, in a warm (preferably sunny) place until the mixture begins to bubble and has a pleasantly sour odor. You may refrigerate the starter at this point or use the entire amount immediately in a bread dough. (In the latter case, be sure to reserve ½ cup of this bread dough for subsequent bakings.)

In the old days, the huge stone bread bowl in which the dough was mixed was never washed between bakings; thus the sour starter was automatically preserved in the bits of dry, crusty dough that adhered after each mixing. To start new bread dough, water was poured into the bowl, the sides of the bowl were scraped, a little flour added, and then the mixture was allowed to sour again.

FINNISH RYE BREAD   Suomalaisruisleipä

This is the favored bread of American Finns and is an adaptation of the original sour rye bread. Rye meal, available in parts of the Midwest and in health-food stores, gives the bread an interesting coarseness.

1 package active dry yeast   1½ cups rye meal
¼ cup warm water   1 tablespoon melted butter
1 cup potato water   1½ teaspoons salt
1 tablespoon brown sugar   2 cups white flour

Dissolve the yeast in the ¼ cup water. Pour the potato water, brown sugar, and 1 cup of the rye meal into a large mixing bowl. Add the yeast mixture, and beat well. Stir in the butter, salt, and almost all the flour. Mix until a stiff dough forms. Sprinkle the remaining ½ cup rye meal on a board. Turn the dough out onto it. Cover with the bowl and let rest for 10 minutes.

Knead until smooth, using the rye meal to ease the stickiness. (The dough may not take the entire amount of rye meal.) Turn the dough into a buttered bowl, cover lightly, and let rise until doubled in bulk. Punch down and shape into a round loaf. Place in a buttered 8- or 9-inch round cake pan and let rise again until almost doubled. Prick all over with a fork. Bake in a moderately hot oven (375°) for 55 to 60 minutes. Brush with butter while hot. Makes 1 loaf.

RYE AND BARLEY BREAD   Hiivaleipä

Hiivaleipä translated literally means "yeast bread." This round loaf is light colored and has a rich whole-grain flavor.

2 packages active dry yeast
¼ cup warm water
2 cups lukewarm milk or potato
  water
1½ teaspoons salt
1½ teaspoons crushed anise seed
  (optional)

1½ teaspoons crushed fennel seed
  (optional)
2 tablespoons melted butter
1 cup rye flour
1 cup barley flour or graham flour
2—3 cups white flour

Dissolve the yeast in the warm water. Pour the milk or potato water into a large bowl, add the yeast, salt, crushed seed, and melted butter. Gradually add the rye and barley or graham flours, mixing well after each addition. Beat until smooth. Slowly beat in the white flour until a stiff dough is formed. Let the dough rest in the bowl for 10 minutes before kneading.

Turn the dough out onto a floured board and knead until smooth. Place in a lightly greased bowl, turn over to grease the top of the dough, and cover lightly. Put into a warm place to rise until doubled in bulk (1 to 2 hours).

Divide into 2 parts and shape each into a ball. Place, smooth side up, on a greased baking sheet or in lightly greased 8- or 9-inch round cake pans. Flatten slightly and let rise again until doubled. Prick all over with a fork. Bake in a moderately hot oven (375°) for 45 minutes or until very lightly golden brown. Brush with butter while hot. Makes 2 loaves.

■⚬◔■⚬◔■⚬◔■⚬◔■⚬◔■⚬◔■⚬◔■⚬◔■⚬◔■⚬◔■⚬◔■⚬◔■⚬◔■⚬◔■

POTATO RYE LOAF   Perunalimppu

This special Christmas bread is fun to make when you understand the reason why the dough seems to get softer during the rising period. The basis for its original character is a malting process that begins in the dough when mashed potatoes are added. During the malting, starches break down to form a simple sugar that liquifies the mixture. The finished bread is a moist, rather heavy loaf, rich in flavor.

1 package active dry yeast
1 cup warm potato water (or plain
    water if you are using instant
    mashed potatoes)
2 cups rye flour
2 cups mashed potatoes

½ cup dark corn syrup (or light
    molasses)
2 teaspoons salt (less if the potatoes
    are seasoned)
2 teaspoons caraway seed (optional)
3½–4½ cups white flour

Glaze
1 tablespoon sugar   1 tablespoon hot water

Dissolve the yeast in the warm potato water and add 1 cup of the rye flour, stirring until well blended. Set aside.

In a saucepan, combine the warmed mashed potatoes with the syrup or molasses, salt, and caraway seed. Stir in the remaining cup rye flour. Beat until smooth. Let stand for 1½ hours in a warm place (the mixture should get thinner during this time).

Combine the two mixtures in a large mixing bowl and beat well. Mix in enough of the white flour to make a stiff dough, beating well after each addition. (The exact amount of flour used will depend on the consistency of the mashed potatoes.) Let the dough rest in the mixing bowl 15 minutes, then turn out onto a lightly floured board and knead for about 5 minutes or until smooth. Place in a lightly greased mixing bowl in a warm place, turning the dough to grease it on all sides, and let rise until doubled in bulk (about 1 hour). Punch down and let rise again until doubled in bulk (about 30 minutes).

Divide the dough into 2 parts and form each into a ball. Place the balls of dough, smooth side up, on a greased baking sheet, and let rise for about 25 minutes or until the loaves look puffy but are not doubled in bulk. Bake in a moderately hot oven (375°) for 35 to 40 minutes or until the loaves sound hollow when tapped with a finger. Brush while hot with the mixture of sugar and water. Makes 2 loaves.

CHRISTMAS RYE LOAF   Joululimppu

During the holiday season in Finland, the everyday sour rye bread is not served. Instead, special breads baked prior to the holidays (which officially begin December 23, the eve of Christmas Eve, and end on Epiphany, January 6) are enjoyed. Most commonly these special breads are *Joululimppu* and *Perunalimppu* (above).

3½ cups boiling water
½ cup sorghum molasses or dark, unsulphured molasses
4 cups rye flour

2 teaspoons salt
1 package active dry yeast
¼ cup warm water
4–5 cups white flour

Glaze
1 tablespoon molasses

1 tablespoon warm water

Mix 1½ cups of the boiling water with the molasses and 1 cup of the rye flour; beat well. Let stand for 30 minutes. Beat in 1 cup of the rye flour and then add another 1½ cups boiling water and beat well. Let stand for 1 hour longer. Add the remaining ½ cup (boiling) water and beat well. Cool until mixture is lukewarm.

Stir in the salt. Dissolve the yeast in the ¼ cup warm water, and add to the flour mixture. Slowly add the remaining 2 cups rye flour and the white flour, beating well after each addition. When the dough is stiff, let it rest in the bowl for 15 minutes.

Turn out onto a floured board and knead until smooth. Place in a lightly greased bowl, turn over to grease the top, cover lightly, and let rise in a warm place until doubled in bulk (from 1 to 3 hours).

Turn out again onto a lightly floured board. Divide the dough in half and shape each portion into a ball, rolling it to a peak on one side (it will be shaped like a huge chocolate drop). Place each loaf, flat side down, on a greased baking sheet. With your thumb, punch the peak down into the loaf as far as possible. Let rise again until not quite doubled. Bake in a moderately hot oven (375°) for 45 to 50 minutes or until the loaves sound hollow when tapped with a finger. Glaze the hot loaves with the mixture of molasses and water. Makes 2 loaves.

■◌۹■◌۹■◌۹■◌۹■◌۹■◌۹■◌۹■◌۹■◌۹■◌۹■◌۹■◌۹■◌۹■

OULU PUMPERNICKEL   Oulunlimppu

This dark, caraway-and-orange-flavored rye bread is traditional in Oulu, a city in northwestern Finland. It is similar to the Swedish rye breads because sweetening is added to it.

1 package active dry yeast	1½ teaspoons salt
¼ cup warm water	2 teaspoons caraway or fennel seed
½ cup dark corn syrup or light molasses	2 cups buttermilk
1 tablespoon grated orange peel	3 cups rye flour
	3–3½ cups white flour

Glaze

1 tablespoon syrup or molasses   4 tablespoons water

Dissolve the yeast in the ¼ cup warm water; set aside. Mix the syrup or molasses, orange peel, salt, and caraway or fennel seed in a saucepan and bring to a boil. Pour into a large mixing bowl and add the buttermilk. Cool to lukewarm. Add the yeast and blend well. Add the rye flour gradually and beat well. Add the white flour, beating well after each addition. When the mixture is stiff, let it rest for 15 minutes before kneading.

Turn the dough out onto a floured board and knead until satiny smooth, then place in a lightly greased mixing bowl, turning to grease the top, cover lightly, and let rise in a warm place until doubled in bulk (about 1 hour). Turn out again onto a floured board and divide into 2 parts. Shape each half into a round fat ball or into a rectangular loaf about 4 by 8 inches. Place on a greased baking sheet and let rise until almost doubled (about 30 minutes).

Before baking, brush the loaves with a mixture of the syrup (or molasses) and water; repeat twice during the baking, and again on removal from the oven. Bake in a moderate oven (350°) for 45 to 50 minutes. Makes 2 loaves.

UNLEAVENED RYE BREAD   Ruisrieska

This is a variation of Unleavened Barley Bread made with all-rye flour. It is slightly chewier than rieska and very tasty.

1 cup milk	1 cup rye flour
½ teaspoon salt	4 tablespoons melted butter
½ teaspoon sugar	

Mix together in a bowl the milk, salt, and sugar. Stir in the flour and beat until smooth. Add the butter, mixing until blended. Pour into a well-buttered

■e⅝■e⅝■e⅝■e⅝■e⅝■e⅝■e⅝■e⅝■e⅝■e⅝■e⅝■e⅝■e⅝■e⅝■

and floured 9- by 12-inch baking pan. Bake in a very hot oven (450°) for about 30 minutes or until slightly browned in spots. Serve hot with butter. Makes about 6 servings.

RYE CRISPBREAD OR HARDTACK   Ruisnäkkileipä

These are large round flat crisp breads with a hole in the center. Sometimes they are made with a soured dough. Näkkileipä is popular in Western Finland. There, these thin crisp loaves are baked and strung up by the hundreds to dry until they are devoid of all moisture.

When we visited Finnish homes, the family breadbasket offered two choices: usually, wedges of sour rye bread, and rye hardtack cracked into large pieces. The Finnish "sandwich table" (see Chapter XII) always has hardtack as a choice for the base of open-faced sandwiches. There is a healthful aspect to this bread too, for Finns lack a selection of crisp foods such as raw vegetables, and hardtack fills this need.

1 package active dry yeast	1 teaspoon salt
2 cups warm water	4½–5 cups rye flour

Dissolve the yeast in the water. Add the salt and gradually beat in 4 cups of the flour. The dough should be soft. Cover lightly and let rise in the mixing bowl in a warm place until doubled in bulk (about 1 hour). Sprinkle a board generously with flour and turn the dough out onto it. Shape into a smooth ball and divide into 4 parts. Form each into a round ball, using flour freely to keep the dough from sticking to your hands or to the board, but be careful not to work the extra flour into the dough. Roll out carefully, powdering any sticky spots with flour, until the dough is about ¼- to ½-inch thick. Keep the shape round. Using a large spatula, remove the round to a baking sheet that has been greased and floured. Prick the round all over with a fork; cut a hole in the center (using a small round cutter about 2 inches in diameter), and let rise in a warm place about 15 minutes. Bake in a very hot oven (450°) for 10 to 15 minutes or until the bread feels firm when touched. The rounds should still bend when they are removed from the oven. Cool on a rack.

For the breads to become properly crisp, they must be dried after cooling. Traditionally, they were strung up on poles to dry. However, you may place them on the racks in the oven after the oven has cooled, and let them dry overnight or for about 6 to 8 hours. To serve, break into pieces and spread with butter. Makes 4 10- to 12-inch rounds of crisp bread.

■᠗᠗■᠗᠗■᠗᠗■᠗᠗■᠗᠗■᠗᠗■᠗᠗■᠗᠗■᠗᠗■᠗᠗■᠗᠗■᠗᠗■᠗᠗■

UNLEAVENED BARLEY BREAD   Rieska

The rieska, or unleavened bread, of Finland is the earliest of all the breads, dating back to the days before the process of fermentation was discovered, and it differs from place to place within the country. *Rieska* is characteristically a round, rather flat loaf that is not crisp but quite soft; it is delicious hot. The farther north you go in Finland, the thinner the traditional rieska of each village becomes.

In the little village of Nivala and the surrounding countryside, rieska was baked in a loaf about 2½ inches thick. Traditionally, it was baked during the Christmas season and saved until the first planting day in the spring. Before baking, three straws were placed in the loaf; if the bread cracked badly during storage, it foretold a bad year for crops.

In some places rieska is baked on cabbage or rutabaga leaves; the bread then takes up the flavor of the leaf. In other places, pieces of bacon, ham, or salt pork are stuck into the dough before baking. In Eastern Finland, rieska is made with cream and buttermilk; in Western Finland, plain milk or water.

Serve rieska hot from the oven with butter and a tall glass of cold buttermilk, as the Finns do, or serve it with tea, coffee, or in place of a hot bread for breakfast, or with a hearty salad for lunch.

½ cup buttermilk (or any other liquid)
½ cup cream
½ teaspoon salt

½ teaspoon sugar
1 cup barley flour (available in health-food stores)
1 tablespoon melted butter

Mix together in a bowl the buttermilk, cream, salt, and sugar. Stir in the flour and beat until smooth. Add the butter.

Pour the batter into a well-buttered and floured 9-inch round cake pan, or spread the dough on raw cabbage leaves and place on a lightly greased baking sheet. Bake in a very hot oven (450°) for about 30 minutes or until lightly browned. Serve hot with butter. Makes 4 to 6 servings.

KYRSA WHOLE-GRAIN BREAD
Vähäkyrön Ohrakyrsä

In the Western Finnish village of Vähäkyrö, this bread called *kyrsä* has been a tradition for generations. A Finn from another part of the country

■෧෨■෧෨■෧෨■෧෨■෧෨■෧෨■෧෨■෧෨■෧෨■෧෨■෧෨■෧෨■෧෨■

would look at a loaf of kyrsä and call it *rieska*. It is very simple to make: there is no kneading and there is only one rising period. The bread originally was made of barley flour, but white flour or whole-wheat flour works well and both make a very good bread.

2 packages active dry yeast	2 teaspoons salt
¼ cup warm water	4 cups barley flour, whole wheat
2 cups milk, scalded and cooled to lukewarm	flour, or white flour

Sprinkle the yeast into the mixing bowl and add the water. Stir until the yeast is dissolved. Add the milk, salt, and part of the flour, stirring well. Add the remaining flour slowly, beating until the dough is smooth and stiff. Let the dough rest in the bowl for 15 minutes.

Turn out onto a lightly floured board and divide into 2 equal parts (the dough will be slightly sticky). Shape each part into a ball and pat out into a round 8 to 10 inches in diameter. Place on a lightly buttered baking sheet. Let rise until the loaves look puffy (about 45 minutes to 1 hour). Prick all over with a fork and bake in a moderately hot oven (375°) for 30 minutes or until lightly browned. Brush with butter while hot. To slice, cut into wedges and split each wedge into 2 parts. Makes 2 loaves.

HEALTH BREAD   Terveysleipä

This bread has a rich, whole-grain flavor, and can be made with or without sugar or salt, and with the kind of shortening special diets prescribe.

1 package active dry yeast	2 tablespoons brown sugar
¼ cup warm water	(optional)
2 cups buttermilk, water, or	½ cup wheat germ
potato water, heated to lukewarm	1 cup rye meal or rye flour
¼ cup melted and cooled butter	2 cups whole-wheat flour
or salad oil	2—2½ cups white flour
1½ teaspoons salt (optional)	

Dissolve the yeast in the ¼ cup water. Add the buttermilk or water, shortening, salt, sugar, and wheat germ, and stir until combined. Stir in the rye flour and the whole-wheat flour gradually, beating vigorously for 1 minute after adding the first cup of whole-wheat flour. Add enough of the remaining flour to make a stiff dough. Turn out onto a board and let rest for 15 minutes.

Knead until smooth (about 10 minutes). Put the dough into a greased bowl, turn over to grease the top, cover, and let rise for 1 to 3 hours or until doubled in bulk. Shape into 2 loaves and place in greased loaf pans.

Let rise again until almost doubled, then bake in a moderately hot oven (375°) for 45 to 55 minutes or until the bread shrinks from the sides of the pan. Brush the loaves with butter while hot, if desired. Makes 2 loaves.

MOLASSES RYE BREAD   Siirappipölkky

Bake this bread in a 4-quart pail or in 4 loaf-sized bread pans. To slice bread baked in a pail, first quarter it lengthwise, then slice each quarter, making triangular-shaped slices.

2 packages active dry yeast
2 cups warm water
1½ teaspoons salt

1 cup light molasses or dark
  corn syrup
4 cups white flour
3 cups rye flour

Dissolve the yeast in the warm water and stir in the salt. Add the molasses or syrup and gradually stir in the white flour, beating with a spoon to keep the mixture smooth. Stir in the rye flour to make a stiff dough. Let the dough rest for 15 to 30 minutes before kneading. Turn out onto a board and knead until the dough is smooth and springy, adding more flour if necessary. Place the dough in a lightly greased bowl, turn over to grease top, and cover. Let rise in a warm place until doubled. Punch down and shape into 1 large smooth loaf or 4 oblong loaves. Place in a greased pail or pans, cover, and let rise again until almost doubled (45 minutes to 1 hour). Bake the large loaf in a moderate oven (350°) for 1 to 1½ hours. Test for doneness with a long wooden skewer or a cake tester. If it comes out clean, the loaf is baked. Or bake in oblong pans in a moderately hot oven (375°) for 45 to 55 minutes, or until the loaves sound hollow when thumped with finger. Brush with butter while hot. Cool on a rack. Makes 1 large or 4 smaller loaves.

GRAHAM PAN BREAD   Grahamvuokaleipä

Beer gives this bread a tangy flavor. It is excellent for cheese and ham sandwiches.

1 package active dry yeast
¼ cup warm water
3 tablespoons molasses
1 teaspoon salt

½ tablespoon finely crushed
  fennel or anise seed
1½ cups beer or kalja (see index)
3½ cups graham flour
1–1½ cups white flour

Dissolve the yeast in the warm water and add the molasses and salt. Add the fennel (or anise) seed to the beer, heat just to lukewarm, then add to the yeast mixture. Slowly stir in 3 cups of the graham flour. Beat vigorously for 1 minute, then stir in the remaining graham flour and the white flour. Let the dough rest for 15 to 30 minutes.

Turn out onto a lightly floured board and knead until smooth. Place in a lightly greased bowl, turn over to grease top, and cover lightly. Let rise in a warm place until doubled in bulk (1 to 3 hours). Shape into 2 loaves and place in two greased 5- by 9-inch loaf pans or the 8- or 9-inch round cake pans. Let rise again until almost doubled. Prick the loaves all over with a fork and bake in a moderately hot oven (375°) for 45 to 50 minutes or until they sound hollow when thumped with a finger. Makes 2 loaves.

OATMEAL BREAD   Kaurahiutaleleipä

This bread has a distinct toasted-oatmeal aroma and flavor when it is toasted. It is one of the simplest breads to make that you can find!

1 package active dry yeast
2 teaspoons salt
2¼ cups warm water

3 cups quick-cooking rolled oats,
   uncooked
3–4 cups white flour

Combine the yeast, salt, and water in a bowl, stirring until the yeast is dissolved. Stir in the oats and let the mixture stand for 30 minutes, or until it is very sticky when stirred. Slowly add enough flour, stirring all the while, to make a stiff dough. Turn out onto a floured board and knead until smooth and elastic. Be sure to add flour until the dough is no longer sticky, for the dough softens while it rises. Place the dough in a greased bowl, turn over to grease the top, and let rise in a warm place until doubled (from 1 to 3 hours). Shape into 2 round loaves, place on a buttered baking sheet, and prick all over with a fork. Let rise again until doubled. Bake in a moderately hot oven (375°) for 45 to 55 minutes or until golden brown. Brush with butter while hot and cool, covered lightly with clean towels, on racks. Makes 2 loaves.

■◯◢■◯◢■◯◢■◯◢■◯◢■◯◢■◯◢■◯◢■◯◢■◯◢■◯◢■◯◢■

WATER RINGS   Vesirinkilät

These rings, raised in hot salted water and then baked, resemble bagels. We were served Water Rings by a Karelian family every morning for breakfast. Serve them split and toasted, with butter and jam.

2 packages active dry yeast
1 teaspoon salt
1 cup warm water

4 tablespoons melted butter
3–3½ cups white flour

Dissolve the yeast and salt in the warm water. Add the butter and some of the flour, beating until the batter is smooth and elastic. Add the remaining flour, a little at a time, beating very well until the dough is stiff. Work in the last part of the flour with your hands—the dough should be very stiff but not dry. Turn it out onto a floured board and knead until smooth. Place in a lightly greased mixing bowl, turn to grease the top, cover lightly, and let rise in a warm place until doubled (from 1 to 3 hours). (You may wish to let the dough rise overnight in a cool kitchen. In that case, you can shape and bake the rings in the morning and serve them as a breakfast treat!)

Turn the dough out onto the board. Pinch off a piece about the size of a small egg and roll it between your hands and the floured board into a strand about 6 inches long. Shape this into a ring and dampen and pinch the edges together. Repeat this process until all the dough is used up. Place the rings on a sheet of lightly greased waxed paper and let them rise for about 30 minutes.

Have ready a kettle of boiling water (use 2 tablespoons salt to each quart of water). Lower the rings into the water one at a time, and place them on a very-well-greased baking sheet. Brush with a mixture of 1 tablespoon water and 1 tablespoon sugar, if desired. Bake in a hot oven (400°) for 20 minutes or until golden brown. Makes 16 to 18.

SALT HORNS   Soulasarvet

These are rich, crescent-shaped dinner rolls that are best served fresh and hot. But you can shape and freeze them, baking them just before serving, if you prefer.

1 package active dry yeast
½ cup warm water
1 cup heavy cream or milk
2 tablespoons butter (1/3 cup
   if you are using milk)
1 teaspoon salt

2½–3 cups white flour
½ cup soft butter (for spreading)
caraway seeds
beaten egg white
coarse salt

■☙■☙■☙■☙■☙■☙■☙■☙■☙■☙■☙■☙■☙■☙■☙■☙■

Dissolve the yeast in the warm water in a bowl. Heat the cream or milk to boiling and add the butter. Remove from heat. Cool to lukewarm, then add to the yeast mixture. Stir in the teaspoon salt and 1 cup of the flour, adding the last gradually, to keep the mixture smooth. Beat vigorously, then add the remaining flour to make a stiff dough. Let it rest for 15 minutes, then turn out onto a lightly floured board and knead until smooth. Put into a lightly greased bowl, turn to grease the top, cover, and let rise for 1 to 2 hours or until doubled.

Turn the risen dough out onto the board and roll out into a 16-inch circle. Spread the dough with the soft butter and cut into 8 wedges. Roll each wedge up, starting with the wide end, and shape into a crescent. Place on a lightly greased baking sheet, brush with the egg white, and sprinkle with the salt and caraway seeds. Let rise for 30 minutes, then bake in a moderately hot oven (375°) for 25 to 30 minutes or until golden. Makes 8.

SAFFRON RAISIN SCONES   Sahrammiskonssit

Golden scones, studded with raisins and topped with a sugary crust, are a breakfast or teatime treat. Or serve them for lunch with a salad.

pinch powdered Spanish saffron
3 tablespoons sugar
½ cup hot milk
2 cups sifted white flour

3 teaspoons baking powder
½ teaspoon salt
¼ cup butter
1 cup raisins

Stir the saffron and sugar into the hot milk until the saffron is completely dissolved and the milk is golden colored. Sift the flour with the baking powder and salt into a mixing bowl. Cut in the butter until the mixture is crumbly, and add the raisins, stirring until they are coated. Add the milk mixture all at once and stir until a stiff dough is formed. Knead lightly on a floured board until the dough is almost smooth. Divide into 2 parts. Shape each into a flat round loaf about 6 inches in diameter and ¾-inch thick. Place on a baking sheet, cut into quarters, and sprinkle with sugar. Separate the wedges slightly. Bake in a moderately hot oven (375°) for 20 to 25 minutes or until the scones are lightly browned but not baked so long that they are dry. Makes 8 scones.

■ᴑᴙᴄ■ᴑᴙᴄ■ᴑᴙᴄ■ᴑᴙᴄ■ᴑᴙᴄ■ᴑᴙᴄ■ᴑᴙᴄ■ᴑᴙᴄ■ᴑᴙᴄ■ᴑᴙᴄ■ᴑᴙᴄ■ᴑᴙᴄ■

BREAKFAST BUNS   Aamiaissämpylät

You can buy these buns at about nine in the morning at bread and milk shops in Helsinki. Finnish breakfast-time is usually from ten to eleven o'clock. Today although homemakers in Helsinki buy these buns still hot from the bakery, in the country the early-rising housewife bakes them herself.

2 cups milk
1 package active dry yeast
¼ cup warm water
½ cup graham flour
6–6½ cups white flour
¼ cup melted butter

3 tablespoons dark corn syrup
  or light molasses
1 teaspoon salt
¼ cup currants or raisins
1 cup (approximately) crushed loaf
  sugar or granulated sugar

Scald the milk; cool to lukewarm. Add the yeast to the warm water, stirring until dissolved. Pour the milk into large mixing bowl with the dissolved yeast. Add the graham flour and about 2 cups of the white flour, beating well. Cover the bowl lightly and let the dough rise in a warm place until spongy (about 45 minutes).

Stir down and add the melted butter, syrup or molasses, salt, and currants or raisins. Add the remaining flour and mix until the dough is stiff. Turn out onto a lightly floured board and knead until smooth. Place in a lightly greased mixing bowl, cover, and let rise again in a warm place until doubled in bulk (about 1 hour).

Turn the dough out onto a floured board, cut off pieces (each about the size of an egg), and shape into buns. Place on well-buttered baking sheets 3 to 4 inches apart, and let rise until doubled (about 30 minutes). Brush the buns with warm water. With a sharp knife or razor blade, cut an X in the top of each bun and sprinkle about 1 teaspoon sugar on each cut. Bake in a hot oven (400°) for 15 to 20 minutes or until golden brown. Brush the buns again with water when they are removed from oven. Makes about 24 buns.

FINNISH BUTTERMILK KORPPU   Piimäkorppu

Varieties of Finnish korppu or rusks are numerous. The most common home-made toast is made from leftover pulla or coffee bread (see *index*) on Saturday, when the new batch of pulla is usually baked. Serve korppu as the Finns do, as an accompaniment to coffee. Finns dunk korppu into coffee

■⁊■⁊■⁊■⁊■⁊■⁊■⁊■⁊■⁊■⁊■⁊■⁊■⁊■⁊■

to best savor the flavor of both the bread and coffee. Dunking is considered quite proper—even in public coffee shops—for the daintiest of coffee drinkers.

1 package active dry yeast
¼ cup warm water
1 cup lukewarm buttermilk
1 egg, beaten
¼ teaspoon salt
1 cup sugar

¼ teaspoon finely crushed
   anise seed
¼ teaspoon finely crushed
   fennel seed
¼ cup melted butter
3–3½ cups flour

Dissolve the yeast in the water in a large bowl. Add the buttermilk, egg, salt, sugar, crushed seed, and butter. Stir in the flour gradually, beating well. When the dough is stiff, turn it out onto a floured board and knead until smooth. Place in a lightly greased mixing bowl turning to grease top, cover lightly, and let rise in a warm place until doubled in bulk (about 1 hour).

Turn the dough out onto the board and shape into 2 loaves about 2 inches in diameter and 10 inches long, place on a greased baking sheet, and let rise again in a warm place for 15 to 30 minutes or until doubled. Brush with milk. Bake in a moderately hot oven (375°) for 20 minutes or until lightly browned. Remove from the oven and cool on a wire rack. Cut the loaves into ½- to 1-inch slices and place these on a baking sheet or wire rack. Return to the oven (which has been turned off) and toast until lightly golden on both sides. Makes about 3 dozen pieces.

RYE SCONES   Ruisskonssit

Rye Scones are quick to make and an ideal suggestion for breakfast or for afternoon coffee or tea. Baking powder is the leavening agent.

½ cup rye flour
1½ cups white flour
2 teaspoons baking powder
½ teaspoon salt

¼ cup butter
1 tablespoon molasses
¾ cup milk

Sift together the rye flour, white flour, baking powder, and salt into a large bowl. Cut in the butter until the mixture is crumbly. Combine the molasses and milk and add, stirring with a fork until the dough forms a ball. Divide into 2 parts. Shape each into a smooth ball and place on a lightly floured board, patting into a thick round loaf about 7 inches in diameter. Place on a lightly greased baking sheet and cut into eighths with a knife. Prick all over with a fork. Bake in a moderately hot oven (375°) for 30 to 35 minutes or until lightly browned. Serve hot with butter and jam. Makes 8 generous servings.

■❧■❧■❧■❧■❧■❧■❧■❧■❧■❧■❧■❧■❧■❧■❧■

QUICK KORPPU   Pienet Vehnäkorput

These tasty rusks are leavened with baking powder and are an ideal addition to the coffee table.

½ cup butter	1½ teaspoons baking powder
1 cup sugar	1 teaspoon grated orange peel
2 eggs	2½ cups flour
¼ teaspoon salt	

Cream the butter and sugar together until light and lemon colored. Beat in the eggs. Add the salt, baking powder, orange peel, and flour to the mixture, beating well. Turn the dough out onto a lightly floured board and knead until smooth (about 2 minutes). Shape into balls the size of large walnuts and place 2 inches apart on lightly greased baking sheets. Bake in a hot oven (400°) for 15 minutes or until lightly browned. Tear the buns apart (like English muffins) while hot, then put them back on the baking sheets, turn the oven down to 350°, and bake until they are dried and lightly browned. Makes about 24 pieces.

CINNAMON KORPPU   Kanelikorppu

Make like Quick Korppu (above), but before the second baking, sprinkle each torn surface with a mixture of ⅓ cup sugar and 1 tablespoon cinnamon.

II. The Coffee Table

The coffee table, elaborately laid out with baked items ranging from yeast coffee breads to fancy filled cakes, is the Finnish way to entertain guests. It is most elaborate if the guests or the occasion is important. The usual custom is to serve seven baked items, the three main items being pulla (a yeast bread), an uniced pound cake, and a fancy filled cake, and the other four an array of cookies balanced in flavor, variety, and richness.

There is a coffee table for every occasion: after sauna, called *sauna kahvi*; after church—*kirkko kahvi*; on Christmas—*Joulu kahvi*; on Easter—*Pääsiäis kahvi*. The coffee table also appears on celebration days such as birthdays, name days, anniversaries, weddings, and christenings—and even after funerals.

■᠔᠔■᠔᠔■᠔᠔■᠔᠔■᠔᠔■᠔᠔■᠔᠔■᠔᠔■᠔᠔■᠔᠔■᠔᠔■᠔᠔■᠔᠔■᠔᠔■᠔᠔■᠔᠔■

It is almost national law that you do not leave a home without being offered a cup of coffee. It is almost equally important that you be offered something to "go with" the coffee. Pulla (the cardamon-flavored, sweet braided yeast bread) is always on hand in the Finnish home; it is always a part of "morning coffee." It may be the sole accompaniment when the coffee table is set for the family or for drop-in guests—but there is always something!

For guests, the coffee table is always set with the finest coffee cups in the house. The settings include a bread-and-butter plate placed beneath the cup and saucer before the person is served, and a tiny coffee spoon. A bowlful of lump sugar, a pitcher of cream, and a vase of flowers make the table complete.

A ritual built through tradition governs the eating. With the first cup of coffee, guests take pulla, along with a cooky or two; with the second cup, the uniced cake and a cooky or two; with the third cup, as a grand finale and the last course, a piece of the filled, decorated cake. With the fourth cup of coffee it is permissible to sample the items missed, or you may simply sip the coffee through a lump of sugar which you hold between your teeth. It is considered polite—and a great compliment to the hostess—to taste all of the items on the table.

APOSTLE'S CAKE   Apostolinkakku

In the past, this cake was made for the Apostle's Days—June 29 and November 30. Today it is classified with the Christmas cake shapes.

Prepare Pulla Yeast Coffee Bread dough (below) and divide into three portions (each will make 1 Apostle's cake). Divide each portion into 2 parts and roll each of these into a thin strand about 36 inches long (the dough is easier to handle if it is chilled overnight). Lay the first strand on a lightly greased baking sheet in the shape of a deep S. Lay the second strand in another S shape crosswise over the first, weaving them together in a lattice fashion (*see illustration*). Let rise for 30 minutes, then brush with beaten egg and bake in a hot oven (400°) for 20 to 25 minutes or until golden. Decorate each cake with 12 candles stuck into the openings. Makes 3 cakes.

APOSTLE'S CAKE

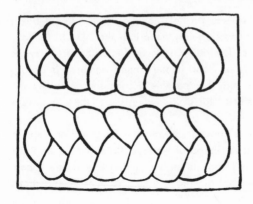

PULLA YEAST COFFEE BREAD

PULLA YEAST COFFEE BREAD   Pulla (Pitko)

Do not expect pulla to be light and fluffy; it is a moist rich coffee bread. It is served without butter and is a delight when it is hot. The Finnish housewife usually bakes on Saturday so there will be fresh pulla for Sunday morning coffee.

A straight braid is the standard form for pulla, but the braided pulla dough is often shaped into a wreath for special occasions such as name days, birthdays, anniversaries, or other honor celebrations. (In Finland, one's "name day" or saint's day—the day that bears the name of the saint after whom one is named—is celebrated by adults instead of the birthday. Children, however, do celebrate birthdays.)

Note: Observe carefully the order of combining the ingredients. The melted butter is added *after* about half of the flour.

1 package active dry yeast
½ cup warm water
2 cups milk, scalded and cooled
   to lukewarm
1 cup (or less) sugar
1 teaspoon salt

7–8 whole cardamom pods, seeded
   and crushed (about 1 teaspoon)
4 eggs, beaten
8–9 cups sifted white flour
½ cup melted butter

Glaze

1 egg, beaten
½ cup chopped or sliced almonds
   (optional)

½ cup crushed lump sugar
   (optional)

Dissolve the yeast in the warm water. Stir in the milk, sugar, salt, cardamom, eggs, and enough flour to make a batter (about 2 cups). Beat until the dough is smooth and elastic. Add about 3 cups of the flour and beat well; the dough should be quite smooth and glossy in appearance. Add the melted butter and stir in well. Beat again until the dough looks glossy. Stir in the remaining flour until a stiff dough forms.

Turn out onto a lightly floured board and cover with an inverted mixing bowl. Let the dough rest 15 minutes. Knead until smooth and satiny. Place in a lightly greased mixing bowl, turn the dough to grease the top, cover lightly, and let rise in a warm place (about 85°) until doubled in bulk (about 1 hour). Punch down and let rise again until almost doubled (about 30 minutes).

Turn out again onto a slightly floured board, divide into 3 parts, then divide each of these parts into 3. Shape each into a strip about 16 inches long by rolling the dough between the palms and the board. Braid the 3 strips together into a straight loaf, pinch the ends together, and tuck under. Repeat for the second and third loaves. Lift the braids onto lightly greased baking sheets. Let rise for about 20 minutes (the braids should be puffy but not doubled in size).

Glaze the loaves by brushing with the beaten egg, and if you wish, sprinkle with the crushed sugar and the almonds.

Bake in a hot oven (400°) 25 to 30 minutes. Do not overbake or the loaves will be too dry. Remove from the oven when a light golden-brown. Makes 3 braids. Slice to serve.

BISHOP'S WIG

BISHOP'S WIG   Papintukka

Prepare Pulla Yeast Coffee Bread dough (see index), divide into 3 portions (each will make 1 Bishop's Wig), and divide each portion into 3 parts. Roll each of these parts into a strand about 18 inches long. Fold the first strand in half and place on a lightly greased baking sheet, curling each end upward. Place the second strand next to the first strand so that the curled ends are just above those of the first. Repeat with the third strand (see illustration). Let rise for 30 minutes, brush with beaten egg, and bake in a hot oven (400°) for 20 to 25 minutes or until golden. If you wish, you may decorate the "curls" with halved cherries or raisins before baking. Makes 3 "wigs."

■෧෨■෧෨■෧෨■෧෨■෧෨■෧෨■෧෨■෧෨■෧෨■෧෨■෧෨■෧෨■෧෨■෧෨■

CHRISTMAS STAR

CHRISTMAS STAR   Joulutähti

Make 1 recipe of Pulla Yeast Coffee Bread (see index). Chill overnight for easy handling. Divide the dough into 3 portions (use 1 portion for each star). Divide each portion of dough into 2 parts, and roll each into a thin strand about 40 inches long. Twist the strands together into a long rope and shape into a star (see illustration). Place on a lightly greased baking sheet, let rise for 30 minutes in a warm place, and bake in a hot oven (400°) for 20 to 25 minutes or until golden brown. Makes 3 stars.

CHRISTMAS CROSSES

CHRISTMAS CROSSES   Jouluristit

Make 1 recipe of Pulla Yeast Coffee Bread (see index) and divide into 3 portions (1 portion will make 24 Christmas Crosses). Pinch off balls of the dough (each about the size of a large walnut) and roll between the palms and board into strands about 5 inches long. To shape each cross, use 2 strands (see illustration). Place the crosses on a lightly greased baking sheet, let rise for 30 minutes in a warm place, and bake in a hot oven (400°) for 15 or 20 minutes or until golden.

GOLDEN CHARIOTS

GOLDEN CHARIOTS   Kultavaunut

Make 1 recipe of Pulla Yeast Coffee Bread (see index). Divide the dough into 3 parts (each part will make 1 cake). Divide each portion of dough into

4 parts, rolling each on a board into a strand about 12 inches long. Place the 4 strands on a lightly greased baking sheet, in spoke fashion and turn ends to curl (*see illustration*). Brush with beaten egg, let rise for 30 minutes in a warm place, and bake in a hot oven (400°) for 25 to 30 minutes or until golden. Makes 3 chariots.

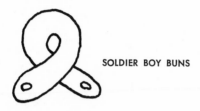

SOLDIER BOY BUNS

SOLDIER BOY BUNS   Sotilaspojat

Make 1 recipe of Pulla Yeast Coffee Bread (*see index*) and divide it into 3 parts (1 portion will make 24 Soldier Boy Buns). Pinch off balls of the dough (each about the size of a large egg), and roll between your palms and the lightly floured board into strands about 12 inches long. Arrange each on a greased baking sheet in a loop (*see illustration*) and press raisins or cherries into the end of the dough. Let rise for 30 minutes, then brush with beaten egg and bake in a hot oven (400°) for 15 to 20 minutes or until golden.

CHRISTMAS "PIGS"

CHRISTMAS "PIGS"   Joulu Porsaat

Make 1 recipe of Pulla Yeast Coffee Bread (*see index*). Pinch off balls of the dough (each about the size of a large egg) and roll between your palms and the lightly floured board into strands about 12 inches long. Arrange these on a greased baking sheet in the form of an S (*see illustration*). Let rise for 30 minutes in a warm place, brush with beaten egg, and bake in a hot oven (400°) for 15 to 20 minutes or until golden. One-third of the pulla dough will make 24 Christmas "Pigs."

CHRISTMAS BUNS

CHRISTMAS BUNS   Joulupulla

Make 1 recipe of Pulla Yeast Coffee Bread (see *index*). Pinch off balls of dough (each about the size of a large egg). For the two-part bun (see *illustration*), divide the pieces of dough in two, and roll each part into a strand about 12 inches long. Place the strands side by side on a greased baking sheet, curling the ends toward the centers. For the one-piece bun, (see *illustration*), shape the egg-sized piece of dough into a single thick strand about 12 inches long, then, with sharp knife, split both ends (for about 4 inches) toward the center. Curl the split ends toward the center and press raisins down the middle of the 4-inch uncut portion of the bun. Place the buns on a lightly greased baking sheet, and let rise in a warm place for 30 minutes. Brush with beaten egg, and bake in a hot oven (400°) for 15 to 20 minutes. One-third of the pulla dough recipe makes 24 buns.

LUCIA'S CROWN

LUCIA'S CROWN   Luciankruunu

This cake represents especially the Swedish-speaking portion of Finland's population, which has many traditions and foods similar to those of Sweden. It is one of the classic cakes served on Lucia's Day, December 10.

Make 1 recipe Pulla Yeast Coffee Bread and divide the dough into 3 parts (you will use 1 part for each cake). Divide each third of dough into 9 parts, and roll each of these into a strand about 15 inches long. Twist 2 of the strands together in ropelike fashion and arrange in a curve (see *illustration*) on a greased baking sheet. Curl up the remaining 7 strands and lay them along the outside edge of the twisted curve of dough. Let rise in a warm place for 30 minutes, brush with beaten egg, and bake in a hot oven (400°) for 25 to 30 minutes or until golden brown. Makes 3 crowns.

Note: This cake is often made of saffron-flavored yeast dough. (See *Saffron Buns in index.*)

FANCY CHRISTMAS CAKES   Joulukakut

Make 1 recipe of Pulla Yeast Coffee Bread (*see index*) and use half of the dough to make any of the following cakes. They are usually served on fancy Christmas coffee tables. The dough is easiest to shape when it is chilled.

I

Divide the pulla dough (half of the total recipe) into 2 parts. Shape 1 part into a large, flat loaf, perfectly round and about 12 inches in diameter, and place on a lightly greased baking sheet. Divide remaining dough into 3 parts, rolling each into a very thin strand about 48 inches long. Cut off a 4-inch piece from the end of each and reserve. Braid the long strands and place onto the flat round in a circle (*see illustration*). Shape each 4-inch piece of dough into an S and place it on the center of the cake. Let rise in a warm place for 30 minutes, brush with beaten egg, and bake in a hot oven (400°) for 25 to 30 minutes or until golden. Makes 1 cake.

FANCY CHRISTMAS CAKES

II

Divide the pulla dough (half of the total recipe) into 7 parts and roll these into strands about 12 inches long. Curl up each strand. Place the first curl in the center of a lightly greased baking sheet and arrange the remaining curls in a closed circle around it (*see illustration*). Let rise in a warm place for 30 minutes, brush with beaten egg, and bake in a hot oven (400°) for 25 to 30 minutes or until golden. Makes 1 cake.

FANCY CHRISTMAS CAKES

■◎◈■◎◈■◎◈■◎◈■◎◈■◎◈■◎◈■◎◈■◎◈■◎◈■◎◈■◎◈■

III

Use half of the total recipe of pulla dough. Reserve about 1 cup of the dough, then roll the remaining dough into a round about 12 inches in diameter. Place on greased baking sheet. Divide the reserved dough into 4 parts and roll into strands 6 inches long. Shape each into an S and arrange around the edges of the rolled-out dough (see *illustration*). Let rise in a warm place for 30 minutes. Brush with beaten egg. With a sharp knife or razor blade, cut lines to simulate the outline of a Christmas tree in the center of the loaf. Sprinkle the cake with crushed loaf sugar and finely chopped almonds if you wish. Bake in a hot oven (400°) for 25 to 30 minutes or until golden brown. Makes 1 cake.

FANCY NAME-DAY RING

FANCY NAME-DAY RING   Hieno Nimipäivärinkilä

The name-day—the day of the saint whose name a person bears—is the day commonly observed in Finland in place of the birthday after, say, the twenty-fifth birthday or so. A name-day celebration is typically more elaborate the older the honored person is.

This fancy bread is braided and shaped into a large wreath (as large as the baking pan will allow). It is traditionally served sliced, with the center filled with pepper cookies.

Make 1 recipe of Pulla Yeast Coffee Bread (see *index*) but increase the sugar to 1½ cups and the butter to ¾–1 cup. Shape the pulla into 1 large ring about 24 inches in diameter (if you have a baking sheet large enough to hold it). Place on a lightly greased baking sheet, brush with the beaten egg, and sprinkle with the sliced almonds and crushed sugar. Bake in a hot oven (400°) for 25 to 30 minutes.

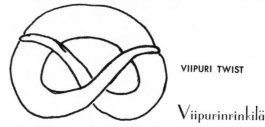

VIIPURI TWIST

VIIPURI TWIST   Viipurinrinkilä

This traditional Christmas bread is named after Viipuri, a city which is now within the Russian border. Karelians still think of Viipuri as "their" city. It was the center of a great world of specialty foods, particularly pastries and pasties.

The authentic method of making the Viipuri Twist was quite difficult. After the strip of dough was shaped into a pretzel-like twist, it was placed in a kettle of boiling water for a few minutes, then removed and baked on clean oat straw. The result was a bread with a hard crust and soft center. The oat straw imparted a special flavor and also kept the bread from sticking to the pan. Today the boiling water and oat straw are omitted, though it may be fun to try using them sometime. The method given here results in a softer-crusted bread.

1 package active dry yeast
¼ cup warm water
2 eggs, beaten
1 cup sugar
2 cups milk, scalded and cooled
2 teaspoons ground cardamom

1 teaspoon ground nutmeg
1½ teaspoons salt
7⅛–8 cups sifted white flour
¼ cup melted butter

1 egg, beaten (for glaze)

Dissolve the yeast in the warm water. In a mixing bowl, combine the yeast with the 2 eggs, sugar, milk, cardamom, nutmeg, and salt. Mix until well blended. Gradually add 4 cups of the flour, beating well to keep the dough very smooth and satiny. Add the melted butter and mix well. Add the remaining flour, mixing with the hands to form a very stiff dough. Knead until smooth on a lightly floured board.

Place the dough in a lightly greased mixing bowl, turning it to grease the top, and let rise in a warm place until doubled (about 1 hour). Punch down and let rise again for about 30 minutes.

Divide the dough into 3 portions; roll each between the palms and board until you have a long strip no more than 1 inch in diameter. Shape each strip into a large pretzel and place on a greased baking sheet. Let rise in a warm place about 15 minutes (not until doubled). Brush with beaten egg and bake in a hot oven (400°) about 25 to 30 minutes or until a light

■૯ঌ■૯ঌ■૯ঌ■૯ঌ■૯ঌ■૯ঌ■૯ঌ■૯ঌ■૯ঌ■૯ঌ■૯ঌ■૯ঌ■

golden-brown. Do not overbake. Serve thinly sliced with tea or coffee, or for breakfast. In Finland, the Viipuri Twist is commonly baked for the Christmas coffee table. Makes 3 twists.

EASTER BREAD   Pääsiäisleipä

Easter foods are rich with dairy products—butter, eggs, and milk. The fruits used in Easter breads vary according to the tastes of families. This bread is baked in straight-sided round pans such as soufflé dishes, or in 1-pound coffee cans or in a 4-quart pail. Pääsiäisleipä is Karelian in origin.

2 packages active dry yeast
¼ cup warm water
3 cups milk, scalded and cooled
   to lukewarm
7–7½ cups white flour
4 egg yolks
1 cup sugar
1 teaspoon salt

2 teaspoons crushed cardamom
3 tablespoons chopped candied
   orange peel
1 tablespoon grated lemon peel
½ cup chopped raisins
½ cup chopped almonds
1 cup butter, melted

Frosting

2 cups sifted confectioners' sugar
4 tablespoons cold water
   (approximately)

few drops almond flavoring

Dissolve the yeast in the warm water. Combine 2 cups of the milk and the yeast mixture. Sift in 2 cups of the flour. Beat until smooth and elastic, cover, and let rise until light and spongy (about 45 minutes). Beat the egg yolks and sugar together until light and fluffy; add to the spongy mixture, mixing well. Add the salt, cardamom, orange peel, lemon peel, raisins, and almonds. Beat in the remaining cup of milk and the melted butter. Add the remaining flour slowly, stirring until a stiff dough is formed. Turn it out onto a lightly floured board and knead until smooth. Place in a lightly greased mixing bowl, turn to grease the top, cover, and let rise in a warm place until doubled in bulk (about 1 hour).

Grease 3 baking dishes or coffee cans and dust with sugar or grease one 4-quart-sized aluminum pail. Fill these only half full and let rise in a warm place until almost even with the rim of the pan (the dough will rise rapidly). Bake in a moderate oven (350°) for 60 minutes or until golden brown. Test for doneness using a wooden skewer or cake tester. Let the loaves cool in the pans.

After the bread is removed from pans they may be decorated with a mixture of the confectioners' sugar, water, and almond flavoring. Drizzle

■❀■❀■❀■❀■❀■❀■❀■❀■❀■❀■❀■❀■❀■❀■❀■❀■

frosting on the top and sides of the loaves. To serve, cut the bread into wedges and cut each wedge into thin slices (crosswise, to form triangular slices). Makes 3 loaves the size of 1-pound coffee cans, or 1 large loaf if you bake it in the pail.

VIENNA BREAD   Vienerleipätaikina

In the Scandinavian countries, Danish pastry, for some curious reason, is called Vienna Bread. The Finnish version is typically less sweet than the same pastry found in the other Scandinavian countries. This pastry can be made in a variety of shapes and fillings. All are fun to make.

Note: This dough is put to rise in a cool place (less than 85°). You may find it difficult to make on a hot day.

1½ cups soft butter	1 cup cold milk
4½–5 cups flour	1 egg
2 packages active dry yeast	3 tablespoons sugar
¼ cup warm water	½ teaspoon salt

Mix together the butter and a ½ cup of the flour until well blended. Let stand in the refrigerator while you prepare the yeast dough.

Dissolve the yeast in the water in a mixing bowl. Add the milk, egg, sugar, and salt, and mix until blended. Stir in enough of the remaining flour to form a fairly stiff dough. Turn out onto a lightly floured board and knead until well mixed and smooth.

Roll the dough out to a rectangle about 6 by 12 inches. Roll out the butter-and-flour mixture to a rectangle about 6 by 6 inches and place this on top of the rolled-out yeast dough, with three of the edges meeting (so that only half the dough is covered). Turn the other half of the yeast dough over the butter-and-flour mixture to encase it. Pinch the edges together to seal them completely. With a rolling pin, lightly pound the dough (to start the stretching), then roll it lightly to a rectangle about 12 by 16 inches. Fold one-third of the dough over the center, and the remaining one-third of dough over that (as you would fold a letter). Chill the dough in the refrigerator for 30 minutes, or in the freezer for 10 minutes (not longer; you must not freeze it). Remove the dough from the refrigerator, pound it lightly on the floured board with the rolling pin, roll it into a 16-inch square, and then fold it into thirds, as before. Chill once more. Repeat the pounding, rolling, folding, and chilling processes three times more. After the final chilling, roll the dough out into a large rectangle (24 by 36 inches). Cut, fill, and bake the dough according to the following directions.

■◎◢■◎◢■◎◢■◎◢■◎◢■◎◢■◎◢■◎◢■◎◢■◎◢■◎◢■◎◢■◎◢■

I. Envelopes (Kirjekuoreet)

Cut the dough into 4-inch squares. Place about ½ teaspoon cold butter in the center of each square and sprinkle with 1 teaspoon sugar. Fold the dough into a rectangular shape over the butter and sugar filling. Place on a lightly greased baking sheet and let rise in a cool place for 45 minutes. Bake in a moderately hot oven (375°) for 8 to 12 minutes. One recipe makes 54.

II. Combs (Kammat)

Cut the dough into rectangles 2 inches by 4 inches. On one of the long sides of each rectangle make several cuts about 1 inch deep and ½ inch apart. Turn the dough so the cut edge fans out, and place on a lightly greased baking sheet. Sprinkle each comb with 1 teaspoon sugar. Let the combs rise in a cool place for 45 minutes, then bake in a moderately hot oven (375°) for 8 to 12 minutes or until golden. One recipe makes 108.

III. Packages (Paketit)

Cut the dough into 4-inch squares. Turn two opposite corners toward the center and dot the dough with ½ teaspoon jam just where the corners meet. Place on a lightly greased baking sheet and let rise in a cool place for 45 minutes. Bake in a moderately hot oven (375°) for 8 to 12 minutes or until golden. One recipe makes 54.

IV. Figure Eights (Pormestarin Palmikat)

Cut the dough into strips about 1 inch wide and 6 inches long. Twist each strip and form it into a figure eight. Place on a lightly greased baking sheet and let rise in a cool place for 45 minutes. Bake in a moderately hot oven (375°) for 8 to 12 minutes or until golden. One recipe makes 12 dozen.

V. Butter Cake (Voikakku)

Use only half of the total dough for this cake.

Cut a round of the rolled-out dough to fit the bottom of a 9- or 10-inch springform pan. Butter the pan lightly and sprinkle it with sugar. Place the dough in the pan. Roll the remaining dough into a rectangle about 12 by 16 inches and sprinkle with a mixture of ¼ cup sugar and 2 tablespoons cinnamon. Roll up like a jelly roll. Slice off 1-inch pieces and place them, cut side up, side by side on top of the dough in the pan. Let the cake rise in a cool place for about 45 minutes, then bake in a moderately hot (375°) oven for 35 to 40 minutes or until golden.

VI. Vienna Horns (Vienersarvi)

Cut the rolled-out dough into long narrow strips (about 16 inches by 3 inches). Fill the strips with a mixture of ½ cup ground almonds, ¼ cup sugar, and ¼ cup soft butter, or with a cup of your favorite jam. Turn the edges of the strips up to keep the filling from overflowing during the baking. Place the strips on a lightly greased baking sheet, curving them into half-circles. Let rise for 45 minutes in a cool place. Bake in a moderately hot oven (375°) for about 30 minutes or until lightly golden brown. One recipe of pastry makes 3 to 5 Vienna Horns, depending on their length.

LENTEN BUNS   Laskiaispullat

These buns appear in the bakeries during Lent. In the old days, the Church prohibited the eating of dairy foods during Lent, so these buns were made to use up all the eggs, butter, milk, and whipped cream still on hand, and they were eaten the day before Ash Wednesday. The custom then was to serve them, filled with almond paste and whipped cream, floating in a bowl of hot (perhaps sweetened) milk, but today they are served as a coffee bread. Curiously, modern Lenten foods are rich in dairy products—just the reverse of the old tradition.

1 recipe Pulla Yeast Coffee Bread *(see index)*   1 egg, beaten,   sugar

Filling

½ cup butter,   1 cup sugar   1 cup heavy cream
1 cup ground almonds   confectioners' sugar

Prepare the pulla dough, let rise as usual, then shape it into buns, using about ½ cup of the dough (a piece the size of a large egg) for each bun. Place the buns, smooth side up, on a lightly greased baking sheet and let rise for 15 to 20 minutes in a warm place. Brush with the egg and sprinkle with a few grains of sugar. Bake in a hot oven (400°) for 15 minutes or until lightly golden brown.

Meanwhile, prepare the filling. Cream together the butter and the sugar until light and fluffy. Add the almonds and mix well. In another bowl, whip the cream until stiff. When the buns are cool, slice about ½ inch off the tops. Pull out a small amount of the inside and fill the cavity with about 1 tablespoonful of the ground-almond mixture. Top with a dab of whipped cream. Cap with the cut-off piece of bun and dust with the confectioners' sugar. Serve with coffee. Makes about 36 buns.

SAFFRON BUNS (LUCIA BUNS)

SAFFRON BUNS (LUCIA BUNS)   Sahrammileipä

The Swedish-speaking population of Finland claims the saffron Christmas breads for its very own. The breads first appear on St. Lucia's Day, December 12, a day of special celebration, when "little Lucia"—each classroom dubs one of its girls "Lucia"—presents her teacher with these special buns, ginger cookies, and coffee at some time during the school day. In villages where Swedo-Finns are in high concentration, there is usually a "Lucia Day Parade," with one girl from the entire community chosen to represent Lucia.

These golden saffron buns are served with coffee during the Christmas season. The dough can, of course, be baked in any shape you desire, including the traditional coffee braid or tea ring.

1 egg	2 cups milk, scalded and cooled to
⅔ cup sugar	lukewarm
1 package active dry yeast	dash powdered saffron
¼ cup warm water	7½–8 cups white flour
1 teaspoon salt	¼ cup melted butter

Glaze
½ cup strong coffee   4 tablespoons sugar

Beat together the egg and the sugar. Dissolve the yeast in the water. Add the salt to the milk, then add the saffron (this is very potent, so use just the smallest amount). Combine the egg, yeast, and milk mixtures in a large mixing bowl. Slowly beat in 4 cups of the flour, keeping the batter smooth and elastic. Stir in the butter, then add the remaining flour, mixing until a stiff dough is formed. Turn out onto a floured board and knead until smooth.

Place the dough in a lightly greased mixing bowl, turning it to grease the top, and let rise until doubled in bulk (about 1 to 1½ hours). Punch down. Cover, and let rise again until doubled.

To shape into Lucia Buns, pinch off pieces of the dough about the size of small oranges and roll into strands about 6 inches long and 1 inch in diameter. With a sharp knife, cut the dough from both ends toward the center, leaving about ½ inch uncut in the center. Turn each end out and up toward the middle; the bun will look like a four-leaf clover. Put a raisin in the center of each "leaf." Place the buns on a lightly greased baking sheet and let rise about 20 minutes or until puffy but not doubled. Bake in a moderately hot over (375°) for 20 to 25 minutes or until golden brown.

Prepare the glaze by bringing to a boil the coffee and the sugar; stir until dissolved. Remove from heat and brush on the buns while they are still hot. Makes 36 buns.

QUICK YEAST COFFEE BREAD   Peltileipä

This coffee bread can be made within two hours from start to finish. It is best served freshly baked and hot.

1 package active dry yeast
¼ cup warm water
2 cups milk, scalded and cooled
    to lukewarm
1 teaspoon salt

1 cup sugar
2 eggs, beaten
5 cups white flour
½ cup melted butter

Topping
¾ cup melted butter
¾ cup brown sugar, well packed

½ cup sifted white flour
½ cup sliced almonds

Dissolve the yeast in the water in a large mixing bowl. Add the milk, salt, sugar, eggs, and 3 cups of the flour. Beat well until smooth and elastic. Add the ½ cup melted butter and beat until it is well combined. Slowly add the remaining flour, beating until very smooth. Cover, and let rise in a warm place for 30 minutes or until almost doubled in bulk. Stir down and turn out onto buttered jelly-roll pan, about 12 by 16 inches.

Spread the ¾ cup melted butter over the dough, then sprinkle it evenly with a mixture of the brown sugar, flour, and almonds. Let rise for about 30 minutes. Bake in a moderately hot oven (375°) for 20 minutes or until golden brown. Cut into squares to serve.

■❦■❦■❦■❦■❦■❦■❦■❦■❦■❦■❦■❦■❦■❦■❦■❦■

YEAST COFFEE CAKE   Vehnäskakku

This is a rich coffee cake made with yeast batter and having a crunchy topping. Serve it hot, or serve it toasted on the second day.

1 package active dry yeast
¼ cup warm water
1 cup light cream or undiluted
  evaporated milk
1 egg, slightly beaten

½ teaspoon salt
¾ cup sugar
4 cups white flour
½ cup soft butter

Topping
2 tablespoons melted butter
cinnamon
sugar

½ cup sliced almonds or chopped
  nuts

Dissolve the yeast in the water in a bowl and add the cream, eggs, salt, and sugar. Stir in half the flour, beating until smooth, then stir in the soft butter and the remaining flour. Beat well. Cover and let rise in a warm place until doubled (about 2 hours). Turn the dough into a buttered fancy mold (about 2-quart size) or one large cake pan (about 9 by 12 inches) or two 5- by 9-inch bread pans that have been well greased and dusted with sugar. Spread the melted butter over the top and sprinkle generously with the sugar, cinnamon, and nuts. Let rise again until doubled. Bake in a moderately hot oven (375°) for 35 to 45 minutes or until the cake is golden brown and has pulled away from the sides of the pan. Makes 1 large or 2 smaller cakes.

CINNAMON AND RAISIN COFFEE BREAD
Kaneli Rusina Pitko

This coffee bread is made with whole-wheat flour and has a swirl of cinnamon and raisins in each spicy slice. The recipe uses no shortening.

2 packages active dry yeast
2 cups warm water
½ cup sugar
1 teaspoon salt
6–7 cups whole-wheat flour
½ cup cream or undiluted
  evaporated milk

3 tablespoons molasses
1 teaspoon ginger
½ teaspoon cloves
1 cup raisins
cinnamon sugar (½ cup sugar
  blended with 2 teaspoons
  cinnamon)

Glaze
2 tablespoons molasses

2 tablespoons water

Dissolve the yeast in the warm water, add the sugar, salt, and half the flour, and beat vigorously. Stir in the cream or milk, molasses, ginger, cloves, and most of the remainder of the flour—add the last slowly—to make a smooth stiff dough. Let it rest for 15 to 30 minutes, then turn out onto a lightly floured board and knead until smooth, adding more flour, if necessary, to keep the dough from sticking. Place in a lightly greased bowl, turn the dough to grease the top, cover, and let rise in a warm place until doubled (about 45 minutes). Turn out again onto a lightly floured board and roll out into a rectangle about 12 by 18 inches. Sprinkle with the raisins and cinnamon sugar, and roll up, jelly-roll fashion. Cut the roll into 2 even pieces and place each in a well-greased oblong bread pan (or cut into 1-inch slices and place them, cut side down, close together in a 12- by 16-inch greased pan), cover, and let rise again until almost doubled (about 45 minutes). Before baking, brush the loaves (or rolls) with the mixture of molasses and water. Bake the loaves in a moderately hot oven (375°) for 45 to 55 minutes (bake the rolls 30 to 35 minutes). Makes 2 loaves (or about 18 pan rolls).

GOOD BASIC SWEET YEAST DOUGH   Vehnänen

This is a good basic dough from which many of the everyday yeast rolls and coffee cakes are made.

1 package active dry yeast	¾ cup sugar
¼ cup warm water	1½ teaspoons salt
2 cups whole milk, light cream, or	6–7 cups white flour
half-and-half cream, scalded and	½ cup butter, melted and cooled
cooled to lukewarm, or 2 cups undiluted evaporated milk,	
heated to lukewarm	

Dissolve the yeast in the water and add the milk, sugar, salt, and half the flour. Beat vigorously for 1 minute. Stir in the butter until well combined and enough of the remaining flour to make a stiff dough. Turn out onto a board and knead until smooth (about 10 minutes). Place the dough in a greased bowl, turn it to grease the top, cover, and let rise in a warm place until doubled (this may take as much as 2 to 3 hours when the weather is cool).

Shape the dough in the manner called for in the following recipes or into the traditional shapes for dinner rolls—cloverleaf, Parker House, fantan, pinwheel, or any of the other classics. Place on a greased baking sheet and let rise until almost doubled. Bake in a moderately hot oven (375°) for 20 to 25 minutes or until golden. Makes about 3 dozen rolls.

CINNAMON EARS   Korvapuustit

These individual, cinnamon-filled rolls are good to serve for breakfast or with coffee.

Roll out 1 recipe of Good Basic Sweet Yeast Dough (above) into a rectangle 24 by 36 inches (or halve the recipe dough and roll out to about 12 by 18 inches). Spread with ½ cup soft butter and sprinkle with your *choice* of the following: ½ cup cinnamon sugar; ½ cup dark brown sugar and ½ cup chopped nuts; ¼ cup ground almonds mixed with ¼ cup sugar; ½ cup orange marmalade; ½ cup glacéed fruits; or 2 apples, peeled and thinly sliced, and ½ cup cinnamon sugar.

Roll up into a firm, log-shaped roll. Cut diagonally to make triangularly shaped pieces measuring about 1 inch on one side and 2½ inches on the other. With the side of your little finger, press down across the center of the rolls so the cut ends spread out, creating two ear-shaped sides. Place the rolls on a greased baking sheet and let rise for 30 minutes. Bake in a moderately hot oven (375°) for about 30 minutes or until golden. Glaze, if you wish, with confectioners' sugar thinned with hot coffee. Makes 36 rolls.

FILLED BUNS   Täytepullat

Serve these light moist buns hot for breakfast or with coffee. If you wish, you can prepare the dough and shape the buns and store them, unbaked, in the freezer. To use, remove from the freezer and let thaw for 1 hour before baking.

Make 1 recipe Good Basic Sweet Yeast Dough (*see index*). Shape the risen dough into a long strand about 2 inches in diameter. Cut this into 2-inch lengths and place the pieces, cut side down, on a greased baking sheet.

Dip your finger or thumb in flour and press a deep hole into the center of each bun. Fill the hole with a dab of butter and your choice of sugar, brown sugar, ground almonds, jam, jelly, marmalade, or glacéed mixed fruits. Let the buns rise in a warm place until almost doubled, then brush with beaten egg. Bake in a hot oven (400°) for 20 to 30 minutes. Cool on racks. Makes about 3 dozen.

BOSTON CAKE   Bostonkakku

Whether or not they actually know this cake in Boston, it is one to be found in every bakery in Helsinki—and quite a popular item. This cake has a double glaze: the first makes the surface shiny; the second is decorative (and optional).

Make Good Basic Sweet Yeast Dough (see index). Divide the dough in half. Roll the first part out as thin as possible. Spread with ½ cup butter, ½ cup cinnamon sugar, and ½ cup chopped nuts. Roll up tightly, and cut into 3-inch pieces. Stand the pieces, cut side down, in a well-buttered tube pan and as close together as possible. Repeat with the second half of dough, making a second cake. Cover and let rise until almost doubled (about 45 minutes in a warm place). Bake in a moderately hot oven (375°) for 45 to 55 minutes or until golden brown. Glaze while hot with 2 tablespoons hot coffee mixed with 2 tablespoons sugar, then drizzle with confectioners' sugar frosting. Makes 2 cakes.

BUTTER POUND CAKE   Murokakku

Serve this rich cake uniced but dusted with confectioners' sugar and thinly sliced. Store it in a cool place; it keeps very well.

1 cup butter	1 teaspoon baking powder
1 cup sugar	¼ teaspoon salt
4 eggs, beaten	2 teaspoons grated lemon peel
3 cups sifted white flour	confectioners' sugar

Cream the butter and sugar until light. Add the beaten eggs and mix until very light and creamy. Sift the flour with the baking powder and salt, and add gradually to the creamed mixture, keeping the batter as smooth as possible. Stir in the lemon peel. Pour into a well-buttered and sugar-dusted tube cake pan. Bake in a moderate oven (350°) for about 1 hour or until a cake tester comes out clean. Before serving, dust with the confectioners' sugar. To serve, cut into ½-inch slices. Serves about 10 at the coffee table.

■୧୬■୧୬■୧୬■୧୬■୧୬■୧୬■୧୬■୧୬■୧୬■୧୬■୧୬■୧୬■୧୬■୧୬■

COLD NUT ROLLS   Kylmät Rullat

This is an old, country recipe. The yeast dough is raised in cold water, and the resulting rolls are light textured and very rich. They have an almond-sugar coating.

1 cup finely chopped walnuts,
   pecans, almonds, or filberts
¾ cup sugar
3 cups white flour
1 teaspoon salt
½ cup butter

¼ cup hot milk
1 package active dry yeast
¼ cup warm water
3 eggs, slightly beaten
1 teaspoon vanilla

Combine the nuts and ½ cup of the sugar and set aside.

In a mixing bowl, combine 1½ cups of the flour with the salt and butter, mixing with a fork or with your fingers until the mixture resembles fine crumbs. Add the hot milk and stir quickly. Dissolve the yeast in the water and add to the flour mixture. Beat in the remaining sugar, the eggs, and vanilla to make a smooth batter, then add the rest of the flour to make a stiff dough.

Have ready a large square clean tea towel. Turn the dough out onto the center of the towel and bring the corners together, fastening them securely with string or a rubber band to make a bag containing the dough. Place the bag in a pan of cold water deep enough to cover the dough completely. Let stand for about 1 hour or until the dough in the bag rises to the surface of the water, then remove and turn out onto a floured board. Scoop up spoonfuls of the dough and drop into the nut-sugar mixture, and shape into fingers about 6 inches long. Twist into S or U shapes and place on a well-greased baking sheet to rise until light. Bake in a moderately hot oven (375°) for 10 to 20 minutes or until golden. Makes 24 rolls.

FIG BUTTER CAKE   Viikunakakku

This cake is most commonly served during the Christmas holidays. It can be stored for a week or more without losing its freshness.

¾ cup butter
¾ cup sugar
3 eggs, beaten
2 tablespoons grated orange peel
1½ cups sifted white flour

1 teaspoon baking powder
½ cup chopped dried figs
½ cup chopped raisins
¼ cup finely chopped walnuts
confectioners' sugar

Cream the butter and sugar until light and lemon colored. Add the beaten eggs and orange peel. Sift the flour with the baking powder. Combine the dried figs, raisins, and walnuts, and dust with about 2 tablespoonfuls of the flour mixture. Add the rest of the flour gradually to the creamed mixture, beating until very smooth. Last of all, stir in the fruit-nut mixture. Pour the batter into a tube pan that has been well buttered and dusted with vanilla wafer crumbs, ground almonds, or sugar. Bake in a moderate oven (350°) for 40 to 45 minutes, or until a cake tester comes out clean. Dust with confectioners' sugar before serving and cut into thin slices.

FINNISH SOUR CREAM CAKE   Kermakakku

This is one cake that American-born Finns still make from their immigrant grandmothers' recipe. It is served as the uniced cake on the coffee table, dusted with confectioners' sugar and sliced very thinly. It has a spicy cardamom flavor.

2 eggs, beaten
2 cups sour cream
2 cups sugar
2–3 drops almond extract
3 cups sifted white flour

1 teaspoon soda
½ teaspoon salt
½ teaspoon cinnamon
½ teaspoon ground cardamom

Combine the eggs, sour cream, sugar, and almond extract. Sift the flour with the soda, salt, cinnamon, and cardamom. Add gradually to the egg mixture, beating until the batter is smooth and well mixed. Pour into a buttered tube pan that has been dusted with cooky crumbs or granulated sugar. Bake in a moderate oven (350°) for 1 hour or until a cake tester comes out clean. Cool for 5 to 10 minutes before turning out of pan.

■◎◑■◎◑■◎◑■◎◑■◎◑■◎◑■◎◑■◎◑■◎◑■◎◑■◎◑■◎◑■◎◑■◎◑■

BUTTERMILK CAKE   Piimäkakku

Bake this spicy cake in a plain or fancy tube pan and cut it thinly to serve it.

2½ cups flour
1½ cups sugar
1½ teaspoons soda
1 teaspoon baking powder
¼ teaspoon salt

1 teaspoon cinnamon
½ teaspoon cloves
½ cup melted butter
1½ cups buttermilk

Sift together the flour, sugar, soda, baking powder, salt, cinnamon, and cloves into a mixing bowl. Stir in the butter, then stir in the buttermilk, mixing until the batter is well combined and smooth. Grease a tube cake pan and dust lightly with granulated sugar. Pour in the batter and bake in a moderate oven (350°) for 1 hour or until a cake tester comes out clean.

ALMOND CAKE   Mantelikakku

This is a rich, almond-flavored pound cake.

4 eggs
2 cups sugar
6 tablespoons melted butter
6 tablespoons heavy cream
¾ cup ground almonds
2 cups sifted white flour

⅛ teaspoon salt
1½ teaspoons baking powder
confectioners' sugar (optional)
whipped cream (optional)
jam or jelly (optional)

Beat the eggs until light and add the sugar; continue beating until thick. Fold in the butter, cream, and ground almonds. Sift the flour with the salt and baking powder and fold carefully and thoroughly into the egg mixture. Turn the batter into a buttered and lightly floured tube pan. Bake in a moderate oven (350°) for 1 hour or until a cake tester comes out clean. Or bake in 2 buttered and lightly floured 8-inch round cake pans for 35 to 45 minutes or until the cakes are golden and beginning to pull away from the sides of the pans. Serve the large cake dusted with confectioners' sugar and sliced. Fill the layer cake with your favorite jam or jelly and top with whipped cream.

RAIJA'S JELLY ROLL   Kääretorttu

A Finnish housewife I knew was so adept and quick at making jelly rolls, she could turn them out in a half-hour flat. In Finland you *never* sit down to "just" coffee; it is considered almost rude not to offer something "to go with" it. So, each housewife has her favorite quick trick. My friend Raija was such a master of the jelly-roll art that I have named this one after her.

3 eggs
½ cup sugar
¾ cup sifted white flour
½ teaspoon baking powder
dash salt

1 teaspoon vanilla
  sugar
1 cup fruit or berry jam
1 cup cream, whipped (optional)
  confectioners' sugar

Beat the eggs until light, add the sugar, and beat until thick. Sift the flour with the baking powder and salt and fold carefully into the egg mixture until well combined. Fold in the vanilla. Line a jelly-roll pan with waxed paper; butter it very well and sprinkle it generously with granulated sugar. Spread the batter evenly in the pan and bake in a moderate oven (350°) for 20 minutes or until the cake is just set. Turn out onto a clean tea towel that has been well dusted with confectioners' sugar and roll up while still hot. Cool slightly, then unroll and remove from the towel. When it has cooled, spread the inside of the roll with the jam and whipped cream. Reroll. Slice to serve. (Note: *Do not* try to fill a still-warm jelly roll with whipped cream; it will melt and run all over the serving plate.)

APPLE SUGAR CAKE   Omena Sokerikakku

A group of Finnish women who were interested in us Fulbrighters (the scholars and their wives) organized a Finnish cooking school for us. This cake is one that was demonstrated and then served to us on a coffee table, together with six other baked items.

¼ cup butter
1 cup sugar
2 eggs
2 cups sifted white flour
1½ teaspoons baking powder
dash salt

¾ cup light cream
2 apples, peeled, cored, and
  sliced
cinnamon sugar (2 tablespoons
  sugar mixed with 1 teaspoon
  cinnamon)

Cream the butter and sugar together until thick and lemon colored. Add the eggs, beating until light. Sift the flour with the baking powder and salt, and add alternately to the batter with the cream. Mix until the batter is smooth. Pour into a well-greased 9- by 12-inch pan and insert the apple slices so that the outer edges are up. Sprinkle evenly with the cinnamon sugar. Bake in a moderate oven (350°) for about 50 minutes or until a cake tester comes out clean.

■❦■❦■❦■❦■❦■❦■❦■❦■❦■❦■❦■❦■❦■❦■❦■

CHRISTMAS CAKE   Joulukakku

A Christmas Cake is typified by a filling of plums or prunes topped with whipped cream—actually a delectable combination. You may, if you wish, use apricot jam instead; this is another good combination with whipped cream, but it is not traditionally Christmassy.

4 eggs
1 cup sugar
1 cup sifted white flour

¼ teaspoon salt
½ teaspoon baking powder
1 teaspoon vanilla

Filling
1 cup red plum jam

1 cup heavy cream, whipped

Beat the eggs and sugar together until thick and creamy. Sift the flour with the salt and baking powder into the egg mixture; fold in until well blended. Divide the batter between two buttered 8- or 9-inch cake pans and bake in a moderately hot oven (375°) for 20 to 25 minutes or just until the cakes begin to pull away from the sides of the pans. Cool on a rack.

Split each cooled cake layer into two parts. Fill the layers with the plum jam topped with a layer of 1 cup heavy whipped cream, but reserve some of the whipped cream to garnish the top of the cake. Refrigerate until serving time.

KERTTU'S DRIED-FRUIT CAKE   Kerttn Kakku

Kerttu, one of our dearest relatives and friends, was one of the sources of enlightenment to us about many ways of Finnish life. She made this cake to serve on the Christmas coffee table. It is simple and good, and the perfect answer for those who do not particularly care for glacéed fruits.

1 cup soft butter
1 cup sugar
4 eggs, beaten
2 cups white flour
2 teaspoons baking powder
¼ teaspoon salt

2 teaspoons grated orange peel
1 cup finely chopped mixed dried
  fruits (prunes, apricots, pears,
  apples, etc.) dusted with
1 tablespoon flour

Cream the butter with the sugar until light and lemon colored. Add the eggs and beat until thick. Sift in the flour, baking powder, and salt, and mix until the batter is well blended and smooth. Stir in the orange peel and fold in the dried fruits so they are well distributed. Turn the batter into a well-buttered 5- by 9-inch loaf pan or into a tube pan. Bake in a moderate oven (350°) for 55 to 60 minutes or until a cake tester comes out clean.

FINNISH FRUITCAKE   Joulunpyhien Kahvikakku

The literal translation of the name for this cake is "Christmas holiday's coffee cake." It is a simple white poundcake that has glaceéd or candied fruits in it. It slices best a day or two after it is baked.

1 cup butter
1 cup sugar
5 eggs, beaten
2 cups white flour
2 teaspoons baking powder

½ teaspoon salt
1½ cups chopped mixed
   candied fruits
½ cup chopped walnuts or pecans

Cream the butter with the sugar until light. Add the eggs, beating until the mixture is very light and thick. Sift the flour with the baking powder and salt, and sift about 2 tablespoons of this mixture over the mixed fruits and nuts, tossing them to coat well. Sift the remaining flour mixture into the creamed mixture and blend until the batter is smooth. Fold in the fruits and nuts. Turn the batter into 2 well-buttered 3- by 8-inch loaf pans that have been dusted with flour (or into 1 tube pan) and bake in a moderate oven (350°) for 1 hour or until the cake begins to shrink from the sides of the pan.

HILMA'S FRUIT SPICE CAKE   Hilman Kakku

I do not know who Hilma is. But her cake is a popular one that appeared on coffee tables throughout Finland when we were visiting friends and relations. It is a large cake that is a really good one for taking to a potluck or a meeting.

3 cups brown sugar, well packed
1 cup melted butter
5 cups sifted white flour
4 teaspoons baking powder
1 teaspoon soda

1 tablespoon mixed spices (cloves,
   cinnamon, and cardamom)
½ teaspoon salt
3 cups buttermilk
½ cup raisins or chopped dates
   (optional)

In the large bowl of your electric mixer, cream together the brown sugar and butter until thick and light, using medium to high speed. Sift the flour with the baking powder, soda, spices, and salt, and add alternately with the buttermilk to the butter mixture. Beat at low speed until the batter is smooth, then fold in the raisins or dates. Turn into a large buttered baking pan about 9 by 13 by 3 inches, or into 2 smaller buttered pans, and bake in a moderate oven (350°) for 55 to 65 minutes or until a cake tester comes out clean. Frost when cool with caramel frosting, if desired.

■❦■❦■❦■❦■❦■❦■❦■❦■❦■❦■❦■❦■❦■❦■❦■❦■

RYE CHOCOLATE TORTE   Ruis Suklatorttu

Crushed rye hardtack or crispbread and grated chocolate make an interesting combination in this easy-to-make but elegant torte.

5 egg yolks	2 tablespoons uncooked farina
¾ cup sugar	½ cup crushed rye crispbread
¼ teaspoon cinnamon	or hardtack
¼ teaspoon cloves	5 egg whites
¼ cup grated semisweet chocolate	2 cups heavy cream

Beat the egg yolks and ½ cup of the sugar together until very light and creamy. Add the cinnamon and cloves and stir until blended. Fold in the grated chocolate, the farina, and the crushed rye crispbread. Beat the egg whites until stiff and gently fold into the batter. Butter and flour two 8-inch cake pans. Pour the batter into the pans and bake in a moderately hot oven (375°) for 30 minutes or until the top springs back when lightly touched. Cool in the pans on a rack.

Whip the cream until stiff and to it add the remaining ¼ cup sugar. Fill the torte layers with part of the whipped cream and spread the remaining cream over the top and sides. Garnish with more grated chocolate. Cut in wedges to serve. Serves about 10.

OLD-FASHIONED CAKE   Vanhanaikojenkakku

The layers in this cake are thin pastry rolled into five different-sized rounds that have been baked, cooled, and then filled with thinly sliced fruit or with jam and whipped cream. The cake is delicate, delicious, and devastatingly rich.

2 cups sifted flour	5 to 6 tablespoons cold water
1 cup cold butter	¼ cup sugar (approximately)

Filling

2 cups heavy cream	2 cups thinly sliced strawberries
¼ cup sugar	or other fruit, or jam

Sift the flour into a mixing bowl. Cut in the butter until the mixture resembles fine crumbs. Sprinkle the water over the mixture, stirring with a fork, until it comes together into a ball. Turn out onto a lightly floured board and divide into 5 parts, ranging in size from a 3-inch ball to a

1-inch ball. Roll these out into rounds (the largest about 10 inches in diameter, and the smallest, 3 inches in diameter). Place on lightly greased baking sheets. Brush each round with water and sprinkle with the sugar. Bake in a moderately hot oven (375°) about 12 minutes or until a light golden brown. Cool.

Whip the cream and to it add the ¼ cup sugar. To assemble the cake, place the largest round of pastry on a serving plate. Cover with a thin layer of the fruit or jam and whipped cream. Top with the next-sized round, and repeat until all 5 layers are stacked and filled. The cake will have a pyramid shape. Refrigerate until serving time. Serves 10 to 12.

CHRISTMAS PRUNE CAKE   Joululuumukakku

At Christmas, this tortelike prune-filled cake is often served as the "last course" at the coffee table in place of a decorated, filled cake. This cake can be stored (preferably in the refrigerator) for several days before using. If it gets too dry, brush it with prune juice or orange juice.

Cake
¾ cup butter   1½ cups white flour
½ cup sugar   1 teaspoon baking powder
2 eggs

Topping
1 cup cooked, puréed prunes   2 tablespoons (approximately) sugar
1 teaspoon grated lemon peel   1 cup heavy cream, whipped

To make the cake, cream the butter and sugar until light. Add the eggs, one at a time, and beat until very creamy. Sift together the flour and the baking powder, and add gradually to the batter, mixing well until a stiff dough is formed. Pat into a well-buttered and -sugared 8- or 9-inch cake pan or a tart pan with a raised bottom. Bake in a moderately hot oven (375°) for 45 minutes or until a light golden-brown. Cool.

To prepare the topping, combine the prunes with the lemon peel and sugar; taste, and add more sugar if necessary. Pour onto the cake to within a half-inch of the edges. Mound the edges with whipped cream. Serves 6 to 8.

■☙■☙■☙■☙■☙■☙■☙■☙■☙■☙■☙■☙■☙■☙■☙■■

FANCY FILLED CAKE   Täytekakku

This cake is served as the grand finale on the coffee table. It has a multitude of variations, depending on the fruits available for filling the cake.

Cake

4 eggs	2 tablespoons cornstarch
1 cup sugar	1 teaspoon baking powder
1 cup sifted white flour	¼ teaspoon salt

Moistening Mixture

½ cup fruit juice or fruit-flavored liqueur	½ cup water
	2 tablespoons lemon juice

Filling

2 cups berries or other fresh, very thinly sliced fruit	1 cup heavy cream, whipped stiff

Glaze

1 tablespoon unflavored gelatin	sliced fruits (apples, melons, grapes, bananas, etc.)
1 cup water	
2 tablespoons sugar	2 cups (approximately) fruit purée or strained baby fruit

To make the cake batter, beat the eggs until light and fluffy. Add the sugar, gradually beating until thick. Sift the flour with the cornstarch and salt and fold carefully into the egg mixture. Pour into 2 well-buttered and floured 8-inch round cake pans. Bake in a moderately hot oven (375°) for 35 to 40 minutes or until the top springs back when touched lightly. Cool on a rack and remove from pans. Split each layer so you have 4 layers in all. Combine the fruit juice, water, and lemon juice to make the moistening mixture.

To assemble the cake, moisten each layer with the moistening mixture. Place the first moistened layer on a serving plate and fill with a layer of the fruit. Top with one-third of the whipped cream. Cover this with the second layer and repeat until all 4 layers are stacked and filled. (The cake may be stored in the refrigerator at this point to be finished the next day, if you wish.)

To make the glaze, soften the gelatin in ½ cup cold water. Heat the remaining ¾ cup water to boiling and stir into the softened gelatin to dissolve it. Add the sugar, stirring until it is dissolved. Chill the glaze until it is slightly thickened.

To complete the cake, arrange the sliced fruits on top, and spoon the half-set gelatin evenly over the fruit, giving it a thin glaze. Frost the sides of the cake with the fruit purée or baby fruit. Chill until serving time. Serves 10 to 12.

KARELIAN CHEESE TORTE   Rahkatorttu

Karelians serve this cake proudly, often topping it with fresh berries in the summertime. Serve it on the coffee table or for dessert.

Crust

2 cups sifted white flour
1 teaspoon baking powder
2 tablespoons sugar

½ cup butter
1 egg

Filling

1 cup (½ pint) creamed cottage
   cheese
1 tablespoon lemon juice
2 teaspoons grated lemon peel
2 teaspoons vanilla
½ cup sugar

½ cup soft butter
2 eggs, slightly beaten
berries (optional)
jam or jelly (optional)
1 cup heavy cream, whipped
   (optional)

To make the crust, sift the flour with the baking powder and sugar into a mixing bowl. Using a fork, cut in the butter until the mixture resembles fine crumbs. Beat the egg and pour over the crumb mixture. With the tips of the fingers, mix until all the ingredients are well blended and a dough is formed. Butter a 9-inch cake pan (preferably one with a removable bottom) or a springform pan. Pat the mixture into the bottom and sides of the pan.

To prepare the filling, whip the cottage cheese until creamy, using a rotary or electric mixer. Add the lemon juice and peel, vanilla, sugar, butter, and eggs. Beat until the mixture is smooth. Pour into the dough-lined cake pan. Bake in a moderate oven (350°) for 40 to 45 minutes or until the filling is set. Cool. If you wish, spread with a thin layer of jam or softened jelly, or cover with sliced berries and serve with whipped cream. Serves 6 to 8.

■◎◢■◎◢■◎◢■◎◢■◎◢■◎◢■◎◢■◎◢■◎◢■◎◢■◎◢■◎◢■◎◢■◎◢■

APPLE-FILLED STRIP   Omenapitko

This is in between a pastry and a cake. Traditionally, it is to be served at the coffee table; however, it is ideal for dessert.

Crust

3 cups white flour	¼ cup sugar
½ teaspoon salt	1 cup butter
1 teaspoon baking powder	⅓–½ cup cold milk

Filling

6 large cooking apples, peeled, cored, and sliced thinly crosswise	3 teaspoons cinnamon
	1–1½ cups sugar

In a bowl, mix the flour with the salt, baking powder, and sugar. Cut in the butter until the mixture resembles fine crumbs. Stirring with a fork, add 1/3 cup of the cold milk. The dough should cling together in a ball (add more milk if necessary).

Roll the dough out on a lightly floured board into a rectangle about 10 inches wide and 20 inches long. Make slightly diagonal cuts about 3 inches long and about 1 inch apart from the outside edges toward the center. Arrange the sliced apples in layers neatly down the center of the dough, dusting each layer with some of the cinnamon and sugar. Fold the cut pieces of dough across the filling, alternating from side to side, so the strip has a "braided" look. Seal the ends so the filling does not run out. Place the filled strip on a lightly greased baking sheet and brush the top with milk. Bake in a moderately hot oven (375°) for about 45 minutes or until the strip is golden brown and the apples are tender. Cool and frost with Coffee Glaze (below). Serves 6 to 8.

Coffee Glaze Filling

Sift and measure 2 cups confectioners' sugar and slowly stir in 2 to 3 tablespoons hot strong coffee to make a smooth thin glaze.

BASIC MERINGUE   Munanvaahtoleivät or Marenki

Eight-inch meringues are handy staples to keep in your kitchen for an unexpected company dessert, or coffee accompaniment. The Finnish housewife knows this well; one of my closest Finnish friends always kept one or two meringue layers on hand stored in an airtight tin. Some of the various ways to serve layer meringues follow this recipe.

⅔ cup egg whites (about 5)   1½ cups sugar

Beat the egg whites with your electric mixer until frothy, then gradually beat in the sugar. Put the bowl over a kettle of boiling water and continue beating at the highest speed until the meringue forms very stiff peaks.

Butter a baking sheet and cover it with brown paper. Coat the paper with cornstarch. Press the meringue mixture through a pastry bag or waxed-paper cone in spiral fashion, beginning at the center of the meringue layer, to make 2 rounds about 8 inches in diameter or 12 small 3-inch meringues. Bake in a very slow oven (200°) for 2 to 4 hours or until the meringues are dried. Or, heat the oven to 475°, put the meringues in, turn the heat off, and leave in the oven overnight or for 6 to 8 hours. Makes two 8-inch layers or 12 small individual-sized meringues.

PINEAPPLE MERINGUE CAKE
Marenki Ananaskakku

1 8-inch Basic Meringue layer
  (recipe above)
1 cup heavy cream, whipped and
  sweetened to taste

2 cups diced fresh pineapple or
  well-drained canned pineapple
  tidbits or cubes
shaved sweet chocolate

Spread the meringue layer with half the whipped cream. Arrange the pineapple attractively over the whipped cream, and garnish the cake with the remaining whipped cream (to be fancy, you can press it through a pastry bag or waxed-paper cone). Garnish the edges with the chocolate. Serve immediately. Serves 6.

STRAWBERRY MERINGUE CAKE
Marenki Mansikkakakku

Follow the directions for Pineapple Meringue Cake (above), but use fresh strawberries, sliced or halved, in place of the pineapple, and omit the chocolate. Serves 6.

PRUNE MERINGUE CAKE   Marenki Luumukakku

Follow the directions for Pineapple Meringue Cake (*above*), but substitute 1 cup puréed cooked prunes for the pineapple and omit the chocolate. Decorate the top of the cake with 12 pitted cooked prunes. Serves 6.

CLOUDBERRY MERINGUE CAKE
Marenki Lakkakakku

If you are fortunate enough to have in your possession some cloudberry jam (imported from Finland and available in some food stores), this is an elegant way to extend its fine flavor. Otherwise you can substitute apricot jam for the cloudberry jam in the recipe.

2 8-inch Basic Meringue layers   1 cup cloudberry jam
   (*see index*)   1 cup heavy cream, whipped

Put the first meringue layer on a serving plate and top it with half of the jam and half of the whipped cream. Place the second layer on the whipped cream and top with the remaining jam. Decorate the cake with the rest of the whipped cream (put it through a pastry bag, or dot it on with a spoon). Serve immediately. Serves 10.

SNOW CAKE   Lumikakku

If you have excess egg whites, this is an excellent way to use them up. The cake starts out and looks like an angelfood, but at the last you fold in melted butter—the ingredient that changes the character of the cake entirely (do not expect an angelfood texture).

8 egg whites (1 cup)   ½ cup butter, melted and cooled
1 cup sugar   ½ teaspoon vanilla or almond
1 cup sifted white flour   extract
1 tablespoon cornstarch

Beat the egg whites until foamy, slowly add the sugar, and continue to beat at high speed until very stiff (but not dry) and the whites stand in peaks. Sift the flour into the egg whites with the cornstarch, folding to combine well. Fold in the cooled butter until it too is well combined, and then the vanilla or almond extract. Turn into a buttered tube or fancy cake pan dusted with sugar or ground nuts. Bake in a moderate oven (350°) for about 1 hour. (This cake does not rise, but will feel firm to the touch when baked.) Turn out of the pan onto a wire rack and cool.

ORANGE TORTE   Appelsiinitorttu

This is an elegant torte that should be served in very thin slices because it is so rich. It keeps well, stored in the refrigerator or in an airtight container in a cool place.

Crust
¾ cup soft butter   ½ cup sugar
1½ cups white flour   1 egg yolk

Filling
1 cup granulated sugar   1 egg white
1 cup finely ground almonds

Frosting
½ cup sifted confectioners' sugar   candied peel for decoration
orange juice

To make the crust, put the butter in a bowl and stir in the flour, sugar, and egg yolk, mixing with your hands until a dough forms. Turn out onto a floured board and roll into a rectangle about 6 by 15 inches.

To make the filling, combine the almonds, sugar, and egg white into a smooth paste (add a drop or two of water if the mixture seems dry). Shape into a log about 13 inches long and center it on the rolled-out dough. Bring the dough up over the filling, moisten the edges, and seal well. Place the log, seam side down, on a baking sheet and bake in a moderately hot oven (375°) for about 15 minutes or until golden. Cool on the baking sheet.

For the icing, add enough orange juice to the confectioners' sugar to make a thin glaze. Frost the torte and press candied peel into the icing before it hardens. Serve, cut in thin slices, on the coffee table.

■◎■◎■◎■◎■◎■◎■◎■◎■◎■◎■◎■◎■◎■◎■◎■◎■

UNBAKED CHOCOLATE TORTE   Keksitorttu

We first tasted this cake when it was served as one of the seven items on the coffee table at the home of one of our relatives in Western Finland. It has become a favorite because it is quick to make and keeps well, in the refrigerator or freezer. The flavor is mild, chocolaty and smooth. The slices are "striped."

Filling

2 tablespoons cocoa
¾ cup sugar
2 teaspoons vanilla
1 tablespoon milk

¾ cup melted butter
18 graham crackers about 2½
   inches square

Mix the cocoa, sugar, vanilla, and milk, then the melted butter. Beat, using high speed on an electric mixer, until light and very thick.

Line a very small (about 3- by 6-inch) bread-loaf pan with waxed paper, and on the bottom spread a layer of the chocolate mixture. Arrange two of the crackers on top, cover them with more of the chocolate mixture, and top with two more crackers. Repeat this process until all the filling is used up, then cover the torte and refrigerate until the filling is set. Unmold onto a serving plate and slice thinly to serve.

PEACH TARTS   Persikkatortut

Serve these fancy little tarts with a peach filling for dessert or as a coffee table item.

Crust

1 cup white flour
½ cup butter

6 to 8 tablespoons water

Filling

6 canned drained peach halves
2 tablespoons sugar
2 tablespoons cornstarch
¼ teaspoon almond extract

dash salt
nutmeg (optional)
ground almonds (optional)

To make the crust, measure the unsifted flour into a bowl and cut in the butter until the mixture resembles fine crumbs. Add the water, a tablespoonful at a time, stirring with a fork until a dough forms. Press this into a ball. Roll the dough out ⅛-inch thick and cut six rounds of dough about 5 inches

■◌◌■◌◌■◌◌■◌◌■◌◌■◌◌■◌◌■◌◌■◌◌■◌◌■◌◌■◌◌■◌◌■◌◌■

in diameter. Arrange the dough rounds into small tart pans (the foil pans from individual frozen pies work fine).

Press the peaches through a sieve or whirl in a blender until puréed. Stir in the sugar, cornstarch, almond extract, and salt. Divide the filling equally among the six tarts. Roll out the leftover scraps of dough, cut them into strips, and lay across the filling in crisscross fashion. Sprinkle the tops of the tarts with nutmeg and ground almonds, if you wish. Bake in a moderately hot oven (375°) for 30 minutes or until golden. Makes 6 tarts.

BLUEBERRY BARS Mustikkapiirakka

The blueberry is one of the berries that grows wild in Finland's low swampy areas. The wild berry has a flavor and tartness that does not come through in the cultivated variety (hence the addition of lemon juice to the berries in this recipe). This pastry is Karelian in origin; it is cut into bars for the coffee table, or in larger squares for dessert.

Crust
2½ cups sifted white flour   ½ teaspoon baking powder
½ cup sugar   1 cup soft butter

Filling
2 cups blueberries   1 tablespoon grated lemon peel
4 tablespoons sugar   2 tablespoons cornstarch
1 tablespoon lemon juice   ¼ tablespoon salt

To make the crust, sift the flour, sugar, and baking powder into a mixing bowl. Using a fork, mix in the butter until the mixture resembles fine crumbs. With the hands, press these together into a dough (the warmth of your hands will make the mixture soften and cling together). Roll the dough out on a lightly floured board to fit a 12- by 16-inch jelly roll pan, reserving about ½ cup of the dough to use as a garnish. (This kind of crumbly dough may tear when it is being lifted into the pan; it can be easily patched by pressing the torn pieces together.) With the fingers, form a ridge around the edge of the dough so the filling will not run over during the baking.

To prepare the filling, pour the blueberries into a small mixing bowl. Mash lightly to produce enough juice to moisten the berry mixture. Stir in the sugar, lemon juice, lemon peel, cornstarch, and salt. Spread the filling over the dough in the pan.

Roll out the reserved portion of dough on a floured board to ⅛- to ¼-inch thickness. Cut in strips and place in a loose lattice pattern on the filling. Sprinkle the top with additional sugar, if desired. Bake in a moderately

■◦■◦■◦■◦■◦■◦■◦■◦■◦■◦■◦■◦■◦■◦■

hot oven (375°) for 25 to 30 minutes or until the crust is a light golden-brown. Cut into squares to serve. Makes 12 dessert-sized (4-inch-square) servings, or 48 coffee-table-sized (2-inch-square servings).

FRUIT SQUARES   Hedelmäkakut

These attractive bar cookies have a rich butter crust and jam topping.

Crust

3 cups white flour
1 cup sugar
1 teaspoon baking powder

1 cup soft butter
3 eggs
1 teaspoon vanilla

Filling

1 cup plum, blackberry, raspberry,
   blueberry, or apricot jam

2 tablespoons sugar

Combine the flour, sugar, and baking powder in a large bowl. Blend in the butter with a fork until the mixture resembles fine crumbs. Add the eggs and vanilla and work into a stiff dough. Reserve one-third of the dough. On a well-floured board, roll out the balance of the dough into a rectangle about 12 by 16 inches and ¼-inch thick. Place the dough on a lightly greased baking sheet and spread the jam evenly over it. Roll out the reserve dough to ⅛-inch thickness and cut in ½-inch strips; place these in crisscross fashion over the jelly to make a diagonal pattern. Sprinkle the 2 tablespoons sugar over the top. Bake in a moderately hot oven (375°) for 20 to 30 minutes. Cut into 1- by 2-inch rectangles. Makes about 80 cookies.

RUNEBERG TARTS   Runebergintorttut

February 5 is the birthday of Finland's national poet, J. L. Runeberg. The flag flies on this special day, as it does on other commemorative days in Finland, and these little cakes appear in bakeries in his honor.

½ cup butter
½ cup sugar
2 eggs

1½ cups sifted white flour
½ teaspoon baking powder
½ cup ground almonds

currant jelly
½ cup sifted confectioners' sugar

1–2 tablespoons hot water

Cream butter and sugar together with an electric mixer until light and fluffy. Add the eggs and beat at a high speed until creamy. Sift together the flour and baking powder, and add gradually to the batter. Beat in the almonds. Butter and sugar small muffin tins or tart pans (the authentic shape for these tarts is a straight-sided cake pan about 2 inches in diameter and 2½ inches deep), and fill about two-thirds full. Bake in a moderate oven (350°) for 20 minutes or until a pale golden-brown. When cool, dot each tart with about ½ teaspoon currant jelly. Outline the jelly, using a force bag, with frosting made by mixing the confectioners' sugar and water together into a paste. Makes about 24 small tarts or 12 medium-sized tarts.

ALEXANDER'S TARTS   Alexanterintortut

Czar Alexander II of Russia was well liked by the Finnish people. It was he who first acknowledged the Finnish language and made it an official language of state. (The official language had previously been Swedish, although the folk tongue was 90 percent Finnish.) Czar Alexander II has a street in Helsinki named after him (Alexanterinkatu), as well as these little, sweet tarts that are sold in coffee shops the year round and are often served on the coffee table. Serve as a cooky choice on the coffee table or as an accompaniment to a fruit soup (see *index*) for dessert.

1 cup sifted white flour	½ cup soft butter
¼ teaspoon baking powder	½ cup jam
¼ cup sugar	

Frosting

½ cup sifted confectioners' sugar	2–3 tablespoons hot water
1 tablespoon cornstarch	

Sift the flour with the baking powder and sugar into a mixing bowl. Using a fork, mix in the butter until the mixture resembles fine crumbs. Then, with your hands, press the crumbs into a ball until the warmth of your hands makes the mixture cling together. Divide the dough into 2 parts. Roll each into a square 8 by 8 inches and about ¼-inch thick. Place the squares on a lightly greased baking sheet and bake in a moderate oven (350°) until very lightly golden brown (about 12 to 15 minutes). When cool, spread both squares with the jam, and place one on top of the other. Ice with a mixture of the confectioners' sugar, cornstarch, and hot water and let stand until the frosting has hardened. Cut with a sharp knife into 1-inch squares. Makes about 64 tarts.

■ ⊘﹢ ■ ⊘﹢ ■ ⊘﹢ ■ ⊘﹢ ■ ⊘﹢ ■ ⊘﹢ ■ ⊘﹢ ■ ⊘﹢ ■ ⊘﹢ ■ ⊘﹢ ■ ⊘﹢ ■ ⊘﹢ ■ ⊘﹢ ■ ⊘﹢ ■ ⊘﹢ ■

BASIC COOKY DOUGH   Perustaikina

The Finnish hostess is always prepared to set a coffee table for she always
has cookies on hand. These she bakes about twice a month, then stores in a
cool dry place. Butter cookies keep well in an airtight tin in a cool cup-
board. A variety of cookies can be made from this Basic Cooky Dough.

2½ cups soft butter   5 cups white flour
1 cup sugar   ¼ teaspoon salt

Using your electric mixer, cream together the butter and sugar. Gradually
add the flour and salt. The mixture will resemble fine crumbs. Work the
crumbs between the palms of your hands until their warmth turns the mixture
into a dough. (If your kitchen is cold, this conversion process is slow. It helps
if you set the bowl in warm water.) Use the dough as directed in the following variations.

NUT COOKIES   Pähkinäkakut

Knead ½ cup ground nuts (almonds or walnuts) into one-quarter recipe
Basic Cooky Dough. Roll the mixture into a log 1 inch in diameter, wrap it
in waxed paper, and chill in the refrigerator. Slice as thinly as possible
(about ⅛-inch thick) and sprinkle with additional chopped nuts and granulated sugar (about ⅛ teaspoon per cooky). Place on lightly greased baking
sheets and bake in a moderate oven (350°) until a light golden brown (about
7 to 10 minutes). Makes about 48 cookies.

DIAGONAL COOKIES   Wienen Tangot

Use one-quarter recipe Basic Cooky Dough. Divide it into four parts. Roll
each into a long log about the thickness of a finger (½ inch) and place on
lightly greased baking sheets. With the side of the blunt end of a knife,
press a dent down the length of each log. Bake in a moderately hot oven
(375°) for 10 minutes. Remove from the oven and fill the dent with your
favorite jam (strawberry, seedless raspberry, cherry, or currant are good
choices). Return to the oven and bake until edges are a very light golden
brown (about 10 minutes more). Remove from oven and brush with a glaze
made of ½ cup sifted confectioners' sugar and 1 tablespoon hot water. Cut
the logs into 1-inch diagonal slices when cool. Makes about 48 cookies.

AUNT HANNAH'S COOKIES   Hanna-tädinkakut

Use one-quarter recipe Basic Cooky Dough. Crumble this and add to it 2 egg yolks, ½ teaspoon baking powder, and ¼ cup sugar. Mix well. Chill. Roll out on a lightly floured board to about ¼-inch thickness. Using a scalloped cooky cutter, cut out rounds, then cut each of these in half so you have scalloped half circles. Place on lightly greased baking sheets and bake in a moderately hot oven (375°) for 10 minutes. Makes about 48 cookies.

ANISE COOKIES   Anisleivät

To one-quarter recipe Basic Cooky Dough add 1 teaspoon ground anise seed and 1 egg. Mix until well blended. Chill. Roll out on lightly floured board to about ⅛-inch thickness. With a crimped-edge pastry wheel, cut the entire surface into diamond shapes. Brush with egg white and sprinkle with more crushed anise seeds. Place on a lightly greased baking sheet and bake in a moderately hot oven (375°) 10 minutes or until lightly golden brown. Do not overbake. Makes about 24 cookies.

S'S   Ässät

To one-quarter recipe Basic Cooky Dough add 2 egg yolks. Mix well until the dough is smooth. Force through the star tip of a cooky press into long strips on a board. Cut the strips into 3-inch pieces. Shape each into an S and place on a lightly greased baking sheet. Bake in a moderately hot oven (375°) about 10 minutes or until a light golden-brown. Makes about 24 cookies.

EGG RINGS   Munarinkilät

To one-quarter recipe Basic Cooky Dough add 2 egg yolks and ½ teaspoon baking powder. Mix well. Roll into strips about ¼-inch thick and cut these into 4-inch lengths. Shape each into a ring and place on a lightly greased baking sheet. Brush with slightly beaten egg white and sprinkle with sugar (for Christmas cookies, sprinkle with colored sugar). Bake in a moderate oven (350°) for 10 minutes or until firm and lightly browned. Makes about 24 cookies.

CINNAMON CARDAMOM NUGGETS
Kaneli-kardamummikakut

To one-quarter recipe Basic Cooky Dough add 1 teaspoon ground cardamom and 2 teaspoons cinnamon, mixing until well blended. Roll out into
strands about the thickness of a finger and chill until stiff. Cut into ½-inch
pieces and place on a lightly greased baking sheet. Bake in a moderately
hot oven (375°) for 10 minutes or until very lightly golden. Cool and dust
with confectioners' sugar. Store in an airtight container in a cool place.
Makes about 50 nuggets.

FORK COOKIES   Haarukkaleivät

To one-quarter recipe Basic Cooky Dough add 1 teaspoon vanilla, ½ teaspoon baking powder, and 1 egg yolk. Knead well to mix the ingredients
thoroughly. Pinch off about 2 teaspoonfuls of the dough at a time and roll
between palms into a ball. Place on a lightly greased baking sheet and
press flat with a fork. The fork tines will make a crisscross design. Bake in
a modern oven (350°) for 10 minutes or until a light golden brown. Makes
about 24.

BROWNED BUTTER COOKIES   Erämaanhiekkaa

The literal translation of the Finnish name for these cookies is "Wilderness
Sands," which is descriptive of the cookies' browned color that comes from
the browned butter used in making them.

1 cup butter	3 cups sifted white flour
1 cup sugar	1 teaspoon soda
3 teaspoons vanilla	strawberry jam

Brown the butter in a heavy saucepan. Cool. Stir in the sugar and vanilla
and mix well. Sift the flour with the soda and slowly add to the butter mixture, mixing until a smooth dough is formed.

To shape, roll about 2 teaspoonfuls of the dough between the palms of
your hands into balls about ¾-inch in diameter, and place on a lightly
greased baking sheet. Bake in a slow oven (375°) for 7 to 10 minutes. The
cookies should be firm but not brown. If they overbake, they become un-
desirably hard. When cool, form the cookies into sandwiches, using the jam
as the filling. Makes about 24 sandwich cookies or 48 single cookies.

TEASPOON COOKIES Lusikkaleivät

Follow directions for Browned Butter Cookies (above), but shape the cookies into ovals by pressing the dough into a teaspoon and leveling it off. Slide the ovals, flat side down, onto a greased baking sheet. Bake in a slow oven (325°) for 7 to 10 minutes.

RYE COOKIES Ruiskakkuja

These dainty cookies are miniature sour rye bread loaves with a hole in the center. Rye cookies are traditionally served on the Christmas season coffee table.

½ cup butter
5 tablespoons sugar

1 cup rye flour
½ cup sifted white flour

Cream the butter and sugar until light and fluffy. Slowly add the rye flour and white flour, mixing until the mixture resembles fine crumbs. Knead until the warmth of your hands turns it into a dough. (You may place the mixing bowl in warm water to speed the process.)

Turn the dough out onto a lightly floured board and roll out very thin (to about ⅛-inch thickness). Cut into rounds and place on a lightly greased baking sheet. Cut a hole slightly off center, using a tiny bottle cap (such as a flavoring- or food-coloring bottle cap) as a cutter. Prick each cooky with a fork and bake in a hot oven (400°) for 5 to 7 minutes or until slightly browned. Makes about 36 cookies.

■౭◈■౭◈■౭◈■౭◈■౭◈■౭◈■౭◈■౭◈■౭◈■౭◈■౭◈■౭◈■౭◈■

LITTLE CHOCOLATE MERINGUES
Suklaamarengit Pienet Murjaanit

These little meringues are neither candy nor cooky but sweet little morsels which are served on the most elegant of coffee tables. The sugar-cocoa-egg-white mixture is rolled out like a stiff cooky dough, then cut into tiny rounds and baked. The meringues pop during the baking so they resemble an open accordion.

2½ cups sifted confectioners' sugar   2 egg whites
2 tablespoons cocoa

Put the sugar, cocoa, and egg whites into the small bowl of your electric mixer. Beat until a very stiff dough is formed. Roll out to about 1/3-inch thickness, on a board dusted with confectioners' sugar, using additional confectioners' sugar as needed to prevent the dough from sticking.

Cut 1-inch rounds (use the center piece of a doughnut cutter or a bottle cap). Place on a very well-greased and floured baking sheet, and bake in a moderately hot oven (375°) for 10 minutes or until the meringues have popped. Makes 24.

SAND TARTS   Hiekka Kakkuja

These buttery little tarts are usually baked in specially shaped tiny fluted molds. If you do not have the molds, you can shape the dough into tiny balls, treating them like cookies.

1 cup soft butter   ½ cup ground almonds
½ cup sugar   3 cups sifted white flour
2 eggs   2 tablespoons finely crushed
2 tablespoons cream   vanilla wafers

Cream the butter with the sugar and add the eggs and cream, mixing until smooth. Stir in the almonds. Sift flour into the creamed mixture, blending in well. Stir in the wafer crumbs and mix until a stiff dough forms.

Press the mixture into tiny fancy molds (sand-tart or French fluted molds) and place on a baking sheet. Bake in a moderately hot oven (375°) for about 10 minutes or until very lightly browned. Remove from the molds while hot. Dot with jam or jelly if you wish. Makes 2 to 3 dozen, depending on the size of the tins.

BISHOP'S PEPPER COOKIES   Rovastinpipparkakut

The traditional Christmas shapes of these pepper cookies are little pigs and little boys, called *Nissu* and *Nassu,* respectively. At other times during the year, the cookies are cut out with a scalloped-edge cutter. Pepper cookies are a universal favorite in Finland; some people like them big, thick, and soft, while others insist they should be thin and crisp. This recipe makes the thicker, softer variety.

1 egg
1 cup sugar
½ cup dark corn syrup
1 cup melted butter
¼ cup finely chopped almonds
2½ cups sifted white flour

1 teaspoon soda
1 teaspoon cinnamon
1 teaspoon ground cardamom
¼ teaspoon allspice
1 teaspoon ginger
¼ teaspoon salt

Beat the egg. Add the sugar and syrup, mixing well. Add the butter and chopped almonds, and beat until well mixed. Sift the flour with the soda, cinnamon, cardamom, allspice, ginger, and salt, and add gradually to the creamed mixture, continuing to mix well until a stiff dough is formed. Chill. Roll out to about ¼-inch thickness. Cut into rounds or animal shapes and place on a lightly greased baking sheet. Bake in moderately hot oven (375°) for 7 to 10 minutes or until the cookies feel firm when touched. Makes about 36.

CHEESE STICKS   Juustotangot

Something salty is often a refreshing treat on the coffee table. These rich cheesy sticks are also nice as a soup accompaniment.

¼ cup butter
2½ tablespoons heavy cream
5 tablespoons grated Cheddar
    cheese

½ cup white flour
1 egg, beaten

Cream the butter until smooth and add the cream slowly. Blend in the cheese and the flour to make a stiff pastry. Roll into ropelike strands about the thickness of your finger, and cut these into 2-inch lengths. Place on a baking sheet, brush with egg, and bake in a moderate oven (350°) for 10 to 12 minutes or until lightly browned. Makes 12.

■◎◈■◎◈■◎◈■◎◈■◎◈■◎◈■◎◈■◎◈■◎◈■◎◈■◎◈■◎◈■◎◈■

COFFEE TRIANGLES   Kahvikolmiot

½ cup butter   ¼ cup cream
1 egg   2 cups white flour
¼ cup sugar   2 teaspoons baking powder
¼ teaspoon salt

Topping
orange marmalade   sugar

Cream the butter well and add the egg, sugar, and salt, beating until light and fluffy. Stir in the cream. Add the flour and baking powder to the creamed mixture and stir until a stiff dough forms. Chill. Roll out to ¼-inch thickness and cut the dough into 2-inch triangles. Place on a lightly greased baking sheet, dot each triangle with orange marmalade, and sprinkle sugar over the top. Bake in a moderately hot oven (375°) for 12 to 15 minutes or until golden. Makes about 3 dozen.

CINNAMON COOKIES   Kaneelikakut

These crisp cookies are traditonally shaped into rounds and are pretty when garnished with a blanched almond half.

1 cup soft butter   2 teaspoons cinnamon
1 cup sugar   2 teaspoons baking powder
2 eggs   3 cups white flour
2 tablespoons cream

1 egg, beaten (for glaze)   cinnamon sugar (½ cup sugar mixed
halved blanched almonds (optional)   with 1 tablespoon cinnamon)

Cream the butter and sugar until light and lemon colored. Beat in the two eggs until the mixture is thick. Stir in the cream, cinnamon, baking powder, and flour to make a stiff dough. Chill. Roll the dough out to about ¼-inch thickness and cut into rounds with a cutter about 2 inches in diameter. Place the cookies on a greased baking sheet. Brush each with beaten egg and sprinkle with about ¼ teaspoon of the cinnamon sugar. If you wish, press a blanched almond half into the center of each cooky. Bake in a moderately hot oven (375°) for 10 minutes or until lightly browned. Makes 3 to 4 dozen cookies.

■◎⌘■◎⌘■◎⌘■◎⌘■◎⌘■◎⌘■◎⌘■◎⌘■◎⌘■◎⌘■◎⌘■◎⌘■◎⌘■◎⌘■

JAM-FILLED COOKIES   Täytettykakut

1 cup soft butter	dash salt
½ cup sugar	apricot, raspberry, or strawberry
1 egg yolk	jam (for filling)
3 cups white flour	

Cream the butter and sugar together until light. Blend in the egg yolk.
Add the flour and salt gradually, until well combined. Shape the dough into
balls the size of walnuts and place on a lightly greased baking sheet. Make
a slight indentation in the center of each and dot with the jam. Bake in a
moderately hot oven (375°) for about 10 minutes or until almost golden.
Makes 36.

FINNISH GINGERSNAPS   Suomalaiset Piparkakut

These are thin, crisp, spicy cookies that are a favorite around Christmastime. They keep well when stored in an airtight container.

½ cup light molasses or dark corn	1 tablespoon ginger
syrup	1 tablespoon cinnamon
½ cup dark brown sugar	3–3½ cups white flour
½ cup soft butter	1 teaspoon baking powder
½ cup heavy cream	½ teaspoon salt

In the bowl of your electric mixer, beat together the syrup, brown sugar,
and butter until mixture is smooth. Add the cream, ginger, cinnamon, flour,
baking powder, and salt, and continue mixing until the dough is stiff. Chill
for several hours.

Roll out small portions of the dough to ¼-inch thickness, and cut into
3-inch rounds. Bake in a moderately hot oven (375°) for about 8 minutes.
Do not overbrown. Makes about 60.

■◦■◦■◦■◦■◦■◦■◦■◦■◦■◦■◦■◦■◦■◦■◦■

SHAVINGS   Lastut

These are delicate, lacelike cookies that are shaped after baking by drap-
ing over a round object. Sometimes these cookies are filled with berries and
whipped cream or ice cream, and served as a dessert; sometimes they are
cut into large rounds (about 8 inches in diameter) and filled with whipped
cream and stacked, to make a torte.

¼ cup butter   ½ cup quick-cooking oatmeal or
½ cup sugar   finely ground almonds
                                      1 tablespoon cream

Melt the butter in a saucepan. Remove from the heat and stir in the sugar,
oatmeal, and cream. Drop by very small teaspoonfuls onto a well-greased
and floured baking sheet. Flatten slightly to uniform thickness. (Be sure to
leave plenty of room between the cookies, as they spread during the baking.)
Bake in a moderate oven (350°) for 5 to 7 minutes or until uniformly browned.
Let the cookies cool for about 15 seconds on the baking sheet, then use a
long sharp knife to remove them, and drape them over a broom handle,
bottle, wooden-spoon handle, or other round object to finish cooling. Store
in a cool dry place. Makes 18 to 24 cookies, or 4 8-inch rounds.

VERY GOOD PEPPER COOKIES   Hyvät Piparkakut

The variations of gingersnaps in the Scandinavian countries are countless.
This recipe makes a crisp spicy cooky that keeps very well.

1 cup dark corn syrup   2 cups butter
2 teaspoons cinnamon   2 cups granulated sugar
½ teaspoon allspice   1 egg
¼ teaspoon black pepper   1 cup heavy cream
1 teaspoon cloves   4 teaspoons soda
1 teaspoon ginger   9 cups white flour

Combine the syrup, cinnamon, allspice, pepper, cloves, ginger, butter,
and sugar in a saucepan, and bring to a boil. Remove from heat and pour
into a mixing bowl. Cool. Stir in the egg, cream, soda, and flour. Chill
overnight.

Roll out very thin, using about ½ cup of the dough at a time, and cut into
any desired shape. Place on a greased baking sheet and bake in a moderately hot oven (375°) for 12 to 15 minutes, or until the cookies are crisp
but not overly browned. Makes about 8 dozen 2-inch-round cookies.

ALMOND-FILLED TARTS Masariinit

These tarts are a favorite on the Finnish coffee table. They are very rich.

Shells

½ cup butter
½ cup confectioners' sugar
1 egg

1 cup white flour
½ teaspoon baking powder

Filling

2 eggs
¾ cup sugar

⅓ cup soft butter
½ cup very finely chopped almonds

To make the shells, cream the butter until light. Add the sugar and egg and beat until thick. Stir in the flour and baking powder. Press the dough into 12 paper-lined cupcake tins.

For the filling, beat the eggs, then add the sugar, butter, and almonds, mixing until all ingredients are thoroughly blended. Fill the unbaked tart shells with this mixture. Bake in a moderately hot oven (375°) for 15 to 20 minutes or until golden. Makes 12.

CARDAMOM BALLS Kardemummapyrökät

These spicy cooky balls are nice to serve with tea or dessert or on the coffee table.

½ cup soft butter
½ cup sugar
1 egg
¼ cup heavy cream
2 cups sifted white flour

2 teaspoons baking powder
¼ teaspoon salt
3 teaspoons crushed or powdered
   cardamom

1 egg, beaten
   (for glaze: optional)

Cream the butter and sugar together until light, then add the egg, beating until thick. Stir in the cream. Sift the flour with the baking powder and salt and add with the cardamom to the creamed mixture, mixing until a stiff dough forms. Chill thoroughly.

Shape the chilled dough into small balls (about 1 inch in diameter) and arrange on a lightly greased baking sheet. Bake in a moderately hot oven (375°) for 10 to 12 minutes or until golden. If you wish, you may brush the cookies with egg before baking to give them a shiny glaze. Makes 48.

■❦■❦■❦■❦■❦■❦■❦■❦■❦■❦■❦■❦■❦■❦■❦■

GRANDMA'S MERINGUES   Isoäidin Marengit

1 cup egg whites (approximately 8)	4 tablespoons lemon juice
3 cups sugar	2 teaspoons grated lemon peel

Grease a baking sheet heavily and have it ready. In your electric mixer, beat the egg whites until foamy and slowly add the sugar, beating at high speed until the mixture is so stiff that a spoonful dropped on the baking sheet keeps its shape. Continue beating the mixture while gradually adding the lemon juice. Drop spoonfuls of the meringue mixture onto the baking sheet. Bake the meringues in a moderately slow oven (325°) for 35 to 45 minutes or until they are tinged with gold and dry. Makes about 4 dozen.

FINNISH COOKY STICKS   Suomalaiset Puikot

These rich, melt-in-the-mouth cooky sticks with an almond coating are made from one of the oldest Finnish cooky recipes. They are nice to serve with ice cream for dessert or on the coffee table.

1 cup soft butter	1 teaspoon almond extract
½ cup sugar	dash salt
1 egg	3 cups sifted white flour

Coating
1 egg, beaten	½ cup finely chopped almonds
sugar	

Cream the butter and sugar together until blended, add the egg, almond extract, and salt. Sift the flour into the mixture, blending it in well. Work the dough with the hands until smooth. Shape into long rolls about ½-inch thick. Cut into 2½-inch lengths and roll first in the beaten egg, then in sugar, then in the chopped almonds. Place on a lightly greased baking sheet. Bake in a moderately hot oven (375°) for 8 minutes or until just barely golden. Makes 6 dozen.

COUNTRY COOKIES   Talonpoikaiskakut

These are rich refrigerator cookies.

1 cup butter	2 cups white flour
1 cup sugar	1 teaspoon soda
2 tablespoons dark molasses	dash salt
¾ cup finely chopped almonds	

Cream the butter and sugar together until light, then add the molasses and nuts. Stir in the flour, soda, and salt until well blended. Chill slightly if the dough is too soft to work with. Shape into 2 rolls, each about 1¼-inches in diameter, refrigerate, and bake at your convenience.

Just before baking, cut ¼-inch thick slices, place on a greased baking sheet, and bake in a moderate oven (350°) for 10 minutes or until very lightly golden. Makes about 100 cookies.

III. Pasties and Pastries

The recipes in this chapter are mostly Karelian in origin. Notice that one basic crust is used for several kinds of pastries, both sweet and savory. Karelian menus, by tradition, are rich with filled savory pasties and sweet pastries. Karelian piirakka—an oval-shaped, open pastry with a rye crust and a potato or rice filling—is about the best known.

Pastries are an important item in the baking schedule of the Karelian homemaker. On the farm, she does her baking all in one day, for it takes several hours to heat up the large brick oven in the tupa of her home, and once heated, it is good for several hours of baking. In one day she may make pasties, both rice- and potato-filled, berry-filled pastries, meat dishes, perhaps a fish casserole, and large thick round loaves of sour rye bread.

Western Finnish cooks seldom make pastries; instead they bake thinly rolled-out dough into crackers and crispbreads.

Kalakukko, which originated in the province of Savo in east-central Finland is one of the most unusual foods of Finland. In Kalakukko (*see index*) small fresh-water fish are baked in a rye crust for several hours at a low heat. In that time, the bones of the fish become soft enough to eat. The kalakukko is then sliced. Each slice has a rye crust surrounding a cross section of the fish packed inside. It has a wonderful flavor.

BASIC YEAST PASTRY   Vehnäleipätaikina

Finns use this dough to encase a variety of fillings.

1 package active dry yeast
¼ cup warm water
1 cup milk, scalded and cooled
   to lukewarm
1 teaspoon salt

1 egg, well beaten
½ cup sugar
4–4½ cups sifted white flour
½ cup soft or melted butter

Dissolve the yeast in the water. Combine the milk, salt, egg, and sugar in a large mixing bowl. Add the yeast, stir in 2 cups of the flour, and beat until smooth and elastic. Stir in the butter until blended, add the remaining flour, and mix until a stiff dough forms. Turn the dough out onto a lightly floured board and knead until smooth. Place in a lightly greased bowl, turn to grease the top, and let rise until doubled (about 1 hour). Punch down and let rise again (about 30 minutes); the dough will be puffy but not doubled). Use the dough to encase fillings as directed in the recipes for Deep Fried Meat Pies, Carrot Pasty, Cabbage Pasty, Blueberry Buns, Mashed Potato Buns, Karelian Cheese-Filled Buns or Salmon Piirakkaa (See *index* for *any of these*).

BASIC POTATO PASTRY   Perunavoitaikina

This dough is used many ways. The potatoes give it its very stretchy quality. It is an excellent pastry for encasing apples or ground-nut fillings. Finns make Potato Crackers and piirakkaa (*see index*) with it.

1 cup cooked mashed potatoes
   (may be leftover)

½ cup butter
1½ cups flour

Put the potatoes into a saucepan and add the butter. Heat until the butter is melted, stirring constantly. Slowly add the flour, beating well to make a smooth, stiff dough. (If the mashed potatoes are dry, the pastry may take less flour, so be sure to add to it gradually.) Let the dough rest for 30 minutes. Roll out small portions of dough at a time on a floured board, and add flour freely as needed. Use this pastry to encase fillings or as directed in the recipes for Meat Potato Pasty and Thin Apple Tarts (*see index*).

■◎■◎■◎■◎■◎■◎■◎■◎■◎■◎■◎■◎■◎■◎■◎■◎■

BUTTER PASTRY   Voitaikina

This pastry is used to make many different kinds of tarts and pies. It is somewhat like French puff pastry, but simpler to make. You make two doughs—one of flour and water, the other of flour and butter—and chill both. You first roll them out separately, then together, folding and rolling the dough as in the method for puff pastry.

2 cups sifted white flour   1 cup soft butter
⅓ cup cold water

Place 1 cup of the flour in a small bowl and gradually add the water, tossing the mixture with a fork until it gathers together into a ball. Smooth the dough out with your hands. Place in the refrigerator and let chill until very cold. In another bowl, cream the butter. Add the remaining cup of flour gradually, stirring well until the dough is smooth. Chill this too until cold (about 1 hour).

Roll out the flour-water dough on a lightly floured board into a rectangle about 12 by 16 inches. Remove the flour-butter dough from the refrigerator and roll it into the same size rectangle. Place the butter dough on top of the flour-water dough. Fold the top third of the doughs down over the center and roll lightly. Fold the bottom third up over the center and roll lightly to about ½-inch thickness. Turn the dough around and repeat the folding and rolling processes until both doughs are completely blended. Roll the dough into a large (about 20-inch) square, keeping the corners squared. Use as directed in the recipes for Ground Meat Pie, Hot Meat Tarts, and Christmas Tarts.

CREAM BUTTER PASTRY   Kermavoitaikina

This pastry is suitable for (see index) various filled pastries. Make it when you do not want to bother with regular Butter Pastry (above), or do not have the time to make Basic Yeast Pastry.

1½ cups heavy cream   3¼ cups white flour
1 teaspoon baking powder   1 cup soft butter
¼ teaspoon salt

Whip the cream until stiff. Sift the baking powder, salt, and flour into the cream, and mix until thoroughly blended. Stir in the butter until blended. Chill the dough for several hours. Use as directed for Christmas Tarts or for other filled pastries (like Deep Fried Meat Pies, Salmon Piirakkaa, and Hot Meat Tarts) that call for a pastry dough.

■⊘∞■⊘∞■⊘∞■⊘∞■⊘∞■⊘∞■⊘∞■⊘∞■⊘∞■⊘∞■⊘∞■⊘∞■

BASIC KARELIAN PIIRAKKAA   Karjalan Piirakkaa

Rye-crusted, filled with creamy rice or a savory potato filling, these thin, oval-shaped pies are served with soup or with cold cuts and cheese for lunch. Karelians who carry lunchboxes eat piirakkaa in place of sandwiches.

Crust

1 cup water
1 teaspoon salt
2 tablespoons melted butter, shortening, or salad oil

1½ cups white flour
1½ cups rye flour

Basting Sauce

½ cup hot milk

2 tablespoons melted butter

To make the crust, mix the water, salt, and liquid shortening in a large bowl and stir in the white flour. Beat until smooth. Add the rye flour and mix until well blended. Turn the dough out onto a floured board and knead until smooth (about 2 or 3 minutes). Shape the dough into a roll about 2 inches in diameter, divide into 12 equal portions, and dust with flour. Pat each into a small round cake, then roll out into a circle about 6 to 8 inches in diameter, keeping the shape as round as possible.

To fill, place 3 or 4 tablespoons of the filling (see recipes following) on each round of dough and spread to within an inch of the edge. Fold two sides of the dough onto the filling, forming an oval shape, but leave an inch-wide strip of the filling exposed. Crimp the edges of the dough. Place the piirakkaa on a greased baking sheet. Bake in a very hot oven (450°) for 15 minutes or until lightly browned, basting twice during the baking with the milk-and-butter mixture. Baste once again upon removal of the piirakkaa from the oven. Cover the pies, while they are still hot, with a clean towel to soften the crusts, or wrap the entire batch in foil, in one package. Serve hot or cold.

KARELIAN RICE PIIRAKKAA
Karjalan Riisi Piirakkaa

Crust

1 recipe Basic Karelian Piirakkaa *(above)*

Filling

1 cup uncooked white rice (not precooked or instant)
1 teaspoon salt

6 cups milk
2 tablespoons butter

Prepare the crust according to the directions for Basic Karelian Piirakkaa. To make the filling, combine the rice, salt, and milk in the top of a double boiler. Cook over boiling water, stirring occasionally, for 2 hours or until the milk is absorbed and the rice is creamy. Stir in the butter. Cool.

Fill and bake the piirakkaa as in the directions for Basic Karelian Piirakkaa, basting with the milk-and-butter sauce. Serve hot or cold, with Egg Butter (see index). Makes 12.

KARELIAN POTATO PIIRAKKAA   Perunapiirakkaa

Serve these piirakkaa with a salad or soup for lunch, or a late evening snack, with tea.

Crust
1 recipe Basic Piirakkaa (above)

Filling
2 cups cooked mashed potatoes
¼ cup hot milk

2 tablespoons melted butter
salt to taste

Prepare the crust according to the directions for Basic Karelian Piirakkaa. Whip the potatoes with the milk, butter, and salt until smooth and fluffy. (If you are using instant mashed potatoes, you may not need to use the milk—the consistency of the potatoes should be about the same as for stiff whipped cream.)

Fill and bake these piirakkaa according to the directions for Basic Karelian Piirakkaa, using the same basting sauce. Serve hot or cold with Egg Butter (see index). Makes 12.

CHEESE PIIRAKKAA   Juustipiirakkaa

These are interesting to make and serve as hors d'oeuvres. Prepare the crust as in the recipe for Basic Karelian Piirakkaa; shape and bake as directed in that recipe, but fill with this mixture: 2 cups grated Cheddar or Swiss cheese, 2 tablespoons white flour, and a dash of white pepper.

To make hors d'oeuvres or appetizers, use half the amount of dough, and roll it out into rounds 3 or 4 inches in diameter. Use about 2 tablespoons of the cheese filling for each piirakka. Makes 24 small piirakka.

BUTTER-FRIED PIIRAKKAA   Keitin Piirakkaa

When a fellow courted a girl in old-time Karelia, he was always intro-
duced to her family early in the game. If the family didn't approve of him,
his first visit could well be his last. If they did approve, the mistress of the
house (the girl's mother or grandmother), assisted by the other women of
the household, would make these piirakkaa for him. No words of approval
or disapproval were exchanged, but the boy would keep his ears open for
the sound of baking utensils as he carried on his conversation with the men
of the house. Today these piirakkaa are still made—but after the daughter
has already announced her engagement.

Shaped like half moons and filled with rice, these rye pasties are cooked
in butter in a skillet. Serve them in place of bread with a salad or soup, or
with a light meal. Or, you can make them very small (2 inches in diameter)
and serve them as hors d'oeuvres.

Crust
1 recipe Basic Karelian Piirakkaa *(see index)*

Filling
3 cups fluffy cooked rice, seasoned   ½ cup butter for frying
   with salt to taste

Make the crust as directed in the recipe for Basic Karelian Piirakka, and
roll out in 6- to 8-inch rounds.

Place about 2 tablespoons of the rice in the center of each round of pastry.
Fold the dough over the filling so you have a half-circle. Using a pastry
wheel (or the edge of a saucer), trim ¼ to ½ inch from the rounded edge,
sealing the filling inside the pastry.

In a frying pan or skillet, melt enough of the butter to cover the bottom
of the pan generously. Heat until it sizzles. Put in as many of the piirakkaa
as the pan will hold comfortably and fry about 2 minutes on each side or
until golden brown. Repeat for the remaining piirakkaa, adding butter as
needed. Or place the piirakkaa in a greased baking pan, brush with melted
butter, and bake in a moderately hot oven (375°) for 25 to 30 minutes or
until lightly browned. Serve hot with tea or coffee, or as suggested above.
Makes 12.

BUTTER-FRIED CHEESE PIIRAKKAA

Make like Butter-Fried Piirakkaa (above) but fill the pastry circles with 2 to 3 tablespoons grated cheese (Edam, Tybo, Swiss, or sharp Cheddar). Seal and fry as directed.

BUTTER-FRIED MEAT PIIRAKKAA

Make like Butter-Fried Piirakkaa (above) but fill the pastry with 2 to 3 tablespoons ground cooked meat (beef, ham, veal, chicken, etc.). Seal and fry as directed.

SALMON PIIRAKKA   Lohipiirakka

2 fresh salmon fillets (about
    2 pounds)
4 tablespoons melted butter
1 recipe Basic Yeast Pastry or
    Cream Butter Pastry (see index)
1 cup cooked rice

2 tablespoons chopped parsley
2 tablespoons minced onion
½ teaspoon salt
5 hard-cooked eggs, sliced
lemon juice
1 egg, beaten

Brown the salmon fillets quickly over high heat in 2 tablespoons of the butter, but do not cook them through; remove from the pan and chill. Prepare the pastry. Roll out half into an elongated oval about 16 by 6 inches. Place it on a lightly greased cooky sheet. Combine the rice, remaining butter, parsley, onion, and salt, and spread the mixture onto the rolled-out dough, coming to about 2 inches of the edges. Arrange half of the egg slices over the rice and top with the salmon fillets; sprinkle with the lemon juice and additional salt, if desired. Arrange the second half of the egg slices over the salmon layer.

Roll out the second half of the dough into another elongated oval (16 by 6 inches). Moisten the edges of the bottom crust and arrange the top crust over the filling. Press the edges together to seal. Brush with the beaten egg. With a sharply pointed knife, cut short slashes into the top crust to make vents for steam to escape. Bake in a hot oven (400°) for 25 to 30 minutes or until golden. Watch it carefully, and if the piirakka begins to brown too quickly, lower the heat and cover lightly with foil or brown paper. Serve hot. Serves 6.

■◌з■◌з■◌з■◌з■◌з■◌з■◌з■◌з■◌з■◌з■◌з■◌з■◌з■

KARELIAN CARROT PIIRAKKAA
Karjalan Pokkanapiirakkaa

Prepare the crust, shape, and bake according to the instructions for Karelian Rice Piirakkaa, but substitute for the rice filling the carrot filling used for Carrot Pasty (see index). Serve hot with Egg Butter (see index).

SULTSINA   Sultsina

Sultsina are made using the same rye pastry as for piirakkaa, but instead of being baked or fried, they are cooked on a hot dry griddle. In Finland, they are cooked directly on top of a wood stove or the flat burner of an electric stove. After it is cooked, each round is spread with a creamy filling, then folded in a special way.

Sultsina are served in Finland instead of sandwiches for breakfast, lunch, or supper. Serve them as the hot bread with a salad or soup, or pack them to take along on outings. They are excellent picnic fare.

Crust
1 recipe Basic Karelian Piirakkaa (see index)

Filling

1½ cups milk	2 tablespoons butter
⅓ cup quick-cooking farina	2 tablespoons sugar (optional)
½ teaspoon salt	1 teaspoon cinnamon (optional)

Prepare the rye crust and roll it out (according to the directions for Basic Karelian Piirakkaa) into rounds 6 to 8 inches in diameter. Cook each round in a hot dry electric skillet (on highest heat) for about 30 seconds on each side. The rounds will resemble flour tortillas.

To make the filling, bring the milk to the boiling point and sprinkle in the farina; add the salt. Stir until smooth, cooking for about 1 minute; cover, and let stand for 2 or 3 minutes more or until thick. Stir in the butter and add more milk if needed to make a smooth, spreadable consistency. Add the sugar and cinnamon, if you wish, to flavor the filling (it is not traditional, but flavored this way, Sultsina makes a fine coffee accompaniment or breakfast bread). Spread 2 tablespoons of the filling onto each cooked Sultsina round and fold three times: twice from opposite sides, then in the middle, toward the center (see *illustration*). Leave the ends open. Serve warm. Makes 12.

FISH IN A CRUST   Kalakukko

This is one of the most identifiably Finnish traditional foods. It is made of bony fish cooked in a heavy rye crust for several hours at a low heat. The tiny bones of the fish become soft enough to eat. Slice Kalakukko to serve it, and add to the menu parsley buttered new potatoes, cucumbers, and tomatoes for a true Finnish meal.

The authentic version of the crust calls for only rye flour and no yeast. However, for American tastes, I have revised the crust slightly. The flavor is still the same, but the crust is lighter and easier to chew.

Crust

1 package active dry yeast	4 tablespoons soft butter
1 cup warm water	1½ cups rye flour
1 teaspoon salt	1½ cups white flour

Filling

1 pound small fish (2 to 3 medium-sized trout or about 14 smelts)	dash pepper
1 teaspoon salt	4 slices bacon, cut in 1-inch pieces

Dissolve the yeast in the water in a bowl. Add the salt and butter. Stir in the flours, both rye and white, slowly, until they are combined well and a stiff dough forms. Knead lightly on a floured board until smooth. Replace the dough in the bowl, cover, and let rise until doubled in bulk. Pat the dough out on the floured board to an oval about ½-inch thick and about 12 inches long and 10 inches wide.

Rub the surface of the pastry with flour to dry it. Clean the fish, removing the heads and tails. Dry thoroughly and arrange on the dough, side by side and/or in layers. Sprinkle with salt and pepper and top with the bacon. Bring the dough up over the mound of fish and cover it completely. Dampen the outside of the dough with water to seal the edges, and smooth the top. If the dough should crack, reseal after moistening broken edge. The Kalakukko should have the shape of a loaf of bread. Place in a well-buttered heavy casserole with a lid, put 2 tablespoons of water into the dish, and cover. Bake in a slow oven (300°) for 4 hours. After the first hour of baking, brush with melted butter. After the third hour, remove the cover, remove the Kalakukko from the oven, wrap it in foil, and return to the casserole to bake 1 hour longer. Let it cool wrapped in the foil. This will soften the crust. Slice crosswise to serve. Serves 6.

MEAT COCK   Lihakukko

This is made like Kalakukko but it is filled with veal and pork instead of fish. Serve with sour cream, if you wish.

1 recipe Kalakukko rye crust
  (see *index*)
2 pounds lean veal, cut in ½-inch
  strips

1 pound pork, cut in ½-inch strips
2 teaspoons salt
2 tablespoons rye flour
¼ cup buttermilk

Prepare the crust as directed for Kalakukko, rolling it out to the same dimensions. Combine the veal, pork, and salt. Arrange the pieces of meat lengthwise on the rectangle of dough. Sprinkle with the rye flour. Fold the sides of dough over the filling and seal to make a loaf-shaped pie about 4 inches high and 8 to 10 inches long. Be sure to seal well, using water to dampen the dough edges. Brush all over with the buttermilk.

Place the kukko in a well-greased baking pan that has sides, and bake in a slow oven (300°) for 3 hours. Then remove from the oven, brush with butter, and wrap in foil. Return to the oven and bake for another hour. Remove from the oven again and wrap well in several layers of paper (newspapers will do) over the foil wrapping. Let stand for 3 to 4 hours. In this time the crust will soften but the kukko will still be warm. (This is an ideal dish for a picnic!) Slice crosswise, into 1-inch-thick slices. Serves 6.

TURNIP AND PORK COCK   Lanttu-Lihakukko

This is a favorite in the Savo region of Finland. It is made in the same manner as Kalakukko. This is an ideal accompaniment for hot soup on a cold day.

1 recipe rye crust for Kalakukko
  (see *index*)
1 medium turnip, peeled and thinly
  sliced
2–3 tablespoons butter

1 teaspoon salt
½ teaspoon sugar
1 pound thinly sliced boneless pork
  (pork steaks cut in strips will do)

Make the rye crust and roll out to the same dimensions as for Kalakukko. Brown the turnip slices in the butter over medium heat until they begin to get limp. Season with the salt and sugar. Layer the turnip slices and pork on the center of the pastry rectangle. Fold the sides of the crust over filling, moisten the edges, and seal well to make a loaf-shaped pie. Put into a well-greased pan, seam side down; brush the crust with additional melted butter, and bake in a slow oven (350°) for 3 hours. Remove from the oven, wrap in foil, and return to the oven; bake for another hour. Remove from the foil and brush heavily with butter. Serve hot, cut into slices. Serves 4 to 6.

FINNISH BUTTERMILK CREPES   Lättyjä

Liina, a great-aunt of ours, is an expert at lättyjä, and turns them out as though it were second nature to make them. In Finland these are a dessert or supper dish, but they are fine for breakfast too. Serve them with Blueberry Soup (see index), blueberries, or lingonberry preserves.

2 eggs
1 teaspoon sugar
¾ teaspoon salt
1 cup buttermilk

2 tablespoons melted butter
1 cup white flour
butter for frying

Beat the eggs and sugar together, add the salt, buttermilk, melted butter, and flour. Let stand for at least 1 hour before baking the pancakes. Heat a pancake pan (a Scandinavian pancake pan is best for these) and butter it well. Make small pancakes, using no more than 2 tablespoons of the mixture at a time. Cook on both sides until golden. Serve hot. Makes about 20.

BLUEBERRY PANCAKE   Mustikkapannukakku

Serve this for dessert or a special brunch.

2 eggs
2 cups milk
1 cup sifted white flour
2 tablespoons sugar
½ teaspoon salt

1 tablespoon butter
2 cups fresh blueberries (or thawed
   and drained frozen blueberries)
1 tablespoon lemon juice
4 tablespoons sugar

Beat the eggs and milk until well mixed. Sift the flour with the sugar and salt into a mixing bowl. Pour in the egg-milk mixture all at once and, using a beater or whisk, mix until smooth. Let the batter stand for 30 minutes before baking. Melt the butter in a 10- by 14-inch baking pan and spread it evenly over the bottom. Pour in the batter and bake in a moderate oven (350°) for 20 minutes. Remove the pancake from the oven and pour the blueberries evenly over the surface. Sprinkle with lemon juice and sugar, return to the oven, and bake for another 10 minutes. Cool very slightly. Using a pancake turner, carefully roll up the pancake and slip onto a serving platter. Serve immediately (but it can be reheated before serving). Slice to serve. Serves 4 to 6.

OATMEAL CREPES   Tsupoi or Tsupakka

Long ago, these Karelian crepes were baked on hot slabs of rock next to an open fire, usually behind the mill house where, after the harvest, the flour was ground. Today they are cooked in butter in a frying pan or crepe pan, rolled up, and served with cream and cinnamon sugar. Serve them for breakfast or for a dessert. Serve with a small dish of heavy cream and a bowl of cinnamon sugar. To eat, dip the roll first into the cream, then into the cinnamon (this is finger food). Or, if you wish, pour cream over the rolls, sprinkle with cinnamon sugar, and eat with a fork.

You can buy oat flour in health-food stores, or make your own by whirling in cooked oatmeal in a blender until it is a fine flour.

1 cup oat flour	3–4 tablespoons butter
½ cup milk	cinnamon sugar (½ cup sugar
2 eggs, slightly beaten	mixed with 3 teaspoons
½ cup heavy cream	cinnamon)
¼ teaspoon salt	cream

Combine the flour, milk, eggs, cream, and salt until smooth and creamy. Let stand for 30 minutes before frying. Melt a little of the butter in a skillet or griddle and heat until it sizzles, but don't burn it. For each crepe use 2 to 3 tablespoons of the batter, making a cake about 3 inches in diameter. Cook until the thin cake is set on top. Do not turn. With a pancake turner, roll up, browned side on the outside, and remove onto a platter. Makes about 16 crepes. Pass the cream and cinnamon sugar.

BAKED APPLE PANCAKE   Omenapannukakku

Serve this baked pancake for dessert or as an accompaniment for coffee. It also makes a nice main dish for breakfast or a brunch when served with fruit juice, smoked sausages, and coffee.

4 eggs	3 tart apples, peeled, cored, and
1½ cups milk	sliced
½ teaspoon salt	3 tablespoons butter
2 tablespoons sugar	cinnamon sugar (½ cup sugar
2 cups sifted white flour	mixed with 3 teaspoons cinnamon)
	cream

Beat the eggs until thick, then add the milk, salt, and sugar. Sift in the flour, mixing it in well. Let the batter stand for 30 minutes. Meanwhile, prepare the apples and cinnamon sugar.

Butter well two 8- or 9-inch round cake pans and sprinkle with part of the cinnamon sugar. Arrange the sliced apples in the pans. Sprinkle the apples with the remaining cinnamon sugar and dot with the butter. Pour the pancake batter over the apples, dividing it evenly between the pans. Bake in a moderately hot oven (375°) for about 30 minutes or until the top of each pancake is golden and set. Serve hot (this is best served immediately, although it can be reheated before serving), cut into wedges, and serve plain or with cream to pour over each serving. Makes 2 pancakes which can be cut into 10 or 12 wedges.

YEAST BATTER OVEN PANCAKE Hiivapannukakku

You can make the thin yeast batter the night before if you plan to serve this for breakfast. In that case, cover and refrigerate it; in the morning, the batter should be bubbly; if it is not, let it stand at room temperature until large bubbles appear on the surface.

1½ teaspoons active dry yeast
2 tablespoons warm water
1½ cups milk, scalded and cooled
   to lukewarm
1 teaspoon salt
3 tablespoons sugar
3 eggs, beaten
2 cups white flour

2 large cooking apples, peeled,
   cored, and thinly sliced
2 tablespoons butter
cinnamon sugar (½—1 cup sugar
   [depending on the tartness of the
   apples] mixed with 2 teaspoons
   cinnamon).

Dissolve the yeast in the water and add the milk, salt, sugar, and eggs. Beat until smooth. Add the flour and beat again until smooth. Cover and let rise in a warm place until the batter has large bubbles.

Butter two 8- or 9-inch round cake pans very well and sprinkle evenly with about 2 tablespoons of the cinnamon sugar. Arrange the apples in a layer over the bottom of the pans and sprinkle with the remaining cinnamon sugar. Dot with the butter. Pour the yeast batter over the apples, dividing it equally between the two pans. Bake in a moderately hot oven (385°) for 30 to 35 minutes or until the tops of the pancakes are golden. Invert onto a plate and cut into 3-inch wedges. Serve hot for breakfast, or serve cold as a coffee accompaniment. Makes about 12 wedges.

"DREAM" OVEN PANCAKE   Unelmapannukakku

The name for this rich, delicately textured pancake probably originated from the nature of its ingredients: whipped cream and beaten egg folded together. It makes an excellent base for fresh fruits like peaches or apricots or berries.

1 cup whipping cream   ½ cup sifted white flour
2 eggs   1½ tablespoons melted butter
2 tablespoons sugar

Whip the cream until stiff and set aside. Beat together the eggs and sugar until very light and lemon colored. Fold in half of the whipped cream (reserve the remainder for a garnish after the pancake is baked). Sift the flour over the cream-egg mixture; fold it in well, then fold in the melted butter. Turn the mixture into a well-buttered 8- or 9-inch round cake pan. Bake in a moderately hot oven (375°) for about 15 minutes. Serve hot (this is best served immediately, but it can be reheated before serving), garnished with the remaining whipped cream and fresh fruit or berries. Serves 6.

DESSERT PANCAKES   Ohukaisia

Cook these pancakes in the special Scandinavian pancake griddle that has 3-inch-round indentations for each cake, or make small pancakes, using about 2 tablespoons of the batter at a time. Serve with whipped cream and fruit soup or fresh fruit.

2 eggs, separated   3 tablespoons melted butter
2 teaspoons sugar   whipped cream
2 cups milk   fruit soup (see index)
¼ teaspoon salt   fresh fruit
6 tablespoons white flour

Beat the egg yolks with the sugar until fluffy, add the milk, salt, and flour, and stir in 1 tablespoon of the melted butter. Heat the pancake pan. Whip the egg whites until stiff and fold into the batter just before cooking. Use the rest of the butter to grease the pancake pan, using just enough to coat each indentation. Pour about 2 tablespoons of the batter into each indentation, brown about 1 minute, turn, and brown the other side. Serve immediately or keep hot until serving. Pass bowls of sugar, whipped cream, and fruit soup (see index) or fresh berries to spoon over the pancakes.

■෨෮■෨෮■෨෮■෨෮■෨෮■෨෮■෨෮■෨෮■෨෮■෨෮■෨෮■෨෮■෨෮■

FINNISH OVEN PANCAKE   Pannukakku

Serve this with jam for breakfast, or with Blueberry Soup (see index) for dessert. Pannukakku also makes an excellent base for fresh berries in season; use it as you would a shortcake.

3 eggs   2 tablespoons sugar
1 cup milk   ¼ teaspoon salt
¼ cup flour

Beat the eggs in the bowl of your electric mixer until fluffy. Add the milk, flour, sugar, and salt, beating continuously. The mixture should have the consistency of thick cream. Pour into 2 buttered 8-inch round cake pans lined with waxed paper. (The batter should be only 1/3-inch deep.) Bake in a very hot oven (425°) for 15 to 20 minutes. Turn out onto a serving dish and peel off the waxed paper. Serve hot. You can make this ahead of time and reheat it before serving, but it is best served immediately after baking. Serves 4.

MIDSUMMER DAY PANCAKES   Savolaiset muurlätyt

In the northern part of the province of Savo the sun does not set on Midsummer Day. These whole-grain pancakes are served during the day's celebration. The pancakes, thin, well flavored, and delicious, are served plain with butter or with berries or fruit soup.

1 cup milk   1 cup barley or whole-wheat flour
1 egg, beaten   (or a combination of the two)
¼ teaspoon salt   butter
                                    fruit soup (see index)

Beat the milk and egg together, add the salt and flour, and let stand for at least 30 minutes before making the pancakes. Heat a griddle or frying pan and coat the bottom with butter. Make small pancakes (they should be very thin) using about 2 tablespoons of the batter at a time. Brown well on both sides and serve immediately with butter and lingonberry, Blueberry, Raspberry, or Strawberry Soup. Makes about 20.

DESSERT WAFFLES   Jälkiruokavohvelit

These waffles are rich, light, and crisp—they melt in your mouth. They are best made with the Scandinavian-type waffle iron that you heat on top of the range. Serve them simply sprinkled with sugar, or use, cold, as a base for a shortcake.

2 cups heavy cream
3 eggs
1½ cups white flour

dash salt
3 tablespoons sugar
¼ cup melted butter

Whip the cream until stiff. In another bowl, beat the eggs until light, then fold the eggs into the cream. Fold in the flour, salt, and sugar, then the hot melted butter. Heat the waffle iron and brush with shortening. Pour on the batter. Cook until golden brown. Serve hot with sugar. Makes twelve 8-inch waffles.

CHRISTMAS TARTS   Joulutortut

These prune-filled tarts are baked in great quantity just before Christmas. At this time there is a great exchange of "coffee" invitations, and of course the ladies like to taste each other's Christmas Tarts.

1 recipe Butter Pastry or Cream
   Butter Pastry (see index)
   rolled to about ¼-inch thickness
1 pound dried prunes

3 cups water
½ cup sugar
2 tablespoons lemon juice

Prepare the pastry. Cook the prunes in water until soft. Drain, remove pits, and press through a wire strainer (or whirl in a blender until puréed). Add the sugar and lemon juice; mix well.

Cut the pastry into 3-inch squares and place a mound of filling in the center of each square. Split each corner from the top to within ½ inch of the center. Fold one-half of each corner of the square to the center, thus forming a star. Place on an ungreased baking sheet. Let stand at room temperature for 10 minutes before baking. Bake in a hot oven (400°) for 7 to 10 minutes or until a very light golden brown. Remove from the pan and cool on a rack. Makes about 24.

DEEP-FRIED MEAT PIES   Lihapiirat

These meat-filled tarts can be prepared in advance and then frozen. Reheat them in the oven before serving.

1 recipe Basic Yeast Pastry or
  Cream Butter Pastry *(see index)*
½ medium onion, finely chopped
¼ cup butter
1 pound ground very lean beef

1 teaspoon salt
½ teaspoon white pepper
4 hard-cooked eggs, chopped
1 cup cooled cooked rice
oil for frying

Make the pastry, and while it is rising, prepare the filling. Sauté the onion in the butter until it is limp; add the ground beef and cook until the redness disappears, stirring constantly. Add the salt, pepper, and chopped eggs. Cool completely. Stir in the rice.

Roll the pastry out to about ¼-inch thickness. Good yeast dough will pull and shrink after cutting, so cut out rounds 5 to 6 inches in diameter (a coffee-can lid is a good cutter). Put 2 to 3 tablespoons of the filling in the center of each round, moisten the edges, and fold over into a half circle, sealing well. Set to rise on a greased sheet of waxed paper dusted with flour.

Pour the oil into a frying pan to a depth of about 2 inches and heat to 375°. Drop in several of the filled pies and fry them for 2½ to 3 minutes (until golden brown) on each side. Turn them only once. Drain. Serve hot. Makes 12 to 16 pies.

HOT MEAT TARTS   Kuumat Piiraset

These savory meat-filled tarts are sold in cafés and kiosks in Finland. You can make these bite size and serve them as hot hors d'oeuvres.

1 recipe Butter Pastry, Basic Yeast
  Pastry, or Cream Butter Pastry
  (see index)
1 pound ground lean beef
½ cup finely chopped onion

1 teaspoon salt
¼ teaspoon pepper
¼ cup finely chopped fresh parsley
½ cup cooked rice
1 egg, beaten

Prepare the pastry according to the directions and roll out to about ¼-inch thickness.

Brown the beef and onion in a frying pan until all the red color is gone. Season with the salt and pepper, add the parsley and rice, and mix well. Cool.

Cut 3-inch rounds or squares of the pastry and place 1 to 2 tablespoons of the filling in the center of each piece of dough. Fold the dough over the filling; moisten the edges and seal. Place the tarts on a lightly greased baking sheet, brush with the beaten egg, and allow to stand at room temperature for 10 minutes before baking. Bake in a hot oven (400°) for about 10 minutes or until a light golden brown. Serve hot. Makes about 24 tarts.

GROUND MEAT PIE   Lihapiirakka

Pour your favorite rich gravy over squares of this pie and serve as a main dish. Any leftover cooked meat—beef, lamb, pork, ham, chicken, or turkey—is suitable for the filling.

1 recipe Butter Pastry (see index)
1½ cups cooked rice
1½ cups cooked ground meat
½ cup heavy cream

1 teaspoon salt (less if the meat
   is salty)
½ teaspoon white pepper
2 tablespoons chopped chives
1 egg, slightly beaten

Prepare the pastry and roll it into a 20-inch square. Mix together well the rice, meat, cream, salt, pepper, and chives. Spread the mixture on half of the rolled-out pastry to within 1 inch of the edges, fold the other half of the dough over the filling, dampen the edges of the dough, and seal. Place on a lightly greased baking sheet and bake in a moderately hot oven (375°) for 20 minutes or until browned. Cut into squares and serve hot with gravy. Serves about 6.

KARELIAN CHEESE-FILLED BUNS   Rahkapiirakat

1 recipe Basic Yeast Pastry
   (see index)
1½ cups creamed small-curd cottage
   cheese
¼ cup sugar
2 tablespoons grated lemon peel

1 egg, slightly beaten
½ cup raisins or currants (optional)
currant, blackberry, or blueberry jam
   for topping (optional)
beaten egg

Make the pastry, and while it is rising, prepare the filling. Force the cottage cheese through a sieve, and combine with the sugar, lemon peel, egg, and raisins or currants.

Divide the yeast pastry into twelve portions. Shape each into a ball, then roll out to about ½-inch thickness, keeping the shape round. Press a ridge around the edge to hold in the filling. Spread 2 to 3 tablespoons of the filling onto each round of dough. Brush the edges with beaten egg; place on a lightly greased baking sheet and let rise for 30 minutes in a warm place. Bake in a hot oven (400°) for 10 to 15 minutes or until golden brown. While still hot, spread with the jam, and serve. Makes 12.

CREAM-CHEESE-FILLED BUNS   Juustokukkoset

1 recipe Basic Yeast Pastry
  (see index)
1 8-ounce package cream cheese
¼ cup sugar

½ cup heavy cream
2 tablespoons lemon peel
1 egg, slightly beaten
dash of salt

Follow the directions for making Karelian Cheese-Filled Buns (*above*) but use this filling. To prepare, cream together the cheese, sugar, and cream, add the lemon peel and salt, and beat in the egg until the mixture is very smooth. Makes 12.

MASHED POTATO BUNS   Perunakukkoset

These interesting buns are from Karelia. You can serve them with soup for lunch or as a first course, or with brown sauce or gravy and a meat and vegetable for dinner.

1 recipe Basic Yeast Pastry
  (see index)
1 cup mashed potatoes
1 egg

salt to taste
pepper to taste
2 tablespoons butter, melted
milk (if needed)

Prepare the pastry according to directions. Combine the mashed potatoes, egg, salt, and butter in a mixing bowl. If necessary, add a little hot milk to make of a spreading consistency.

Divide the pastry into twelve parts, roll each into a bun shape, then flatten. Pinch up the edges to hold the filling in, and spoon 2 to 3 table-spoons of the filling onto each. Brush the edges with milk and let rise for 30 minutes in a warm place. Bake in a hot oven (400°) for 10 minutes or until lightly browned. While still hot, spread with extra butter, if you wish. Makes 12.

■ ᏸᎩ■ ᏸᎩ■ ᏸᎩ■ ᏸᎩ■ ᏸᎩ■ ᏸᎩ■ ᏸᎩ■ ᏸᎩ■ ᏸᎩ■ ᏸᎩ■ ᏸᎩ■ ᏸᎩ■

MEAT-POTATO PASTY   Lihaperunapiirakka

Serve these as a main dish for dinner, on the *voileipäpöytä* (bread-and-butter table), or as an accompaniment with soup.

1 recipe Basic Potato Pastry *(see index)*	2 hard-cooked eggs, chopped
1 pound ground lean beef	½ cup small-curd cottage cheese, drained
½ cup finely chopped onion	2 teaspoons salt
1 cup cooked rice	

Prepare the pastry, divide the dough in half, and roll to about ¼-inch thickness. Fit into a lightly greased jelly-roll pan, about 12 by 16 inches.

Brown the meat in a frying pan, add the onions, and cook until soft. Stir in the rice, eggs, cottage cheese, and salt. Mix well. Spread this filling evenly over the rolled-out pastry to within 2/3-inch of the edge of the dough. Roll out the second half of dough for the top crust, place over the filling, moisten the edges, and seal well. Prick the top of the pastry with a fork. Bake in a very hot oven (425°) for 20 minutes or until a light golden-brown. Brush with butter immediately and serve hot, cut into 3-inch squares. Makes about 16 squares.

POTATO CRACKERS   Perunakeksiä

Prepare 1 recipe Basic Potato Pastry *(see index)* and roll out as thinly as possible about 1/16-inch thick. Place on a lightly greased baking sheet. Bake in a moderately hot oven (375°) about 12 minutes or until there are patches of golden-brown color on the pastry. Remove from the oven and immediately cut into squares or triangles. (This gets crispy as it cools.) Store in an airtight container. Serve with dips, soups, or cheeses. Makes about 4 dozen 3-inch-square crackers.

THIN APPLE TARTS   Omenatorttuja

Prepare 1 recipe Basic Potato Pastry *(see index)* and roll out to ⅛-inch thickness. With a cooky cutter, cut out rounds of dough, place on lightly greased baking sheets, and bake in a moderately hot oven (375°) for about 10 minutes or until very lightly browned. Remove from the oven, cool, and sandwich 2 together at a time with apple butter or apply jelly. Serve with coffee.

NOTE: These tarts will soften on standing. So fill them shortly before serving. Makes about 24.

BLUEBERRY BUNS   Hedelmäkukkoset

Serve these with coffee or as a special breakfast treat.

1 recipe Basic Yeast Pastry
  (see index)
1 cup mashed blueberries, fresh,
  canned (drained) or frozen
  (defrosted)

2 tablespoons lemon juice
1 egg, beaten
½ cup sugar (or more, depending
  on the tartness of the berries)

Prepare the pastry according to directions. Divide into 12 parts, flatten, and shape each into a round about 4 inches in diameter. Turn up the edges slightly to hold in the filling. Combine the blueberries, lemon juice, egg, and sugar. Use about 2 tablespoons of this mixture to fill each round of dough. Let the buns rise for 30 minutes, brush the edges with milk, and bake in a hot oven (400°) for 10 minutes or until lightly browned. Serve hot or cold. Makes 12.

CABBAGE PASTY   Kaalipiirakka

This filling has a delightful sweet-sour cabbage flavor. It is an old favorite—I found this recipe in a Finnish cookbook published in 1909. Serve it as an accompaniment to soup, on the *voileipäpöytä* or bread-and-butter table, or as a side dish with a meal.

1 recipe Basic Yeast Pastry
  (see index)
6 tablespoons butter
1 small head cabbage, shredded
2 cups water

1 teaspoon salt
3 tablespoons sugar
1½ teaspoons wine vinegar
1 hard-cooked egg, finely chopped

Prepare the pastry according to directions. Divide it into two parts. Roll out half the dough to fit a well-buttered jelly-roll pan about 12 by 16 inches.

Melt 3 tablespoons of the butter in a large pan or skillet. Add the cabbage and toss with a fork. Cook until the cabbage is wilted and portions of it are browned. Add the water and simmer until the cabbage is tender. Add the salt, sugar, and vinegar; mix well; drain.

Place the cabbage in the pastry-lined pan, dot with the remaining butter, and sprinkle with the egg. Roll out the second half of the pastry to fit the top. Moisten the edges and seal well. Prick the top with a fork and brush with milk. Bake in a moderately hot oven (375°) for 30 to 35 minutes or until golden brown. Cut into 3- or 4-inch squares to serve. Serves 12 to 16.

CARROT PASTY   Porkkanapiirakka

This recipe is from the same old Finnish cookbook as Cabbage Pasty (*above*), and is still a well-liked dish among the Finnish oldtimers. Serve it as you would the Cabbage Pasty—with hot soup, for lunch, or as a side dish.

1 recipe Basic Yeast Pastry
   (*see index*)
1 pound carrots, cooked and
   mashed (about 2 cups)

1 cup cooked rice
1 teaspoon salt
½ teaspoon allspice
3 tablespoons butter

Prepare the pastry according to the directions. Divide it into two parts. Grease a 12 by 16-inch jelly-roll pan and roll out half the dough to fit it.

Combine the carrots, rice, salt, and allspice. Spread evenly over the dough in the pan. Dot with the butter. Roll out the second half of the pastry and fit over the filling. Moisten the edges and seal well. Prick the top with a fork and brush with milk. Bake in a moderately hot oven (375°) for 30 to 35 minutes. Cut into 3- or 4-inch squares. Makes 12 to 16 servings.

APPLE PASTRY   Omenapiirakka

In Finland, this delicacy is served with coffee, but it makes a wonderful dessert when topped with ice cream or whipped cream.

3 cups sifted white flour
1 cup butter
¾ cup cold water
6 medium-sized tart apples

¾–1 cup sugar (depending on the
   tartness of apples)
2 teaspoons cinnamon

Sift the flour into a bowl. Cut in the butter until the mixture resembles coarse crumbs. Sprinkle in the cold water until the dough comes away from the sides of the bowl and forms a ball. Chill. Roll the dough out to fit a 12- by 16-inch baking sheet, turning up the sides of the pastry to hold the filling in.

Peel, core, and slice the apples into a bowl. Add the sugar and cinnamon, tossing until all slices are coated. Arrange the apple slices in neat rows, overlapping the slices slightly, on top of the pastry. Bake in a hot oven (400°) for 15 to 20 minutes or until the crust is nicely browned and the apples are tender. Cut into squares to serve. Makes 12 to 16 squares.

OATMEAL PASTRY   Kaurapiirakka

Serve this rich pastry for dessert with a scoop of ice cream on top.

Crust

½ cup soft butter
¼ cup sugar

1 cup sifted white flour
⅔ cup uncooked oatmeal

Topping

2 tablespoons butter
⅓ cup uncooked oatmeal

2 tablespoons sugar
¼ teaspoon cinnamon

Cream the butter and sugar. Sift the flour into a small bowl. Combine with the 2/3 cup oatmeal. Stir the flour-oatmeal mixture into the butter-sugar mixture until it resembles coarse crumbs. Pat this crumbly mixture into a lightly greased 8- or 9-inch square pan.

Melt the 2 tablespoons butter in another pan over high heat, stir in the 1/3 cup oatmeal, and heat until the oatmeal is evenly browned, stirring constantly. Remove from heat and add the sugar and cinnamon. Sprinkle evenly over the dough in pan. Bake in a moderately hot oven (375°) for 20 to 25 minutes, or until lightly browned. Cut into bars. Makes about 16.

RYE CRACKERS   Ruiskeksit

1 cup rye flour
1 cup white flour
1 teaspoon sugar

½ teaspoon salt
½ cup butter, melted and cooled
½ cup milk

Stir together the flours, sugar, and salt in a bowl. Combine the butter and milk and pour over the dry ingredients, stirring with a fork until they are evenly moistened. Gather the dough into a ball and knead lightly on a floured board until smooth. Pinch off pieces of dough the size of marbles. Roll each out until very thin, and about 3 to 4 inches in diameter. Prick with a fork and place on a lightly greased baking sheet. Bake in a hot oven (400°) for 10 minutes or until lightly browned. Makes about 48 (3-inch-round) crackers.

GRAHAM CRACKERS   Grahamminäkkileipä

Follow the recipe for Rye Crackers (above), substituting graham or whole wheat flour for the rye flour.

CARAWAY RYE CRACKERS
Kumina-Ruisnäkkileipä

Follow the recipe for Rye Crackers, adding 1 tablespoon caraway seed to the dough. Sprinkle the crackers with salt (preferably coarse) before baking.

MAY DAY CRULLERS OR BIRDS' NESTS
Tippaleipä

Finnish people are quiet—so quiet that there is almost perfect silence even in an overcrowded bus. In department stores, soft music plays in the background as people bustle about. After the church service on Sundays, the congregants quietly leave through the exit as the pastor scurries out the chancel door. This quietness lasts for 364 days. The one remaining day of the year is May Day (May 1). Suddenly the whole country reverberates with a steady roar. Grownups and children alike carry huge colorful balloons, purchased from a sidewalk vendor who has a blimp-shaped bunch of balloons bobbing above him, all tied by their strings to his belt. The May Day celebration is led by the university students, who dance all day and all night, and sing and shout. It is a relief to have the long cold winter over, the summer ahead.

On May Day people invite each other to their homes for *sima* and *tippaleipä*. Sima (*see index*) is the lemon-flavored May Day beverage; tippaleipä is a cruller made of a thin batter drizzled into hot fat that resembles a bird's nest.

2 eggs
1½ teaspoons sugar
½ package active dry yeast
2 tablespoons warm water
1 cup milk, scalded and cooled
  to lukewarm

½ teaspoon salt
2 cups white flour
shortening or cooking oil for frying
confectioners' sugar

Blend the eggs and sugar, but do not beat them. Dissolve the yeast in the water and mix with the milk. Combine with the egg-sugar mixture. Stir in the salt and flour. Beat well. Place in a warm place to rise until bubbly (about 45 minutes to 1 hour).

Heat the shortening or oil (it should be about 4 inches deep) in a heavy pan to about 375°. Cut the corner of a plastic bag to make an opening about ⅛-inch in diameter. Put about 1 cup of the batter into the bag and squeeze it through the opening into the hot fat, moving the bag in a continuous round, to form a bird's nest shape about 3 or 4 inches in diameter. Fry for about 1 minute on each side (use a slotted fork or spoon to turn the cruller). Remove from the fat and drain on paper toweling. When cool, sift confectioners' sugar over it. Makes about 15.

BLINIS
Blinit

Karelian Finns traditionally serve these yeast-risen pancakes with *mäteen-mäti* (the roe of ling cod) on Shrove Tuesday. Serve these with caviar, or sardine, anchovy, or salmon paste, or with slices of smoked salmon (lox), melted butter, and sour cream.

½ package active dry yeast
¼ cup warm water
1¾ cups milk, scalded and cooled to lukewarm
3 cups sifted white flour

2 tablespoons sugar
3 eggs, separated
6 tablespoons melted butter
½ teaspoon salt

Dissolve the yeast in the water. Add the milk. Add 1 cup of the flour to the mixture. Stir in the sugar. Cover and let rise in a warm place until doubled (about 30 minutes). Beat the egg yolks slightly and add to the batter, then stir in the butter, salt, and remaining flour, mixing well. Beat the egg whites until stiff and fold into the batter. Let the batter stand in a warm place for about 30 minutes.

Heat a Scandinavian "Plette" pan (the kind with 6 or 7 round indentations) or a griddle, and butter it well. If you are using the Scandinavian pan, pour 2 to 3 tablespoons of batter into each indentation; if you are using a griddle (or skillet), pour on about 2 to 3 tablespoons of the batter for each cake (the blinis will be slightly larger than the 3-inch traditional size, but close enough to it). Cook until golden brown, then turn and brown the other side. Serve hot. Makes about 25 blinis.

BUCKWHEAT BLINIS
Tattariblinit

Follow the recipe for Blinis (*above*) but substitute ½ cup buckwheat flour for ½ cup of the white flour.

OATMEAL CRACKERS   Kauranäkkileipä

¾ cup uncooked oatmeal
½ cup milk
4 tablespoons melted butter
1 tablespoon sugar

¼ teaspoon salt
1 teaspoon vanilla
¾ cup sifted white flour
2 teaspoons baking powder

Place the oatmeal in a bowl and pour the milk over it. Let stand for 5 to 10 minutes. Add the butter, sugar, salt, and vanilla, and mix well. Sift the flour with the baking powder into the mixture. Stir until a smooth dough forms. Turn out onto a lightly floured board and roll out to ¼-inch thickness. Prick the dough with a fork all over. Cut out 2- or 2½-inch rounds and place on a lightly greased baking sheet. Bake in a hot oven (400°) for 10 to 15 minutes or until almost golden brown. Do not overbake. Store in an airtight container to retain crispness. Makes about 24.

IV. Soups and Stews

A hearty hot soup or stew can be the main course in a Finnish meal. So important are these in everyday meals that every household has a complete set of both company and family soup dishes or ramekins. These are usually about luncheon-plate size, and about 1 inch deep.

One group of American Finns calls both the meat stews and fish stews by the name of *mojakka*. It is a mystery to me where the name originated, for nobody in Finland knew what I meant by the word *mojakka*. The proper Finnish name for soups and stews is *keitto*.

CREAM OF CARROT SOUP   Porkkanasosekeitto

Serve this soup piping hot with toast wedges, rye crispbread or hardtack, and assorted cheeses and cold cuts.

1 bunch (about 1 pound or
    4 or 5 large) carrots
1 cup beef broth
2 tablespoons butter
2 tablespoons flour

4 cups milk
1 tablespoon sugar
dash pepper
chopped parsley
nutmeg

Scrape or peel the carrots. Cook until soft in the beef broth, adding water if needed. Drain, reserving the stock, and strain or mash the carrots to make a smooth purée. Heat the butter in a saucepan, add the flour, and stir until blended. Add the milk gradually, stirring to keep the mixture smooth. Heat to the boiling point and simmer for 10 minutes. Add the reserved stock, carrot purée, sugar, and pepper. Garnish each serving with parsley and a dash of nutmeg. Makes 4 to 6 servings.

POTATO CREAM BROTH   Klapsakkaa

An old Finnish story concerning this soup goes *"Illala perunavoi, aamulla klapsakkaa—ei emäntä kulta siillä jaksakkaa."* "In the evening, mashed potatoes, in the morning, potato broth—no, my dear woman, that isn't enough." The wife would plan her evening meal in order to make this broth for breakfast, and the men insisted it was not substantial enough. . . . But it is so easy!

1 cup mashed potatoes   dash allspice
2 cups whole milk   parsley
1 cup light or heavy cream   butter
salt and pepper to taste

Mix together the potatoes, milk, and cream, and whip until very smooth. Add salt to taste, pepper, and allspice. Heat to boiling, then simmer for 5 minutes. Serve hot, with a sprig of parsley and a dot of butter in the center of each serving. Serves 4 to 6.

FINNISH CREAMY PEA SOUP   Hernerakkaa

2 cups dried whole green peas   ½ teaspoon hot mustard
12 cups water   salt
3 tablespoons butter   pepper
1 tablespoon flour   1 cup heavy cream

Wash the peas well, then soak in the water overnight. Bring to a boil and cook until tender. Force through a wire strainer, or whirl in a blender to make a very smooth purée. Melt the butter, stir in the flour, then add the puréed peas and the cooking liquid, stirring to make a smooth mixture. Cook over medium heat, stirring constantly, for 10 minutes. Add the mustard, and salt and pepper to taste. Whip the cream, and just before serving stir into the hot soup, blending well. Serve garnished with toast cubes or croutons. Serves about 6.

SUMMER VEGETABLE SOUP   Kesäkeitto

Properly, this soup can be made during only a few days of the year, for its ingredients are the succulent young vegetables: baby carrots, tiny peas, sweet new onions, tiny green beans. For those of you who are vegetable gardeners, this soup is not impossible; however, a second-best choice is to use all the fresh vegetables that are available, whether large or small. And it is good even with frozen vegetables.

15 tiny new (or 2 or 3 larger) carrots	1 tablespoon sugar
1 cup sweet new peas	1 teaspoon salt
2 cups tiny snap beans (or larger beans cut into 2-inch pieces)	2 tablespoons flour
3 sweet new onions, chopped	4 cups milk (or for an elegant version, half-and-half cream)
2 cups tiniest new potatoes (or larger potatoes, cubed)	2 tablespoons butter
	chopped parsley

Clean the carrots (cut large carrots into 2-inch sticks and quarter them lengthwise). Scrub the new potatoes to remove the thin peel, but peel the larger ones. Put the carrots, peas, beans, onions, and potatoes into a pot. Add boiling water just to cover. Cook for 5 minutes or until the vegetables are almost tender. In another pot, combine the sugar, salt, flour, and milk and bring to boil. Pour into the pot of vegetables and simmer for 10 minutes. Pour into a soup tureen, dot with butter, and garnish with the parsley. Serve hot. Serves 4 to 6.

BEET-CABBAGE SOUP   Punajuurikaalikeitto

This borschtlike soup is hearty enough to be a main course, served with a meat-filled piirakka (see index).

4 cups beef broth	1/8 teaspoon pepper
1 small head cabbage, shredded	sour cream
3 large beets, peeled and grated	lemon slices
1/8 teaspoon caraway seeds	

Bring the broth to a boil and add the cabbage, beets, caraway seeds, and pepper. Cook until the cabbage is almost tender (about 15 minutes). Cover, and turn the heat to low until ready to serve. Serve, steaming hot, with the sour cream and lemon slices. Serves 4 to 6.

KARELIAN BORSCHT   Borschkeitto

This well-flavored beet-and-cabbage soup is well known in Russian cuisine; however, it is so much a favorite of Karelians (Eastern Finns), and such a fine soup, I am including it here.

4 medium beets, peeled and grated
2 tablespoons butter
1 teaspoon salt
4 tablespoons flour
2 tablespoons vinegar
1 small head red cabbage, shredded
1 bay leaf
1 clove garlic
2 carrots, peeled and cut up
1 tablespoon sugar
8 cups meat broth
½ pound spicy sausages (choritzo, Polish sausage, or frankfurters)
sour cream
lemon slices

Brown the beets in the butter over medium to high heat until limp. Add the salt, flour, and vinegar and mix until blended. Put into a large pot with the cabbage, bay leaf, garlic, carrots, sugar, and meat broth, and simmer for at least 2 hours, adding water as needed if too much stock cooks away.

Before serving, slice the sausages and add; serve when heated through. Serve in a soup tureen; pass a bowl of sour cream and a plate of sliced lemons. Serves about 6.

SAUERKRAUT SOUP   Hapankaalikeitto

Serve this soup as a main course with meat piirakkaa (see index) on a cold day—it is ideal for a soup-supper menu—or you might serve smaller portions as the beginning course for a winter meal. Serve with sour rye bread, rye crispbread, cheese, and cold cuts, and pass a bowl of sour cream to spoon into it.

12 cups water
1 pound lean pork, cubed
1 ham bone
4 cups sauerkraut
9 whole allspice
salt
pepper

Combine the water, pork, ham bone, sauerkraut, and allspice in a pot and simmer for 2 to 3 hours or until the pork is tender. Add salt and pepper to taste. Serve hot. Serves 10 to 12.

KLIMP SOUP   Klimppisoppaa

Klimps are the dumplings in this soup. This national favorite comes from Satakunta, a province in Western Finland. In a village farther north, there is served a soup by this same name, but the liquid used is milk instead of beef broth.

8 cups clear rich beef broth   ½ teaspoon salt
½ cup milk   ¼ teaspoon pepper
1 cup flour   2 eggs, slightly beaten

Heat the broth to boiling. Combine the milk, flour, salt, pepper, and eggs in a small bowl, mixing until smooth. Drop by very small spoonfuls into the simmering broth. Cover, and simmer for 15 minutes more. Serve hot. Serves about 6.

CREAM OF CABBAGE SOUP   Maitokaali

1 small head cabbage, shredded   3 tablespoons flour
6 cups water   1 tablespoon butter
2 teaspoons salt   1 teaspoon sugar
8 cups milk

Place the cabbage in the water (it should just cover the cabbage), add the salt, and cook until the cabbage is almost tender (about 15 minutes). Combine the milk and flour and add to the boiling cabbage; cook for 20 minutes more. Add the butter, stir in the sugar, and serve hot. Serves about 6.

MEAT AND POTATO STEW   Lihakeitto

This dish has plenty of hot, clear broth so it is especially welcome on a cold blustery winter day. Serve it as the Finns do, with rye crispbread, cheese, and bologna.

1 pound stewing beef   2 chopped onions
1 tablespoon bacon dripping or   5 medium carrots, peeled and cut
   other shortening   in 1½-inch chunks
2 teaspoons salt   5 medium potatoes, peeled and cut
4 cups boiling water   in chunks
5 whole allspice

Brown the beef in the fat until all sides are rich brown in color. Add the salt, boiling water, and allspice, and simmer slowly for at least 1 hour or until the meat is tender. Add the onions, carrots, and potatoes, and cook on low heat for 1 hour longer. Add more water, if necessary. Serve hot. Serves about 4.

DRY STEW   Lapskoda

This is called "dry" because you do not add liquid as such. Another fitting name would be "Stove Top Casserole." Serve with rye bread, rye crispbread or hardtack, sliced cheese, and buttermilk. You might add a salad and cooked vegetable to balance the menu.

½ pound thinly sliced salt pork   2 medium onions, peeled and sliced
½ pound thinly sliced veal   1 teaspoon whole allspice
5 large potatoes, peeled and sliced

Heat a heavy—preferably cast-iron—cooking pot, a Dutch oven, or frying pan. Rub the bottom with a piece of the salt pork. Layer the meat, potatoes, and onions, beginning with the salt pork and ending with potatoes, and sprinkle with the allspice. Cover and cook on the lowest heat possible, without stirring, for 4 to 5 hours (because cooking ranges vary so much, you will have to use your judgment—the heat should be high enough to cook it through but not burn it). Or, place in a slow oven (300°) for 4 to 5 hours. Serves about 6.

LAPLAND CHIPS   Lapinliuske or Lapinliuttu

Try this dish with venison unless you have the good fortune to have the real thing—frozen reindeer meat. Serve with sour rye bread, butter, and cheeses.

1 pound frozen reindeer meat   ¼ teaspoon pepper
   or venison   4 cups water
1 teaspoon salt

Slice the frozen meat paper-thin (it will resemble chips). Add the salt and pepper to the water, and bring to a boil. Drop the meat chips slowly into the boiling water, keeping the liquid boiling. Cook for 5 minutes. Serve the chips hot in their liquid over mashed potatoes. Serves 3 to 4.

FISH STEW   Kalakeitto

American Finns would call this *kalamojakka*. This recipe can be made with any fresh-water fish, but it is better to save the very bony fishes for kalakukko (see *index*). Serve this stew Finnish style, with a choice of rye bread, rye crispbread, or hardtack, and with butter, milk, and cheese.

1 pound cleaned fish (such as perch, pike, or trout)	3 to 4 medium potatoes, peeled and diced
2 teaspoons salt	2 cups milk
1 medium onion, chopped	2–3 tablespoons butter
½ teaspoon dillweed	chives or fresh dill
4 cups water	

Cut the fish into 2-inch pieces. Place the fish, salt, onion, and dillweed in a large pot and cover with the water. Bring to the boiling point and simmer (without boiling) until the fish flakes when pierced with a fork but does not fall apart. Drain, reserving the liquid to use as stock for boiling the potatoes. Put the potatoes in a saucepan, add the fish stock, and cook until tender. Pour the potatoes and stock back into the pan with the cooked fish and add the milk. Simmer slowly (do not boil) for about 20 minutes. Pour into a tureen dish and dot with butter. Garnish with the cut chives or fresh dill top. Serves about 6.

SELJANKA FISH STEW   Seljankakeitto

This is a Finnish version of bouillabaisse. Serve it with Karelian Rice Piirakkaa (see *index*) for lunch or supper, or as a first course.

½ pound whitefish	¼ cup sliced mushrooms
½ pound bass	1 tablespoon flour
8 cups water	1 8-ounce can tomato sauce
1 bay leaf	1 small dill pickle, chopped
6 whole allspice	1 thinly sliced lemon
½ teaspoon celery seed	salt
2 medium onions, chopped	pepper
1 tablespoon butter	fresh or dried dill

Skin and fillet the fish, and cut the fillets into 1-inch pieces. Make a stock by simmering the water, bones, head, and skin of the fish, the bay leaf, 6 of the allspice, and the celery seed for 30 minutes; strain. Sauté the onions in the butter for about 5 minutes or until limp, add the mushrooms, then add the flour, and stir until blended. Gradually add the fish stock. Add the tomato sauce, the remaining allspice, the fish, and pickle. Cover and simmer until the fish is done (about 10 to 15 minutes); it will flake easily. Add the lemon, salt, and pepper to taste. Serve hot, garnished with the dill. Serves 4 to 6.

ONION SOUP WITH A CRUST

Kuoritettu Sipulikeitto

4 large onions, peeled and sliced
¼ cup butter
6 cups rich beef stock, or
   3 10½-ounce cans beef broth
   and 2 cups water
1 bay leaf

salt
pepper
6 thick slices French bread
4 tablespoons grated Parmesan
   cheese

Brown the onions in the butter in a heavy pot over medium heat. Add the beef broth and bay leaf. Taste, and add salt and pepper accordingly. Cover and simmer for 30 minutes. Remove the bay leaf. Pour the soup into an ovenproof casserole and cover with the bread slices. Sprinkle with the cheese. Transfer to a hot oven (400°) and cook until the cheese has melted and is slightly browned. Serve immediately. Serves 6.

CARROT BROTH   Porkkanavelli

This milky soup, *velli* in Finnish, has a consistency similar to broth. Serve as a first course, or for lunch or supper.

4 medium carrots, peeled and sliced
1 cup water
3 cups milk
1 teaspoon salt
1 tablespoon sugar

dash fresh or dried dill
1 tablespoon flour mixed with
   1 tablespoon water
butter

Cook the carrots in the water until tender; drain. In a separate saucepan, heat the milk to simmering, add the salt, sugar, and dill. Stir in the flour-water mixture and cook until thickened. Add the carrots. Serve hot and top each serving with a pat of butter. Serves 4.

BEEF STEW WITH ROOT VEGETABLES
Lihajuuresmuhennos

This stew is even better the second day.

1 pound beef stew meat, cut in
  1-inch cubes
2 tablespoons butter
4 cups water
4 whole allspice
1 small rutabaga, peeled and cubed

3 medium potatoes, peeled and
  cubed
2 onions, peeled and halved
3 carrots, peeled and cut in 1-inch
  pieces
1–2 teaspoons salt
¼ cup chopped parsley

Brown the beef well in the butter. Add the water and allspice, and simmer until the beef is tender (about 1 hour). Add the vegetables and salt, and continue to simmer for about 30 minutes or until the vegetables are done but not mushy. Serve hot. Serves 6.

VEGETABLE BROTH   Kasvisliemi

This is a clear broth that you can use in recipes in place of chicken or beef broth. It is slightly pinkish in color and has lots of flavor.

1 carrot, peeled
2 medium celery roots, peeled, or
  4 stalks celery
2 medium parsnips, peeled
12 small radishes
¼ head of a medium cabbage
4 cups fresh peas in the pod
1 bunch parsley
2 cups chopped, peeled Jerusalem
  artichokes

1 large onion, washed but not
  peeled
2 leeks or 6 green onions
1 small beet, peeled
6 whole allspice
6 whole black peppercorns
2 bay leaves
3 quarts water
salt to taste

Wash or scrub the vegetables thoroughly, removing all stems and roots. Put the vegetables, allspice, peppercorns, and bay leaves into a large pot. Add the water, cover, and simmer slowly—do not boil—for 2 to 3 hours. Strain. (Save the vegetables for another use, if you wish.) The broth should be very clear. Add salt to taste and serve hot, as you would bouillon, or use in recipes as a substitute for beef or chicken broth. (Or pour the boiling broth into sterilized jars and seal; they will keep, like any home-canned food, as long as the seal remains intact. Unsealed, they will keep in the refrigerator for 2 to 3 weeks.) Makes about 2½ quarts.

LEEK SOUP   Purjokeitto

This is a thick golden-brown soup that is ideal for lunch, served with a filled piirakka (*see index*) or sandwiches.

5 leeks or medium white onions,
   peeled and quartered
2 medium potatoes, peeled and diced
3 cups rich beef broth

1 egg yolk
½ cup heavy cream or milk
chopped chives

Put the leeks (or onions), potatoes, and 1 cup of the beef broth in a heavy pot and simmer over medium heat for about 30 minutes or until the potatoes are tender. Press through a strainer or whirl in a blender until smooth.

Add the remaining beef broth and bring to a boil. Stir the egg yolk into the cream or milk until blended, and pour into the boiling soup, stirring vigorously. Cook until slightly thickened. Serve hot sprinkled with the chives. Serves 4.

CRAYFISH SOUP   Rapukeitto

Crayfish are available in parts of the United States during certain times of the year. If you can not obtain them, use crab meat, either canned or fresh, as a substitute.

2 tablespoons butter
4 tablespoons flour
3 cups fish stock or chicken
   consommé
salt
pepper

paprika
½ cup heavy cream or sour cream
1 egg yolk
1 cup cooked crayfish meat
1–2 tablespoons lemon juice
chopped parsley

Melt the butter in a large pan and stir in the flour to make a *roux*. Slowly add the fish or chicken stock, stirring all the while to keep the mixture smooth, and cook over medium to high heat until thickened. Add salt, pepper, and paprika to taste. Mix the cream and egg yolk together and add to the boiling mixture, stirring quickly to keep the mixture smooth. Add the crayfish, add lemon juice to taste; garnish with parsley and serve immediately. Serves 4.

BEER SOUP   Kaljakeitto

There are many versions of this off-beat soup; some are richer, some have a higher proportion of beer to milk. It is perfectly innocent—if its alcohol content worries you, remember that all the alcohol evaporates when the soup comes to a boil. Even the little old ladies in Finland enjoy Kaljakeitto!

3 cups milk
2 cups beer or "near beer" or
  kalja (see index)
4 tablespoons flour
water

4 teaspoons sugar
½ teaspoon salt
½ teaspoon or more ground ginger
crisp bread cubes or croutons

Heat the milk and beer in separate pots. Add enough water to the flour to make a smooth paste; stir it into the hot milk, keeping the mixture smooth. Add sugar, salt, and ginger (to taste) to the hot beer, then beat this mixture slowly into the hot milk, using a whisk. Whip until frothy. Serve immediately, garnished with crisp bread cubes. Serves 4.

LAPLAND FOOL   Lapinpila

This dish is so named because only a Lapp could make something that tastes and looks so good out of leftovers! It is best of all if you have some smoked meat, such as ham or bacon, you can use. Serve with pickled beets, rye crispbread or hardtack, and sliced cheese.

1½—2 pounds (about 4 cups) leftover meat (ham, veal, tongue, etc.)
4 slices bacon or ham
4 cups mashed potatoes
2 bay leaves

6 whole allspice
6 whole black peppercorns
salt
3 cups meat stock

Put the meat through a food chopper, using a medium blade. Mix with the potatoes; add the bay leaves, allspice, peppercorns, and meat stock; salt to taste. Heat slowly, stirring constantly, until the mixture boils. Cover, turn the heat off, and let stand for about 10 minues. Serves 6 to 8.

■෨෨■෨෨■෨෨■෨෨■෨෨■෨෨■෨෨■෨෨■෨෨■෨෨■෨෨■෨෨■෨෨■

TOMATO POTATO SOUP   Tomaattiperunakeitto

½ pound fresh tomatoes, peeled
6 cups Vegetable Broth *(see index)*
  or water
3 medium potatoes, peeled and
  cubed
4 medium onions, peeled and diced

3 tablespoons butter
3 tablespoons flour
salt
pepper
1 cup heavy cream
chopped parsley

In a large pot, combine the tomatoes, broth or water, potatoes, and
onions. Cook over medium heat until the vegetables are tender. Press through
a sieve or whirl in a blender until smooth. Melt the butter in a saucepan and
add the flour, stirring until smooth, then pour in the hot puréed soup, stirring vigorously to keep the mixture smooth. Cook until thickened. Taste, and
add salt and pepper. Serve hot (this can be reheated), and just before
serving, stir in the cream and garnish generously with parsley. Serves 6.

CUCUMBER BISQUE   Kurkkukeitto

Cucumbers are abundant in Finland. The favorite way to serve them is
simply sliced and salted; but this is my favorite.

2 medium onions, peeled and
  chopped
2 medium cucumbers, peeled and
  chopped
6 tablespoons butter
2 cups chicken broth or water
2 tablespoons flour

2 egg yolks
½ cup heavy cream
1 medium cucumber, peeled and
  diced
salt
pepper
chopped parsley

Cook the onions and chopped cucumbers in 4 tablespoons of the butter
until the onions are transparent. Add the broth or water and cook until the
vegetables are tender. Press through a sieve or whirl in a blender until
smooth. In the pan, melt the 2 remaining tablespoons butter and stir in the
flour until it is well blended. Pour in the puréed vegetable mixture and stir
vigorously until smooth. Cook until thickened, stirring constantly. Beat the
egg yolks and cream together and stir into the hot soup. Turn the heat
down and simmer for 5 minutes. Just before serving, stir in the diced raw
cucumber, season with salt and pepper, and garnish with the parsley.
Serves 4.

CREAM OF CAULIFLOWER SOUP
Kukkakaalikeitto

This creamy soup is very nice served as a first course, or with sandwiches or piirakkaa for lunch.

1 large head cauliflower, cut up	1 egg yolk
4 cups water	dash of basil, tarragon, or cayenne
2 teaspoons salt	(optional)
1 cup cream	parsley

Put the cauliflower into a saucepan, add the water and salt, and cook until tender. Press through a sieve or whirl in a blender to make a smooth purée. Return to the pot. Combine the cream and egg yolk and beat into the puréed cauliflower. Simmer for 5 minutes. Add the basil, tarragon, or cayenne. Serve hot. Garnish each serving with a sprig of parsley. Serves 8.

BEEF RAGOUT   Palapaisti

This is universally popular in Finland today. Neighborhood meat markets carry palapaisti meat, already cubed, in a large pan next to the two grades of ground meat.

1½ pounds lean stewing beef, cubed	1½ cups beef broth
2 medium onions, sliced	½ cup sour cream
¼ pound mushrooms, sliced	salt
4 tablespoons butter	½ teaspoon white pepper
1 tablespoon flour	1 tablespoon chopped parsley
1 teaspoon hot mustard	

Brown the beef, onions, and mushrooms in butter. Stir in the flour, mustard, and beef broth. Cover, and simmer for about 1 hour or until the meat is tender. Stir in the sour cream, add salt to taste, and the pepper and parsley. After adding the sour cream, do not boil but keep warm until serving time. Serves about 6.

FINNISH BEEF STROGANOFF   Stroganoffin Pihvi

This is one of the most popular items served in a Finnish *ruokala* café. It is served with mashed potatoes or hot fluffy rice.

1½ pounds top round steak
1½ teaspoons salt
¼ teaspoon white pepper
2 tablespoons flour
4 tablespoons butter
½ medium onion, sliced
water or beef broth

½ cup heavy cream
2 tablespoons tomato paste or
  catsup
2 teaspoons prepared hot mustard
  or Finnish-Style Mustard *(see index)*
2 dill pickles, finely minced

Pound the meat with a mallet until flattened. Cut into 1-inch squares, sprinkle with the salt, pepper, and flour, coating the meat evenly, and brown well in the butter over medium to high heat. Brown the onion in the drippings in the pan. Add enough water or broth to cover the bottom of the pan, scraping the brownings up into the meat. Cover and simmer for 30 minutes or until the meat is tender. Just before serving, combine the cream, tomato paste, mustard, and dill pickle and stir evenly into the meat mixture. Serve hot. Serves 4 to 6.

FARMER'S MEAT STEW   Talonpoikaiskeitto

You can vary the meat (use veal, pork, lamb, or venison, round steak, or a combination of any of these) in this recipe, which is a stew, yet not a stew. You do not add liquid to the pot, but cook the meat and vegetables at a very low temperature for a long period of time. In the country, this dish is made on a wood stove and simmered on its very edge all day long.

2 pounds round steak, cut in
  3-inch squares
4 medium potatoes, peeled and
  sliced
4 medium carrots, peeled and sliced

2 large onions, peeled and sliced
2 teaspoons salt
½ teaspoon pepper
2 tablespoons butter

Lay the squares of steak on the bottom of the pot, top with a layer of potatoes, a layer of carrots, and a layer of onions, sprinkling each layer with some of the salt and pepper. Dot with the butter, cover, and cook over very low heat for about 4 hours or until the meat is tender and the vegetables are cooked. This is a one-pot meal with very little if any gravy. Serves 4 to 6.

KARELIAN RAGOUT   Karjalan Paisti

The Karelian homemaker, in the days of the wood stove, would set this
meat dish to simmer early in the morning, and it was ready for the evening
meal. It was especially good to make on baking days, for then the huge
brick ovens remained hot for several hours, and the ragout could be simmered in a covered pot in the oven all day.

1 pound beef chuck, cubed	3 teaspoons salt
1 pound lamb shoulder or breast, cubed	2 teaspoons ground allspice
	6 whole allspice
1 pound pork shoulder, cubed	4 cups beef broth or water
5 medium onions, sliced	

Layer the cubed meats and onions in a 3-quart heavy casserole or Dutch
oven with a tight-fitting lid. Season each layer with the salt and ground
allspice; distribute the whole allspice throughout. Heat the broth or water
to boiling and pour over the meat. Cover, and cook in a very slow oven
(275°) for about 5 hours or until the meat is tender. Karelian Ragout is delicious in a dinner including Baked Mashed Potatoes, Lemon Leaf Lettuce
Salad, Finnish Rye Bread with Butter, Fresh Berry Soup, Milk, and coffee
(see index for all). Serves 6 to 8 generously.

LAMB WITH DILL   Tilliliha

This Scandinavian favorite is a classic in Finland, too; you find it quite
commonly on the menus of small restaurants.

2 pounds lean lamb, cubed	2 teaspoons chopped fresh or
3 tablespoons butter	dried dill
4 cups water	2 tablespoons flour
1½ teaspoons salt	1 tablespoon sugar
	1 tablespoon vinegar

Brown the meat very well in 2 tablespoons of the butter; add the water,
salt, and dill, and simmer for 45 minutes to 1 hour or until the meat is
tender. Remove the meat from the liquid and keep hot. In another pan, melt
the remaining 1 tablespoon butter, and stir in the flour, sugar, and vinegar
to make a smooth paste. Slowly add the cooking liquid from the meat,
stirring constantly to keep the gravy free of lumps. Continue to cook until
smooth and thickened. Arrange the meat cubes on a platter, surround with
buttered new potatoes, sprinkle lightly with more dill, and serve hot with
the sauce either poured over it or in a gravy boat. Serves 4 to 6.

FINNISH SIMMERED LAMB
Suomalainen Lammasmuhennos

Onions and allspice give this lamb stew typical "Finnish" flavor. Serve with a green salad and crisp bread.

2½ pounds lean lamb shoulder or breast, sliced
4 medium potatoes, peeled and cubed
3 medium carrots, peeled and cut in 1-inch pieces

2 medium onions, peeled and cut in eighths
1½ teaspoons salt
¼ teaspoon pepper
2 cups water (approximately)
1 tablespoon chopped parsley
6 whole allspice

Make a layer of the meat in the bottom of a heavy large cooking pot or Dutch oven. Top with the potatoes, carrots, and onions, and sprinkle with the salt and pepper. Add just enough water to cover the meat, sprinkle the parsley and allspice over it, cover, and simmer very slowly for 1 to 1½ hours or until the meat is tender and the vegetables are cooked but not mushy. (Or cover and bake in a moderate oven [350°] for 1 to 1½ hours.) Serve hot. Serves 8.

PORK AND TURNIPS   Sianliha Naurisvatkuli

1 pound pork, cubed
2 medium onions, peeled and quartered
½ cup flour
2 teaspoons salt

8 cups 1-inch turnip cubes (from about 12 small or 3–4 large turnips)
¼ teaspoon white pepper
2 cups boiling water
chopped parsley

Brown the pork and onions together in a heavy pan or Dutch oven (without added fat), stirring constantly. Sprinkle with part of the flour and half of the salt. Top with a layer of turnip cubes and sprinkle with more flour and salt. Repeat this layering process until the turnip cubes and flour are all used. Sprinkle pepper over the top and pour in the boiling water. Cover. Simmer for 1½ to 2 hours or until the meat is very tender and the turnip cubes are well cooked. Garnish with the parsley. Serve hot. Serves 4.

STEWED LAMB WITH HORSERADISH
Lammasviillokki

Tender lamb cubes are served in a smooth sauce that is flavored with fresh grated horseradish (you can buy the latter in a jar). Serve with boiled new potatoes or mashed potatoes. This is also delicious served with buttered egg noodles.

2½ pounds lean stewing lamb
oil or butter
2 cups water
2 teaspoons salt

½ teaspoon white pepper
2 teaspoons chopped fresh or
   dried dill

Sauce
1 tablespoon butter
3 tablespoons flour
broth from the lamb

salt
2 tablespoons grated horseradish

Cut the lamb into cubes and brown well in just enough oil or butter to cover the bottom of the pan. Add the water, salt, pepper, and dill. Cover and cook until the lamb is tender (for 45 minutes to 1 hour). Remove the meat to a serving platter and keep hot. Reserve the broth in which it was cooked.

To make the sauce, melt the butter in a pan and stir in the flour. Gradually stir in 2 cups of the broth in which the lamb was cooked (add water if necessary to make 2 cups), keeping the sauce smooth, and cook until thickened. Taste and add salt. Stir in the horseradish. Pour the sauce over the lamb, and serve immediately. Serves 6.

SIMMERED VEAL   Vatkuli

This is delicious served with mashed potatoes.

2 pounds stewing veal, cut in
   small cubes
2 tablespoons butter
2 tablespoons flour
1½ teaspoons salt

½ medium onion, sliced
1 bay leaf, crushed
12 whole allspice
boiling water

Brown the veal in the butter, sprinkle with the flour, and toss in pan lightly to coat evenly. Add the salt, onion, bay leaf, allspice, and enough boiling water barely to cover the veal. Cover and cook over low heat for 45 minutes to 1 hour, or until the veal is tender. Serve hot. Serves 4 to 6.

V. Fish

In Finland you cannot hope to escape the fish. Fortunately whether it is served smoked, salted, pickled, raw, cold, hot, in patties, cutlets, or creamed dishes, it is almost invariably delicious.

It is true that fish plays an important part in the cuisine of the Scandinavian countries. However, in Finland, because of her 50,000 lakes, freshwater fish are more important than in Sweden, Norway, and Denmark, where the majority of the fish recipes call for salt-water fish. The small Baltic herring called *silakka* (pl. *silakkaa*) is the most abundant, inexpensive, and important in Finland. Next in line are larger species of herring.

Here is a selection of the best of the Finnish fish dishes. But the success of these dishes depends on how fresh the fish is that you are cooking.

COBBLER'S SALMON   Suutarinlohi

Real salmon is very expensive in Finland. Since the poor cobbler never has quite enough money to buy it, he makes this traditional dish of *silakkaa* (Baltic herring). The name "Cobbler's Salmon" in itself typifies Finnish humor in its comparison of extremes.

Because Baltic herring, sometimes called "sprats," are not available in the United States, I have substituted salted herring in this recipe with the sanction of Finns who know the original.

1 large salted herring (about 1–1½ pounds)	2 tablespoons minced fresh onion
½ cup white wine vinegar or cider vinegar	1 teaspoon sugar
¼ cup water	¼ teaspoon ground allspice
	dill or parsley (optional)

Soak the herring in water overnight in the refrigerator to remove as much of the salt as possible. Cut the fish into fillets, removing the backbone, head, fins, and tail *(see Voileipäpöytä Herring recipe for method)*. Cut each fillet into 1-inch pieces. Arrange in a deep serving dish.

Bring the vinegar and water to a boil and add the onions, salt, sugar, and allspice. Pour over the fish. Cool, then chill and serve, garnish with sprigs of dill or parsley. Makes about 12 to 16 pieces, depending on the size of the herring.

■🌀■🌀■🌀■🌀■🌀■🌀■🌀■🌀■🌀■🌀■🌀■🌀■🌀■🌀■

PICKLED FISH ROLLS   Silakkakääryleet

In Finland, these are made with *silakkaa* (Baltic sprats); however, I have found smelts an excellent substitute. They are about the same size as the silakkaa and they are excellent when pickled.

1 pound fresh smelts, boned so they
  lie flat
2 teaspoons salt
¼ teaspoon allspice
1 medium onion, minced

1 cup white wine vinegar or cider
  vinegar, or ½ cup vinegar and
  ½ cup dry white wine
1 teaspoon sugar
fresh dill

Carefully wash and drain the fish. Mix the salt and allspice with the minced onion and sprinkle about 1½ teaspoons of this mixture on each fish. Roll, with skin side on the outside, and place in a baking dish, seam side down. Combine the vinegar and sugar and pour over the fish rolls; bake in a moderate oven (350°) for 15 minutes. Remove from the oven, let cool for 30 minutes, and drain. Store, covered, in the refrigerator until serving time. To serve, garnish with sprigs of the dill. Makes about 12 rolls.

HERRING WITH APPLE AND SOUR CREAM
Omenasilli

1 medium fresh or salted herring
2 medium onions, grated
1 small tart apple, grated

1 cup sour cream
1 teaspoon dry mustard
½ teaspoon sugar

If you are using salt herring, soak it overnight in the refrigerator in skim milk, cold tea, or water to remove the excess salt. Fillet the fish, removing the head, tail, fins, and skin. Cut the fillets into half-inch strips. Arrange on a serving dish and sprinkle with the grated onions and apple. Mix the sour cream with the mustard and sugar and spread over the whole or put through a cake decorator to garnish the fish.

SPICED HERRING   Maustesilli

1 pound fresh herring, trout, or
  salmon
1 medium onion
1 cup white wine vinegar
½ cup water
¼ cup sugar

10 whole allspice
1 teaspoon salt
1 bay leaf
¼ teaspoon dry mustard
½ teaspoon dill seed
fresh sprigs dill (optional)

Clean and fillet the herring *(see Voilepäpöytä Herring for method),* and cut the fillets into 1-inch pieces. Slice the onion and layer the herring and onions into a wide-mouthed quart jar, serving crock, or serving dish. Heat the vinegar, water, sugar, allspice, salt, bay leaf, dry mustard, and dill seed to boiling. Simmer for 10 minutes. Cool to lukewarm. Pour over the fish. Cover and store in the refrigerator for 1 to 2 days before serving. The fish will keep for several weeks; however, it may attain a stronger vinegar flavor than desired. To serve, garnish with the dill. Makes about 24 pieces if the herring are about 8 inches long.

HERRING À LA RUSSE   Venäläisen Silli

4 herrings, filleted	¼ teaspoon sugar
1 cup mayonnaise	2 tablespoons cream
½ teaspoon hot mustard	¼ teaspoon paprika

Garnish

1 tablespoon (approximately) capers	chives
1–2 sliced, hard-cooked eggs	beet slices
dill	

Cut the herring fillets into half-inch slices, and transfer the pieces to a serving dish, arranging them neatly so they have the appearance of the original fillets. Combine the mayonnaise, mustard, sugar, cream, and paprika, and spread over the herring. Garnish with any or all of the suggested garnishes.

VOILEIPÄPÖYTÄ HERRING   Suolasilli

Soak good quality salt herring overnight in the refrigerator in skim milk, cold tea, or water to remove excess salt. Clean each fish and remove the skin, fins, head, and tail. Remove the backbone by gripping it at the head end with thumb and forefinger, then run the forefinger of your other hand down the top side of the backbone, holding the flesh of the fish back with same hand and pulling the backbone and attached bones slowly outward. Or, remove the backbone and bones from one half of the fish and at the same time pull out the individual bones on other side. You will have two fillets. Cut the fillets crosswise into thin slices, and using a spatula, arrange on a long, narrow serving dish into a fish-shaped form. Garnish with onion rings, chopped chives, or chopped dill. Serve on the *voileipäpöytä* (bread-and-butter table) or with boiled potatoes for lunch. One fish serves 1 to 4 people.

■🐟■🐟■🐟■🐟■🐟■🐟■🐟■🐟■🐟■🐟■🐟■🐟■🐟■🐟■

GLASS MASTER'S HERRING   Lasimestarin Silli

This is a traditional pickled herring that is to be served on the *voileipä-pöytä* (bread-and-butter table). I have found that fresh brook trout works as well as a substitute for the salted herring although it has a firmer texture. If you use it, omit the soaking step.

4 salted herrings, cleaned and
  filleted
2 teaspoons whole allspice
3 whole bay leaves
2 teaspoons mustard seed
6 whole cloves
1-inch piece of fresh ginger

1-inch piece fresh horseradish or
  1 tablespoon grated horseradish
1 small carrot, peeled and cut up
3 red onions, peeled and sliced
  crosswise
2½ cups white wine vinegar
¾ cup sugar

Soak the herring fillets in water overnight in the refrigerator, drain, and cut into 1-inch pieces. Layer the herring with the spices and carrot and onions in a glass crock, about 2-quart size. Bring the vinegar and sugar to boiling, stirring until the sugar is dissolved. Cool. Pour over the herring in the jar. Cover and refrigerate for 2 days before serving. This fish keeps about 2 weeks under refrigeration. Serves 8 for the voileipäpöytä, or 4 when it is the main course. The pieces are also nice as appetizers; be sure to provide toothpicks.

HERRING IN TOMATO SAUCE
Silli Tomaattikastikkeessa

2 salted herrings or fresh brook trout
milk for soaking
8 tablespoons white wine vinegar
3 tablespoons salad oil

5 tablespoons tomato catsup or
  tomato sauce
1 small onion, minced
dash of sugar

Clean and fillet the herring (*follow the method in Voileipäpöytä Herring*) and place in a shallow bowl. Pour in just enough milk to cover the fish and let stand overnight in the refrigerator. (If you make the recipe with fresh brook trout you can eliminate this step.) Remove fillets from the milk, rinse in water, and dry. Cut the fillets into half-inch pieces, and arrange attractively in a serving dish. Combine the vinegar, oil, catsup, onion, and sugar, mixing well. Pour over the herring, cover, and refrigerator for 4 to 6 hours (refrigerate fresh brook trout in the marinade for 24 hours). Serve with rye bread and butter. Makes about 48 pieces if the herring are about 8 inches long.

■🌊■🌊■🌊■🌊■🌊■🌊■🌊■🌊■🌊■🌊■🌊■🌊■

HERRING IN ASPIC   Silakkahyytelö

This herring dish is almost always served on the *voileipäpöytä* (bread-and-butter table), but it is ideal for a first-course dish, prepared in individual molds and served on lettuce leaves.

1 pound fresh Baltic herring or 6-inch smelts	¼ cup water or white table wine
fresh dill sprigs	1½ cups water (or half water, half dry white table wine)
1½ teaspoons salt	1 teaspoon vinegar
1 package unflavored gelatin	

Clean and fillet the fish, removing head and backbone (*see Voileipäpöytä Herring for method*). Put a sprig of dill on each fillet, roll up and fasten with a toothpick. Sprinkle with the salt. Soften the gelatin in the ¼-cup water and set aside. Bring the 1½ cups water and vinegar to a boil and place the fish rolls in the water. Lower the heat and simmer for about 10 minutes, or until the fish flakes when probed with a fork. Remove the fish rolls from the broth and arrange them in a ring mold (about 3-cup size) or in 6 individual molds. Strain the fish broth and stir the softened gelatin into it; bring to a boil again and stir until gelatin is dissolved. Cool; pour over the fish rolls and chill until set. Unmold to serve.

HERRING "CAVIAR"   Sillikaviaari

Use this as a topping for sandwiches, mixed with salad dressings, or as a *voileipäpöytä* (bread-and-butter table) dish.

1 salted herring	chopped onion
heavy cream, whipped	pepper

Soak one salted herring in cold water for several hours to remove salt. Drain. Remove the skin and fillet the fish, being sure all the bones are removed. Chop into very small pieces with a sharp knife. Add enough whipped cream to the chopped herring to make a paste. Season to taste with the onion and pepper.

■₠₠■₠₠■₠₠■₠₠■₠₠■₠₠■₠₠■₠₠■₠₠■₠₠■₠₠■₠₠■₠₠■₠₠■

CHILLED POACHED FISH WITH SAUCE
Kylmä Keitetty Kala

3 pounds fish (approximately)
  such as sea bass, white cod,
  halibut, swordfish, or salmon

Broth (for 3 pounds of fish)

1 quart water
2 tablespoons salt
½ cup white wine vinegar

9 whole allspice
2 slices onion
1 bay leaf

Sauce

1 teaspoon fresh dill or dried dillweed
½ cup mayonnaise

½ cup sour cream
salt
lemon juice

Garnish

lemon slices
parsley
chives

lettuce
tomatoes

Allow about ½ pound of fish per person. Use either whole fish or fish steaks.

Heat the water, salt, vinegar, allspice, onion, and bay leaf to boiling. Carefully place the fish in this broth, one piece at a time, adjusting the heat so that the broth simmers, not boils. Cover, and simmer gently until the fish flakes easily (about 10 minutes). Remove from the liquid with a slotted spoon or spatula and place on a serving tray. Chill.

To make the sauce, combine the dill, mayonnaise and sour cream, and add salt and lemon juice to taste. Chill. Serve in a small bowl at the table.

Garnish the chilled fish steaks attractively with your choice of the items suggested above.

HOT POACHED FISH   Keitetty Kala

3 pounds fish (approximately), such as sea bass, white cod, halibut, swordfish, or salmon.

Broth

1 quart water
½ cup vinegar or 1 cup white wine
  and 1 tablespoon vinegar
1 tablespoon salt
1 teaspoon sugar

9 whole allspice
1 bay leaf
1 sliced onion
½ carrot
1 teaspoon fresh dill, chopped

■ⓔⓢ■ⓔⓢ■ⓔⓢ■ⓔⓢ■ⓔⓢ■ⓔⓢ■ⓔⓢ■ⓔⓢ■ⓔⓢ■ⓔⓢ■ⓔⓢ■ⓔⓢ■

Garnish
parsley or dill   lemon wedges

You can cook the fish either whole, or cut into steaks.

Combine the water, vinegar or wine, salt, sugar, allspice, bay leaf, onion, carrot, and dill in a large flat pot or deep frying pan. Bring to a boil. Place the fish in the broth and simmer, covered, for about 10 minutes, or until it flakes easily. Remove from the broth to a hot platter, garnish with parsley or dill and lemon. Serve with Finnish Hollandaise Sauce *(see index)*.

HOLIDAY LUTEFISK   Keitetty Lipeäkala

Lutefisk is the Swedish word, *lipeäkala* is the Finnish name for this special codfish. Lipeäkala is an important food at Christmastime to Finns. It is made by soaking a large fried codfish in water for 1 week, changing the water every day, and for 3 to 5 days (or until the meat of the fish is shiny) in a strong solution of raw soda and ashes mixed with water. The fish is then soaked in fresh water for 7 days more, during which time the water is changed every day. In all, it takes about 3 weeks to prepare the raw fish. But this process is now done commercially, and today you can buy lutefisk ready for cooking. Look for it in your fish market, or order it through your fish man. On Christmas Eve the fish is cooked and served with a rich sauce.

2 pounds lutefisk (bought from a   1 recipe White Sauce *(see index)*
   Scandinavian market)   melted butter
2 quarts water   allspice
2 tablespoons salt

Cut the fish into large pieces and tie in a cheesecloth or clean towel. Pour the water into a large pot (do not use an aluminum pot or it will discolor), add the salt, and bring to a boil. Lower the fish into the water and cook for about 10 minutes, keeping the water at a simmer all the while. Remove the fish to a serving platter(but one that is not silver). Sprinkle the fish with allspice and serve with the White Sauce and melted butter.

RYE-FRIED FISH   Paistettue Kala

Rye-flour-coated fish, fried in butter, have a delicious nutty flavor. Smelts, sole, trout, etc.—any fish that you would ordinarily fry—are good this way.

Dip the cleaned and boned fish first into a mixture of 1 egg beaten with ¼ cup cream, then into rye flour. Fry in butter until golden on both sides. Serve immediately.

■◎◆■◎◆■◎◆■◎◆■◎◆■◎◆■◎◆■◎◆■◎◆■◎◆■◎◆■◎◆■◎◆■

FANCY FISH LOAF   Kalamureke

You can bake this fish loaf in a fancy mold, if you butter it well. Serve with Mushroom Sauce (see index).

1 pound boned fish (perch, sole,   1 teaspoon salt
  or whitefish)   ¼ teaspoon allspice
3 finely chopped anchovy fillets   ¼ teaspoon sugar
1 tablespoon cornstarch   3 egg whites, beaten stiff
3 egg yolks   parsley
1 cup cream

Grind the fish (it will be easier to grind if it is partially frozen), using a coarse blade. Mix the ground fish with the anchovies, cornstarch, egg yolks, cream, salt, allspice, and sugar. Fold in the egg whites. Turn into a very well-buttered and floured 2-quart fancy ring mold. Place the mold in a pan of water and bake in a moderate oven (350°) for 60 to 65 minutes, or until a light golden brown. While the loaf is baking, make the sauce. To serve, invert on a serving plate, garnish with parsley, and serve immediately with Mushroom Sauce. Serves about 4.

BAKED FISH ROLLS WITH TOMATO
Tomaattikalakääryleet

The original recipe for this dish calls for small Baltic herring—silkakkaa—fish about the size of smelts. Actually, any small fish that you can successfully fillet and roll (including brook trout, sole, or smelts) is good cooked this way. Serve the fish rolls with boiled tiny new potatoes and sliced cucumbers.

2 pounds fresh small-fish fillets   5 medium tomatoes, peeled and
⅓ cup (approximately) cold butter   diced
fresh dill sprigs or dried dill   3 tablespoons flour
2 teaspoons salt   3 tablespoons water

Lay each fish fillet out flat and dot with the butter, using at least ¼ cup. Put a sprig of fresh dill or a dash of dried dill onto each fillet and sprinkle with half the salt. Roll the fillets up and arrange them in a single layer in a 2-quart casserole or baking dish. Sprinkle with the remaining salt. Spread the diced tomatoes evenly over all and dot with 1 tablespoon butter. Bake in a hot (400°) oven for 20 to 25 minutes or until the fish flakes easily when probed with a fork.

Drain the liquid from the fish rolls. You should have 2 cups (add water if necessary to make that amount). Mix the flour and water into a smooth paste and stir into the liquid; cook, stirring constantly, over medium heat until thickened. Serve the fish rolls hot with this gravy. Serves about 6.

BAKED STUFFED WHITEFISH   Paistettu Siika

This fish stays juicy right up to eating time; it is basted during the baking with butter, cream, and boiling water.

1 3-pound whitefish or large lake
   trout

salt
vinegar

Stuffing
1½ tablespoons butter
3 tablespoons chopped dill
2 tablespoons chopped parsley
1 tablespoon chopped onion

4 medium tomatoes, peeled and
   chopped
½ teaspoon salt
1 tablespoon lemon juice
¼ teaspoon white pepper

Topping
1 beaten egg
bread crumbs or cracker crumbs

Basting Ingredients
¼ cup melted butter
½ cup boiling water
1 cup light cream

Clean the fish, removing the scales, fins, and bones, but do not remove the skin or separate the two fillets. Sprinkle lightly with salt and rub with enough vinegar to coat the whole fish lightly inside and out; let stand for 30 minutes.

To make the stuffing, combine the butter, dill, parsley, onion, tomatoes, salt, lemon juice, and pepper. Fill the fish with this mixture and truss or fasten it with string or toothpicks to keep it closed. Lay the fish in a buttered casserole, brush with the egg, and cover evenly with the crumbs. Bake in a moderate oven (350°) for 10 minutes, then brush with the melted butter; bake for another 10 minutes and baste with the boiling water; bake for another 10 minutes and pour the light cream over it. Continue baking until the fish flakes when probed with fork (about 20 minutes more). Serve hot. Serves 4 to 6.

■෯෧■෯෧■෯෧■෯෧■෯෧■෯෧■෯෧■෯෧■෯෧■෯෧■෯෧■෯෧■

SOLE ROLLS IN DILL   Tilliliemessäkeitetytkalakääryleet

2½ pounds sole fillets
1 teaspoon salt
abundant fresh dill
6 cups water

2 tablespoons salt
1 teaspoon white wine vinegar
4 tablespoons flour
½ cup water

Chop about 4 tablespoons of the dill. Rinse the fillets with cold water, and dry them. Sprinkle with the teaspoon salt and the chopped dill. Roll up each fillet and fasten with a toothpick. Pour the water into a large pot, add the 2 tablespoons salt, more dill, and the vinegar; bring to a boil. Gently place the fish rolls in the water, one at a time, and let them simmer —do not let them boil—for about 10 minutes or until the fish flakes easily. Remove the rolls with a slotted spoon to a warm serving dish. Strain the broth, heat to boiling again, and stir into it a paste made of the flour and ½ cup water. Stir quickly until the sauce is smooth. Add fresh dill lavishly to the sauce before serving immediately. Serves about 6.

SMOKED FISH AU GRATIN   Savukalalaatikko

8 to 10 smoked herrings
4 to 5 tablespoons chopped fresh
   or dried dill
1 cup heavy cream

2 tablespoons lemon juice
2 tablespoons butter
½ cup grated sharp Cheddar cheese

Clean the fish, removing the bones and skin. Place in the bottom of well-buttered 1½-quart casserole. Sprinkle with dill. Mix the cream and lemon juice and pour over the fish. Dot with butter and sprinkle the cheese evenly over the top. Bake in a hot oven (400°) for 15 minutes, or until the cheese has melted and bubbles. Serves 4 to 6.

FISH-POTATO SCALLOP   Silakkalaatikko

This is one of the most popular everyday casseroles in Finland. Serve it with sliced pickled beets, salted cucumbers, rye bread, and cheese.

1 pound fresh small fish (herring,
   trout, or smelts)
4 large potatoes, peeled and sliced
1 onion, cut into thin slices
1 tablespoon salt
3–4 slices bacon

2 cups milk
1 egg
¼ cup fine dry bread crumbs
2 tablespoons butter
salt

Clean the fish, removing the backbone. In a well-buttered 2-quart casserole arrange alternate layers of potato, fish, and sliced onion (begin and end with the potatoes), and sprinkle salt throughout. Lay the bacon on top. Mix together the milk and egg and pour over all. Sprinkle the top with bread crumbs and dot with butter. Bake in a moderately hot oven (375°) for 1 hour or until the potatoes are done. Serves 4 to 6.

SALMON SCALLOP   Laxlada

Properly made, this dish has fresh salmon as an ingredient. This version, however, is one that our grandmothers made in the United States, using canned salmon.

1 can (1 pound) salmon or 1 pound fresh salmon cut in cubes	2 tablespoons butter
6 large potatoes, peeled and sliced	2 cups milk
1 onion, thinly sliced	1 egg
1 teaspoon salt	¼ cup fine dry bread crumbs
	salt

Remove the skin and bones from the salmon and break into chunks. In a well-buttered 2-quart casserole, arrange layers of the potatoes, fish, onion, and salt. (Begin and end with potatoes.) Dot with the butter. Mix together the milk and egg and pour over the whole, and sprinkle bread crumbs on top. Bake in a moderately hot oven (375°) for 1 hour or until the potatoes are done. Serves 4 to 6.

CREAMED WHITEFISH   Kalamuhennos

3 pounds whitefish or cod fillets or lutefisk	1 teaspoon sugar
3 tablespoons butter	2 cups boiling water
3 tablespoons flour	2 tablespoons lemon juice
1½ teaspoons salt	1 egg yolk
6 whole allspice	3 tablespoons cream

Cut the fish fillets into slices about 1½ inches wide. Arrange them in a well-buttered Dutch oven or other heavy pot. Dot with the butter. Combine the flour, salt, allspice, and sugar, and sprinkle evenly over the fish. Pour the boiling water over the whole and simmer for about 15 minutes or until the fish flakes when probed with a fork. Remove the fish to a serving plate. Combine the lemon juice, egg yolk, and cream, and stir it into the fish stock. Bring to a boil, stirring constantly, and cook until the sauce is thickened. Strain if necessary. Pour over the fish and serve immediately. Serves about 8.

■◎■◎■◎■◎■◎■◎■◎■◎■◎■◎■◎■◎■◎■◎■

FISH CUTLETS   Wieninleike Kalasta

You can use either fresh or frozen fish fillets in this recipe. Serve with buttered fresh green peas and new potatoes.

1 pound fresh or frozen sole or
  cod fillets
1 teaspoon salt
4 tablespoons flour
1 egg, beaten

½ cup fine dry bread crumbs
¼ cup butter
lemon slices
anchovy fillets
capers

If you are using frozen fillets, thaw them before cooking. Cut the fillets into pieces as close to 3 inches square as possible. Combine the salt and flour and roll the fillets in the mixture to coat them evenly. Dip the fillets in the beaten egg and then in the bread crumbs. Melt the butter in a heavy frying pan and fry the fish, turning to brown on both sides. Cook until it flakes when probed with a fork but is not overdone or dry. Remove to a serving platter, and garnish each piece with a slice of lemon, an anchovy fillet, and a few capers. Serve immediately. Serves 3.

FISH AND VEGETABLE CASSEROLE
                                        Kalakasvisvouka

Serve this family-type casserole with buttered potatoes and a leafy green salad.

1 pound frozen cod or sole fillets
  or fresh fish
1 teaspoon salt
⅛ teaspoon pepper
1 package (10 ounces) frozen mixed
  vegetables

½ cup cream
2 tablespoons flour
½ cup grated cheese (Swiss,
  Cheddar, or mild jack)

If you are using frozen fish, thaw before using. Arrange the fish fillets evenly over the bottom of a 1½- to 2-quart casserole and sprinkle evenly with the salt and pepper. Spread the uncooked, frozen mixed vegetables on top. Mix the cream and flour together and pour over all so the vegetables and fish are completely covered. Top with the cheese. Bake in a moderately hot oven (375°) for about 45 minutes or until the casserole bubbles and fish is cooked but not dry. Serves about 3.

LILJA'S SMOKED FISH CASSEROLE
Lilja-Tädin Kalavuoka

Our great-aunt Lilja makes this recipe as she goes along. It is different every time, but always delicious. In my notes I have: "Put rice into a bowl and add an egg and enough milk to make it juicy; mix in enough smoked fish to make it taste good, and some onion and salt and pepper and peas for color, and just enough tomato purée or catsup to give it a pinkish color; sprinkle cheese over top so that it looks appetizing."

That is the recipe as I received it from Lilja. It is one that you can "take off" on if you wish, adding more or different fish, another kind of vegetable, or rice or cheese.

2 cups cooked rice	1 teaspoon salt
1 egg	dash of pepper
1 cup milk	1 10-ounce package frozen peas
2 cups smoked fish (in pieces)	2 tablespoons catsup or tomato purée
1 small onion, minced	½ cup grated sharp Cheddar cheese

Combine all the ingredients except the cheese, and mix thoroughly. Turn into a deep casserole dish and top with the melted cheese. Bake in a moderate oven (350°) for 45 minutes to 1 hour. Serves 4 to 6.

HERRING HASH   Sillipöperö

This is a breakfast or *voileipäpöytä* (bread-and-butter-table) fish dish. Serve it the Finnish way, with boiled new potatoes, or you might prefer it served over toast as an open sandwich.

1 salted herring, filleted	½ cup heavy cream
milk	½ teaspoon sugar
2 tablespoons butter	dash of pepper
2 tablespoons fresh bread crumbs	

Soak the herring fillets in milk overnight in the refrigerator. Drain and wipe dry. Chop very fine with a sharp knife, or put through a food chopper with a medium blade. Heat the butter in a frying pan and add the chopped herring and bread crumbs. Cook, stirring, until the herring turns white and flakes. Add the cream, stirring it in to mix well. Season with the sugar and pepper. Serve hot. Makes 2 servings.

■❦■❦■❦■❦■❦■❦■❦■❦■❦■❦■❦■❦■❦■❦■

MUSHROOM-STUFFED BAKED FISH Täytetty Kala

On the shores of the Finnish lakes, Finns enjoy their *mökkis* or summer homes. Summer is the time to fish—and to eat fish fresh, prepared in various ways. This recipe is heavy with the summer flavors of tomatoes, mushrooms, and chives (chives grow wild in Finland, as do mushrooms).

1 large fish (about 2 pounds mini-
    mum)—pike, pickerel, or white-
    fish
salt
pepper
1 cup fresh or canned mushrooms,
    chopped
2 tomatoes, peeled and chopped

2 tablespoons butter
2 tablespoons minced parsley
2 teaspoons chives or grated onion
lemon juice
1 recipe Finnish Hollandaise Sauce
    (see index)
2 tablespoons fine dry bread crumbs
    (optional)

Clean the fish, but leave the head on if you wish. Sprinkle the cavity and the outside lightly with salt and pepper.

Put the mushrooms and tomatoes into a frying pan with the butter and cook over medium heat, stirring, until heated through. Add the parsley and chives, and sprinkle lemon juice over all. Stuff the fish with this mixture and use toothpicks or skewers to close the cavity. If you have any stuffing left over, put it into the pan alongside the fish or sprinkle it over the top. Or, if you wish, you may sprinkle the fish with bread crumbs to give it a nice crust while baking. Bake in a moderately hot oven (375°) for 30 minutes or until the fish is tender but not overcooked. Serve hot with the hollandaise sauce and pan drippings. Serves 4 to 6.

HERRING-MEAT BALLS   Sillipalleroita

These delicately flavored tiny balls make an excellent appetizer.

2 salted herrings, cleaned and
    filleted
cold water
1 cup cold mashed potatoes
½ pound ground lean beef

1 tablespoon flour
⅛ teaspoon white pepper
milk
1 recipe Sweet-Sour Sauce (see
    index)

Soak the herring in cold water overnight in the refrigerator to remove as much of the salt as possible. Remove all bones and chop the fillets fine with a sharp knife, or put through a meat chopper with a medium-to-coarse blade. Combine the herring with the mashed potatoes, ground beef, flour, pepper, and enough milk to make a consistency right for shaping into tiny balls (about 1 inch in diameter). You may use teaspoons to give the balls a nice oval shape, if you wish. Cook in butter over medium heat until browned. Serve hot with the Sweet-Sour Sauce. Makes about 24 balls.

FISH WITH SPINACH   Kala Ja Pinaatti

Whitefish and sole are especially good combined with spinach flavor. You cook the fish and spinach separately, but serve them together with a special sauce.

2½ pounds whitefish, sole, or
   cod fillets
2 cups water
1 onion, halved
1 bay leaf
1 sprig parsley

1 pound fresh spinach
2 tablespoons butter
¼ teaspoon salt
2 cups Basic Sauce for Poached Fish
   (see index)

Arrange the fish fillets in a large frying pan and pour the water over them. Add the onion, bay leaf, and parsley. Bring to a boil and cook until the fish flakes easily (about 10 minutes).

Meanwhile, clean the spinach, and steam it in a small amount of water. Drain, and add the butter and salt to it. Put the cooked spinach on a serving platter and arrange the fish fillets over it. Pour the sauce over it and serve immediately. Serves about 6.

EAST KARELIAN FISH STEW
Laatokankarjalainen Muikkukeitto

In the part of old Eastern Finland surrounding Lake Ladoga (in Karelia), this dish is traditional. It is made of a fish called *"muikku,"* a species of whitefish about 12 inches long. You are to eat the cooked fish first, and drink the broth afterward. (The Finns pour the broth into the bowls in which the fish was served. If you object to drinking the broth in this fashion, serve it in mugs.)

6 whitefish, each about 12 inches
   long, or trout, fresh or frozen
water to cover

3 teaspoons salt
3 tablespoons butter

Clean the fish and remove the head, tail, and fins. Place them whole in a large pot. Pour over them boiling water to cover; add the salt and butter. Bring to the simmering point and cook for 10 minutes. Serve hot. Serves 6.

■◎◈■◎◈■◎◈■◎◈■◎◈■◎◈■◎◈■◎◈■◎◈■◎◈■◎◈■◎◈■

FISH BAKED IN A BREAD LOAF   Limppukukko

This is an old traditional recipe that is almost "slang" in the art of Finnish cookery. Probably some busy housewife decided to cut a few corners, so she scooped out the soft part of a loaf of bread, filled the cavity with fish, and accomplished a version of Kalakukko that is quick and acceptable, and ideal picnic fare.

1 large round loaf light or dark bread, unsliced	4 slices bacon, diced salt
1 pound smelts, trout, or other small fish	1–2 tablespoons soft butter

Cut off lengthwise a "lid" about 1½ inches from the top of the loaf of bread. Pull out some of the interior, making a cavity large enough to hold the fish.

Clean the fish well, removing scales, insides, fins, tails, and heads. Layer them in the loaf with the diced bacon and sprinkle salt over them. Put the lid back on the loaf, butter the outside well, and wrap securely in foil. Bake in a moderately slow oven (325°) for 3 hours. Do not unwrap, but let stand for 1 hour after removing from the oven. Cool. Cut in crosswise slices. Serves 4 to 6 as lunch or picnic fare.

FISH POT PIE   Patakukko

Related to Kalakukko, this is a very old traditional Karelian recipe. The versions of it vary with the provinces: some Finns use butter in abundance when preparing the dish, others serve melted butter with it, instead. Undoubtedly, this recipe was evolved to provide a way to prepare small bony fish; for because of the long slow cooking time, the bones become soft and can be eaten. Serve hot or cold with melted butter, a green salad and potatoes.

2 pounds fresh bony small fish (trout, smelts, fresh sardines, etc.)	2 teaspoons salt 6 strips bacon

Crust

½ cup cold water	1 cup rye flour
1 teaspoon salt	4 tablespoons butter
½ cup white flour	

Clean the fish, cut off their heads, rinse, and drain on paper toweling. Cut the bacon into half-inch strips. Layer the fish and bacon in a well-buttered 3-quart heavy casserole.

To prepare the crust, pour the water into a mixing bowl, add the salt, and stir in both flours. Mix until the dough is smooth, then pat it into a round that will fit the top of the casserole. Butter both sides of the dough well and place over the fish, pressing down firmly. Seal onto the rim of the dish. Bake in a very slow oven (275°) for 5 hours. Brush top of pastry with water, turn heat up to 300° and bake 1 hour longer. Cover the casserole tightly or wrap in foil and let stand for at least 1 hour, until the crust has softened. Serves 6.

COOKED CRAYFISH   Keitetyt Ravut

July 20 through September 20 is crayfish season in Finland. During this time, restaurants decorate their dining halls in "crayfish red," and the Finns noisily enjoy crayfish-in-the-shell. (See Chapter XIII—the special section on menus—for a Crayfish Supper.)

30 live crayfish
3 quarts water
¼ cup salt
3 tablespoons dill seed

3 tablespoons dill weed or chopped
   fresh dill
fresh dill in abundance

Be sure that all the crayfish are alive. Rinse them well. Pour water into a large kettle and add the salt, dill seed, dried dill weed, and a bunch of fresh dill. Boil until the liquid has a distinct dill flavor (about 5 to 7 minutes; taste it.) Remove the fresh dill and drop the crayfish, a few at a time, into the rapidly boiling water (be sure to keep it boiling). When all the crayfish have been added, cover the surface of the water with more fresh dill, place the lid on the kettle, and cook about 7 minutes longer. Do not overcook the crayfish or the meat will be tough.

Remove the crayfish and place them in a large bowl that has been lined with fresh dill. Strain the stock and pour over them. Let stand until cool, then serve them immediately (at room temperature) or place in the refrigerator to chill. If they are to be served chilled, refrigerate them for at least 12 hours. They are best if refrigerated for 1 to 2 days. To serve, pile the crayfish high on a platter garnished generously with dill, and serve with melted butter for dip. Serves 6.

■C✦■C✦■C✦■C✦■C✦■C✦■C✦■C✦■C✦■C✦■C✦■C✦■C✦■C✦■C✦■C✦■

FISH SMOKED IN PAPER   Paperissasavustettukala

This method for smoking fish is one to remember when you are on a fishing trip. It is very easy. You need only a sheet of waxed paper and a newspaper.

Clean and scale the fish (you may smoke more than one at a time), rub with salt inside and out. Let stand 1 to 2 hours. Wrap in waxed paper and then in several layers of newspapers. The thickness of the newspapers should be about four times the thickness of the fish. Thoroughly dampen the package and place in the embers of a campfire (or on the barbecue grill). Let the newspapers smolder (but be sure they do not burst into flame) until the packet has burned down to the waxed paper layer. Whenever the packet does begin to flame, squirt water on it. The outside wrapping should burn away in from 30 minutes to 2 hours, depending on the thickness of the package. It takes 2 pounds of fish about 25 minutes to cook; however, the longer and slower the smoldering process, the richer the smoke flavor in the fish.

VI. Meat Dishes

In old-time Finland, when an animal was slaughtered, it was always for household use, and every bit of it was used in one way or another. Thus, recipes for such dishes as blood puddings, pancakes, bread and sausages, headcheese, and various types of pressed or jellied meats were developed. These dishes lost popularity in late years—perhaps because the ingredients are less easily come by it and they are therefore made less often today.

Not so long ago, every family had a pig called the *talous porsus*—the "house pig." This pet was fed table scraps and was healthy and fat, and from it, later (though agonizingly, for the children) came the pork for table use. (If the children had grown especially fond of the pig, neighbors or friends would sometimes swap hogs before the killing.) Still today, it is common for families jokingly to name one of their members the *talous porsus,* the "house pig" who cleans the pot—or for one of the members of the family to call himself that!

Meat dishes in Finnish restaurants and homes are always excellent, even when the dish is just a version of a popular European recipe. Among the traditional Finnish meat dishes are Karelian Pot Roast, Finnish Meat Balls, Cabbage Rolls, and Pork Gravy. (This last is considered by some farm people to be their best meat dish, and it does include pieces of salt pork!)

FINNISH MEAT BALLS   Lihapyöryköitä

Serve these on the *voileipäpöytä* (bread-and-butter table) or for family or guest meals, accompanied by lingonberries, or cranberry sauce, sliced beets, pickles, and fluffy mashed potatoes.

¾ cup soft bread crumbs
1 cup cream
1½ pounds ground lean beef
1 onion, minced
1 egg, beaten

2 teaspoons salt
½ teaspoon ground allspice
2 tablespoons butter for frying
2 tablespoons flour
1½ cups milk

Soak the bread crumbs in ½ cup cream. Mix together the meat, onion, and bread crumbs. Add the beaten egg, salt, and allspice, and combine well. Shape into balls (make them tiny, using about a teaspoonful of mixture) if they are to be served as an appetizer or on the voileipäpöytä, or about walnut size if they are for a family meal. Melt the butter in a frying pan and put in the meat balls, a few at a time. Shake the pan to roll the meat balls so they brown on all sides.

After all the meat balls are browned and removed from the pan, brown the flour in the drippings. Mix with a fork until smooth; then slowly add the second ½ cup cream and 1½ cups milk, stirring well until smooth. Add water if the mixture gets too thick. Return the meat balls to the pan, cover, and cook for about 25 minutes on low heat. Serve hot. Serves 4 to 6.

SEAMEN'S BEEF   Merimiespihvi

2 pounds ground lean beef
2 teaspoons salt
¼ teaspoon white pepper
1 cup cold mashed potatoes
½ cup cream or milk
1 egg

butter
2 large onions, finely sliced
8 medium potatoes, peeled and
   sliced
2 cups beef broth

Combine the ground beef, salt, pepper, mashed potatoes, cream, and egg, mixing until thoroughly blended. Shape into patties about 3 inches in diameter. Melt the butter in a frying pan and brown the patties on both sides. Remove the meat from pan and brown the onion slices in the same pan. Layer the potatoes, onions, and beef patties in a well-buttered 2-quart casserole, beginning and ending with the potatoes. Pour the beef broth over all and bake in a moderate oven (350°) for 45 minutes to 1 hour or until the potatoes are tender. Serves 6 to 8.

■◍◍■◍◍■◍◍■◍◍■◍◍■◍◍■◍◍■◍◍■◍◍■◍◍■◍◍■◍◍■◍◍■◍◍■

CABBAGE ROLLS   Kaalikääryleet

Sometimes called "Pigs in Blankets," this universal favorite is also a favored dish in Finland. Serve with boiled or mashed potatoes and cranberry or lingonberry sauce.

1 large head cabbage
2 teaspoons salt
water
½ cup cream
½ cup fresh bread crumbs
1 teaspoon salt

½ teaspoon allspice
1 pound ground lean beef
1½ cups cooked pearl barley
   or cooked rice
½ cup dark corn syrup
2 cups boiling water (approximately)

Cut the core out of the cabbage and place the head in salted boiling water in a large pot. As the outer leaves of the cabbage become tender, peel them off. Let cool.

In a bowl, mix together well the cream, bread crumbs, ½ cup water, 1 teaspoon salt, allspice, and ground beef. Add the cooked barley or rice. Place 1 to 2 tablespoonfuls of the filling on each cabbage leaf. Wrap the leaf around the filling and tuck in the ends. Place the rolls seam side down, in a buttered heavy casserole, and drizzle the corn syrup over them (brush the rolls lightly to distribute the syrup evenly). Cover and bake in a hot oven (400°) for 20 minutes, then remove the cover and pour in about 2 cups boiling water or enough to almost cover the rolls. Leave the casserole uncovered, lower the oven heat to 350°, and continue baking for 1 hour. Serve hot. Makes 12 to 16 rolls.

STUFFED MEAT ROLLS   Lihamurekekääryleet

In this recipe, the meat mixture is patted out into a large square, cut into smaller squares, filled, and rolled up.

½ cup bread crumbs
½ cup milk
1½ pounds ground lean beef
1 teaspoon salt
¼ teaspoon pepper
1 egg

sliced raw apple or uncooked,
   pitted prunes or ½-inch-diameter
   cheese sticks or pickle sticks
   (for stuffing)
fat for frying
½ cup boiling water
½ teaspoon salt
2 teaspoons Worcestershire sauce
parsley

Soak the bread crumbs in the milk and add to the ground meat. Mix in the salt, pepper, and egg. Dampen a sheet of waxed paper and pat the mixture out to a 16-inch square. Cut this into 4-inch squares. Place a slice of apple, 2 pitted prunes, a cheese stick, or a pickle stick in the center of each square. Using a spatula, roll the meat to encase the filling. Brown each roll in hot fat in a frying pan, then place in a large flat greased casserole. When all the rolls are browned, pour the water into the pan, and stir to mix in the drippings. Add the salt and Worcestershire, and pour over the rolls. Bake in a hot oven (400°) for 15 minutes. Serve hot. Garnish with the parsley just before serving. Serves about 6.

VEGETABLE-FILLED MEAT-LOAF RING
Lihamureketta Vihaneksen Kera

This is a very attractive dish. The idea is simple: You bake a meat loaf in a ring mold and fill the center of the ring with cooked vegetables. A word of warning: If you have never used your ring mold for baking, grease it very well so the meat loaf does not stick, or better yet, line it with strips of waxed paper.

Meat Loaf
1½ pounds ground lean beef
½ pound ground lean pork
½ cup soft bread crumbs
¾ cup heavy cream

1 egg
1 small onion, minced
2 teaspoons salt
¼ teaspoon allspice

Filling
2 cups freshly shelled peas or
    1 10-ounce package frozen peas
½ head cauliflower, separated into
    flowerets, or 2 packages frozen
    cauliflower

butter
salt
pepper
1 recipe Mushroom Sauce or Finnish-
style Mustard (see index)

Combine all the ingredients for the meat loaf and knead with your hands until they are very well blended. Turn the mixture into a well-buttered large (2-quart) ring mold, and bake in a moderately hot oven (375°) for 45 minutes to 1 hour. Remove from the oven and invert on an ovenproof serving platter. Slip under the broiler for a few minutes to brown the top. While the meat loaf is in the oven, prepare the vegetable filling.

Cook the peas until just tender (do not overcook), and in another saucepan, cook the cauliflower until tender-crisp. Season with the butter, salt, and pepper. Arrange in the center of the meat-loaf ring, and serve hot with the sauce or mustard. Serves about 6.

MEAT-CABBAGE CASSEROLE   Lihakaalilaatikko

One of our relatives told me that she makes Lihakaalilaatikko when she really feels like having Kaalikääryleet (Cabbage Rolls) because the flavors are about the same—but this is so much easier. Serve this with lingonberries, cranberry sauce, or currant jelly.

1 small head cabbage, shredded
2 tablespoons butter
2 tablespoons dark corn syrup
2 teaspoons salt
¼ teaspoon ground marjoram

1 pound ground lean beef
1 cup bread crumbs
½ cup milk
2 eggs, beaten

Cook the cabbage (in enough boiling water to cover) for about 5 minutes or until tender-crisp. Drain. Add the butter, syrup, salt, and marjoram. In another bowl, mix the ground beef, bread crumbs, milk and eggs. Butter a 2-quart casserole and layer the cabbage and meat mixture in it, beginning and ending with the cabbage. Bake in a moderate oven (350°) for 1 hour or until the meat is done. Serves 6 to 8.

BEEF-MUSHROOM LOAF   Sienilihamureke

Wild mushrooms grow in abundance in Finland, and they are used in many different ways. This meat loaf is one example.

½ pound mushrooms, sliced
1 medium onion, chopped
3 tablespoons butter
1 cup bread crumbs
1½ cups milk

2 pounds ground lean beef
2 eggs, beaten
1 cup mashed potatoes
1½ teaspoons salt
½ teaspoon marjoram

1 recipe Horseradish Sauce (see index)

Brown the mushrooms and onions in butter. Cool. Soak bread crumbs in the milk. Mix the beef with the mushrooms and onions, then add the bread crumbs, eggs, potatoes, salt, and marjoram. Butter a 2-quart baking dish or mold. Turn the mixture into it, and bake in a moderate oven (350°) for 1 hour. Turn onto a serving dish and serve hot with Horseradish Sauce. Serves about 6.

■෨෨■෨෨■෨෨■෨෨■෨෨■෨෨■෨෨■෨෨■෨෨■෨෨■෨෨■෨෨■

GROUND BEEF PIE IN A CRUST   Jauhelihapiiras

Crust
1 recipe crust for Meat With Sour Cream Crust (*above*)

Filling
2 pounds ground very lean beef   ½ teaspoon black pepper
2 tablespoons minced onion   pinch marjoram
2 teaspoons salt   1 egg

Prepare the crust according to the directions in the recipe.

Combine all the ingredients for the filling and mix together with the hands until they are thoroughly blended. Fill and decorate the pie as directed in Meat Pie With Sour Cream Crust. Bake in a moderate oven (350°) for 55 minutes to 1 hour or until golden. Serve hot and pass sour cream to spoon over it. Serves 6.

MEAT SOUFFLÉ   Lihakohokas

You can use leftover cooked meat for this recipe. Do not let the word "soufflé" frighten you away; anyone who can whip eggs can whip up a soufflé. This one should fall very shortly after you take it out of the oven—but it is supposed to! It will be very soft and creamy in the center.

2 tablespoons butter   2 teaspoons salt
¼ cup flour   ¼ teaspoon white pepper or allspice
2 cups rich milk   1½ cups cooked ground meat (ham,
6 eggs, separated   veal, beef, or lamb)

Melt the butter and stir in the flour until blended. Slowly add the milk, and stir to dissolve any lumps. Cook over low to medium heat, stirring constantly, until the mixture comes to a boil. Stir a part of the hot mixture into the egg yolks, beating well, then return the egg yolk mixture to the pan. Add the salt and pepper; cook, stirring constantly, until thickened and smooth. Set aside.

In a large bowl, whip the egg whites until stiff but not dry. Fold in the cooked mixture and the ground meat quickly but carefully, trying to retain as much fluffiness in the mixture as possible. Pour into a buttered 2-quart soufflé dish or casserole, and bake in a moderate oven (350°) for 35 to 40 minutes. Serve immediately. Serves 4 to 6.

■᠔᠔■᠔᠔■᠔᠔■᠔᠔■᠔᠔■᠔᠔■᠔᠔■᠔᠔■᠔᠔■᠔᠔■᠔᠔■᠔᠔■᠔᠔■

FINNISH BEEF TARTARE   Raakapihvi

This Scandinavian favorite is also a restaurant favorite in Finland. Served on toast, this is considered a sandwich; served with crackers, it is an appetizer; and served on a dinner plate garnished with vegetables, it is a main dish. Serve a variety of dark breads with Finnish Beef Tartare—dark rye, pumpernickel, hardtack, rye crispbread, etc.—or serve it with French bread.

2 pounds very lean sirloin, tenderloin,   very finely chopped pickled beets
    or top round (use high quality   egg yolks
    fresh meat only)   chopped parsley fresh
very finely chopped onion

Scrape the meat with a knife so it is finely pulverized, or put it through a meat grinder several times, using a fine blade, until it is very smooth.

For dinner servings, divide the meat into 4 to 6 equal parts, molding each in a rounded cereal bowl to make a smooth mound. Turn each mound of beef out onto a plate and surround it first with a ring of the onion and then a ring of the pickled beets. Sprinkle with the parsley. Top each mound with a whole raw egg yolk, centering it perfectly. Offer salt and pepper. Serves 4 to 6.

For lunch portions, divide the meat into 8 parts, again molding each in a cereal bowl. Unmold on a thin slice of pumpernickel or on toasted buttered French bread. Surround with the onion and beets, and top with a raw egg yolk. Serves 8.

For an appetizer, press the beef into a fancy mold or bread pan that has been rinsed out with cold water, then unmold on a tray. Sprinkle with the onion and beets, and surround with salted crackers.

MEAT-LOAF CAKE   Lihamurekekakku

2 pounds ground lean beef   2 tablespoons butter
2 teaspoons salt   thinly sliced sweet onion
¼ teaspoon pepper   sliced tomatoes
2 eggs   chopped parsley
2 tablespoons minced onion   ½ cup cream
½ teaspoon sweet basil

Combine the ground beef, salt, pepper, eggs, minced onion, and basil until well mixed. Divide into two parts. Shape each part into a flat cake about 6 inches in diameter. Melt 1 tablespoon of the butter in a frying pan and cook 1 of the meat cakes until it is well browned on both sides and the center is done as you like it. Arrange on a heatproof serving dish and keep warm. Repeat for the second cake. Put a layer of the thinly sliced onion on the first meat cake, lay the second cake on the onion, and top with the sliced tomatoes and parsley.

To make the gravy, add the cream to the drippings in the pan and cook, stirring, until all the brownings are scraped up. Season to taste with salt and pepper. Serve the meat-loaf cake hot and cut in wedges, as you would a two-layer cake. Serve the gravy separately in a bowl. Serves 4 to 6.

MEAT PIE WITH SOUR CREAM CRUST
Lihamurekepiiras

This meat loaf with a crust around it can be made in two ways. The first version uses leftover ground cooked meat, the second (recipe following) uses uncooked ground beef. Either one dresses up an otherwise ordinary-looking ground-meat dish. Offer sour cream to spoon over it.

Crust

2 cups white flour
1 teaspoon salt
¾ cup butter

1 egg
½ cup sour cream

Filling

4 cups ground cooked meat (beef, ham, lamb, or veal)
2 tablespoons minced onion

½ cup shredded Cheddar, Edam, or Swiss cheese
1 4-ounce can chopped mushrooms, juice and all

To make the crust, measure the flour and salt into a bowl and cut in the butter until the mixture resembles fine crumbs. Combine the egg and sour cream and stir into the flour mixture, working with the fingers until a stiff dough forms. Divide the dough into two parts and roll each out to make a rectangle 14 inches long and 6 inches wide. Place one of these in a jelly-roll pan.

To make the filling, combine the meat, onion, cheese, and mushrooms. Arrange this mixture in a loglike shape down the center of the dough in the pan. Place the second rectangle of the dough over the filling. Moisten the edges of the crusts and seal well. Prick the top of the pie to make holes for the steam to escape. Roll out the excess scraps of dough and cut into strips. Brush the pie with milk and arrange the strips over the top in a fancy pattern. Brush again with milk. Bake in a moderately hot oven (375°) for 25 minutes or until the pie has browned. Serve hot, cut in slices. Serves about 6.

RACK OR LEG OF LAMB FINLANDIA

Lampaanpaisti

2–2¼-pound rack of lamb or
   6-pound leg of lamb
onions, thinly sliced
10 whole allspice
beef broth, chicken broth, or water

2 tablespoons flour
4 tablespoons water
salt (optional)
pepper (optional)

Place the lamb in a baking pan and cover completely with the onions. Put the allspice into the pan, and add just enough liquid to cover the bottom of the pan. Insert a meat thermometer into the thickest part of the meat. Roast the rack of lamb in a moderately hot oven (375°) for 55 to 60 minutes and the leg of lamb in a moderately slow oven (325°) for approximately 3 hours (until the thermometer registers 170° to 180°). Add liquid as needed to the pan during the roasting, basting the meat frequently so the onions do not burn. Remove the meat to a serving platter and keep warm.

To thicken the pan juices, combine the flour with the water to make a thin paste. Pour into the pan and cook, stirring constantly, over medium heat until thickened. Taste, and correct the seasonings. Serve the gravy in a separate bowl. The rack of lamb serves 2 to 3 persons; the leg of lamb serves 6 to 8.

LAMB SHANKS AND RICE

Lampaankyljykset Ja Riisi

6 lamb shanks (5–6 pounds)
mustard
salt
pepper
3½ tablespoons butter

1 cup long-grain rice
1 large onion, thinly sliced
1 8-ounce can tomato sauce
1 10½-ounce can beef broth
1 cup water

Rub the lamb shanks with mustard and sprinkle with salt and pepper. Brown in 2 tablespoons of the butter until golden on all sides (this takes about 20 minutes). Melt the remaining butter in a heavy saucepan and add the rice. Cook over high heat, stirring constantly, until the rice is partially browned and some of the grains turn white (about 5 minutes). Add the onion, tomato sauce, and beef broth to the rice. Bring to a boil, turn the heat to low, cover, and cook for 20 minutes (the rice will have absorbed the liquid during this time).

Turn the rice into a buttered 2-quart casserole. Pour the water over. Arrange the lamb shanks on the rice, topping each with a few rings of the onion. Cover and bake in a moderate oven (350°) for 1 hour; remove the cover and continue to bake until the lamb shanks are tender (for 1 to 1½ hours). Serves 4 to 6.

LIVER-RICE CASSEROLE   Maksalaatikko

This flavorful, all-year-round favorite is, by tradition, always served at Christmastime in Finland. Even non-liver-lovers go back for seconds! Serve with melted butter to pour over the individual portions, and lingonberries or cranberry sauce.

3 cups cooked rice
2½ cups milk
1 egg, beaten
2 tablespoons butter
1 medium onion, chopped
4 tablespoons dark corn syrup

3 teaspoons salt
½ teaspoon white pepper
½ teaspoon ground marjoram
1 cup raisins
1 pound liver, sliced

Mix together the rice and milk, add the egg. Heat the butter in a frying pan, brown the onion in it, and add to the rice-milk mixture. Stir in the syrup, salt, pepper, marjoram, and raisins. Put the liver through a meat chopper (this is easier to do when the liver is partially frozen), using a coarse blade, or use a sharp knife to chop it very fine. Stir the liver into the rice mixture and pour the whole into a buttered 2-quart casserole. Bake in a moderate oven (350°) for 1 hour or until the casserole is set. Serve hot. Serves about 6.

HAM-LIVER POT   Herkkumaksapata

¼ pound ham, thinly sliced
1–2 tablespoons butter (optional)
1 pound liver, thinly sliced
1 medium onion, thinly sliced
1 teaspoon salt

1 teaspoon pepper
1 tart medium apple, cored and
   thinly sliced
1 cup water (approximately)
½ cup heavy cream

Brown the ham quickly in a hot frying pan (if the ham is lean, brown it in the butter) and lift it out of the pan immediately. Brown the liver and onion slices in the fat left in the pan, and sprinkle with the salt and pepper. Lay the ham and apple slices on top, and add enough water to cover. Simmer for 20 to 25 minutes, then pour the cream over all and serve immediately. Serves about 4.

AUNT LILJA'S LIVER PANCAKES   Maksaplättyjä

Aunt Lilja said that she could not remember where she first got the idea for this recipe, but she has been serving liver pancakes for many years—they are a great favorite in her family! Serve with tart cranberry sauce or currant jelly and melted butter to pour over them.

1 pound liver, sliced	1 medium onion, minced
½ cup bread crumbs	1 teaspoon salt
¼ cup cream	¼ teaspoon pepper
1 egg	2 tablespoons butter (approximately)

Put the liver through a meat chopper (this is easier to do if the liver is partially frozen), using a coarse blade, or chop very fine with a sharp knife. Combine with the bread crumbs, cream, egg, onion, salt, and pepper. Beat well. Heat the butter in a frying pan, and using about 2 tablespoons of the mixture at a time, spoon into the pan to make the pancakes. Brown about 2 minutes on each side. Serve hot. Serves 4.

LIVER PÂTÉ OR LIVER LOAF   Maksapasteija

This is almost a "must" item for the *voileipäpöytä* (bread-and-butter table). It makes an excellent appetizer when served on a platter surrounded with salty crisp crackers; and it is excellent as a sandwich filler.

1 pound calf's liver, sliced	1 teaspoon sugar
2 tablespoons butter	1 teaspoon ground ginger
1 small onion, grated	½ teaspoon white pepper
1 cup light cream	3 tablespoons anchovy paste or
4 tablespoons dry bread crumbs	2 teaspoons minced anchovies
2 eggs, lightly beaten	(optional)
2 teaspoons salt	thinly sliced bacon

Put the liver through a meat chopper with a fine blade (this is easier to do if the liver is partially frozen) or remove all the membranes and whirl in a blender until fine but not foamy. Heat the butter in a frying pan, brown the onion, and add to the liver with the cream, bread crumbs, eggs, salt, sugar, ginger, pepper, and anchovy paste or minced anchovies. Mix until thoroughly combined. Line a 5- by 9-inch bread pan with bacon, being sure to cover all surfaces completely. Pour in the liver mixture. Cover the top of the pan securely with waxed paper or foil and tie the covering on with string. Set in a pan of water and bake in a moderate oven (350°) for

1½ hours. Let cool in the water bath with the cover on, then remove the cover and turn the loaf out onto a serving platter. Chill. Cut in slices to serve. Serves 8 to 10 as an appetizer spread; as the main course, serves 3 to 4.

CHRISTMAS HAM   Joulukinkku

These directions (freely translated) for preparing a fresh ham are taken from an old Finnish cookbook:

> Start two weeks before Christmas Eve. Take one whole fresh ham with the skin on and make gashes through the entire surface. Rub with a mixture of equal portions of salt, sugar, and saltpeter. Force salt from the bony end of ham as far as possible into the meaty portion. Allow to stand in a cool place overnight. On the following day, place the ham into a 20 percent salt solution. Let stand in this for 2 weeks. Check the water and turn the ham over several times during this time. Remove the ham from the water; discard the water. Make a very thick dough, using rye flour and water. Roll the dough out to ¾-inch thickness and use it to completely encase the ham, sealing very well. Bake in a slow oven for 1 hour for the first two pounds and 45 minutes for each additional pound. When the ham is done, remove the rye crust and remove the skin with a sharp knife.

To make "sauna-smoked" ham, the ham was not encased in dough; it was smoked on a rack over the stove in the smoke sauna for 2 to 5 days. Sauna-smoked hams have a delicious flavor and are still sold in some country villages in Finland today. To finish the preparation of the sauna ham for the Christmas dinner, bake the smoked uncooked ham allowing 30 minutes for the first 2 pounds and 30 minutes for each additional pound. Remove the skin and spread the surface with an eighth-inch coating of Finnish-Style Mustard (see index). Sprinkle with bread crumbs and sugar, patting them down firmly. Then brown in a moderate oven (350°) for about 30 minutes. Garnish the ham with cooked prunes. Each pound of ham should serve 3 people.

■❦■❦■❦■❦■❦■❦■❦■❦■❦■❦■❦■❦■❦■❦■

COBBLER'S ROAST   Suutarinpaisti

I can only guess at the reason for the name for this recipe, which is composed of two of the ingredients most easily available in the country—small Baltic herring and salt pork. Here, I have taken the liberty of substituting bacon for the side pork and smelts or trout for the herring because these ingredients are more readily available in the U.S. Serve with potatoes boiled in their jackets and rye bread (to be traditional).

½ pound thinly sliced bacon
15 small fresh smelts (or 10–12
   brook trout)

1 cup water
salt to taste

Cut the bacon into 3-inch strips and fry until browned and crisp. Drain off all but 1 tablespoon of the fat. Clean and fillet the fish and add to the pan with the bacon. Pour in the water, cover, and simmer for 10 minutes or until the fish flakes easily. Add salt to taste. Serve hot. Serves about 3.

ROAST PORK WITH PRUNES   Paistettu Sianselkä

This is a very-well-flavored pork roast. Serve it with mashed potatoes, and pour the gravy over all.

1 pork-loin roast (3–5 pounds)
2 tablespoons lemon juice
1 teaspoon salt

¼ teaspoon white pepper or allspice
½ pound pitted prunes
1 cup water

Gravy
2 tablespoons flour
2 tablespoons prepared mustard

2 tablespoons water

Rub the surface of the roast with the lemon juice, salt, and pepper or allspice, and put into a roasting pan. Insert a meat thermometer into the thickest portion of the roast. Arrange the prunes on the bottom of the pan, and pour in the water. Roast, uncovered, in a moderately slow oven (325°) for 3 to 3½ hours or until the thermometer registers 185°. Add water during this time if needed to keep the prunes moist.

Remove the roast from the pan onto a serving platter. Arrange the prunes around the roast. Make a paste of the flour, mustard, and water, and stir into the meat drippings. Cook over medium heat, stirring until thick and smooth. Add more water if the gravy is too thick. Strain, and pour into a gravy boat. Serves about 6 to 10 persons per pound of meat (figured with the bone in).

■◌▨■◌▨■◌▨■◌▨■◌▨■◌▨■◌▨■◌▨■◌▨■◌▨■◌▨■◌▨■◌▨■

LIVER WITH GREEN BEANS   Maksa Papupata

1 pound beef liver, sliced
2 tablespoons flour
1 teaspoon salt
butter

1 10-ounce package frozen green
   beans
½ cup water
¼ cup cream
1 can French-fried onions (optional)

Cut the liver into strips about one-quarter inch wide (this is easiest to do when the liver is partially frozen)—use your kitchen shears for the job. Sprinkle the flour over the liver and toss the strips lightly to coat, then sprinkle them with salt. Melt enough butter in a frying pan to coat the bottom well. Brown the liver strips in the butter, turning them with a fork, but be sure not to let them cook through. Arrange the strips in a buttered casserole in alternate layers with the green beans: first put in the beans, then the liver, then another layer of the beans, and, last of all, another layer of liver. Pour the water over all. Bake in a moderately hot oven (375°) for 25 to 30 minutes or until the green beans are tender. Pour the cream over the casserole, garnish with the onions, and serve immediately. Serves 4.

PORK LOAF WITH APPLES
Sianlihamureke Ja Omenia

Ground pork makes an interesting meat loaf with layers of apple in it. Serve with new potatoes and a green salad.

1 egg, beaten
1 pound ground lean pork
1 pound ground lean beef
1 small onion, minced
½ cup grated raw carrot
1 tablespoon cornstarch
2 teaspoons salt

½ teaspoon ground ginger
1 cup water
3 tart medium apples, cored,
   unpeeled, and sliced
1 tablespoon butter
2–3 tablespoons finely chopped
   parsley

Beat the egg in a large bowl. Add the ground meats, carrot, onion, cornstarch, salt, ginger, and water, and mix thoroughly. Arrange a layer of about one-third of the apples on the bottom of a greased 1½-quart casserole. Top it with half of the meat mixture. Arrange another layer of apples over the meat, and spread the remaining half of the meat mixture over that. Top with the remaining apple slices. Dot with the butter, sprinkle with the parsley, and bake in a moderately hot oven (375°) for 1 hour or until the meat is cooked. Serve hot. Serves 4 to 6.

■◠◡◠■◠◡◠■◠◡◠■◠◡◠■◠◡◠■◠◡◠■◠◡◠■◠◡◠■◠◡◠■◠◡◠■◠◡◠■

PRUNE-STUFFED PORK ROLLS
Luumulihakääryleet

Thin slices of pork are wrapped around pitted prunes, browned well, and served with a creamy gravy made from the pan drippings. Add potatoes, pickles, and a salad for a delicious meal.

1½ pounds boneless pork, cut into thin slices about 3 inches square	½ pound pitted prunes
1 teaspoon salt	butter
¼ teaspoon white pepper	water

Gravy
2 tablespoons flour   salt
½ cup heavy cream   pepper

Sprinkle the meat slices with salt and pepper. Put 2 or 3 pitted prunes on each slice, roll up, and fasten with toothpicks or tie with string. Brown the rolls in the butter in a frying pan over medium heat. Add about 1 cup water (just enough to keep the bottom of the pan moist) cover, and simmer for 1 hour or until the meat is tender, adding more water if necessary.

Remove the meat from the pan. Add enough water to scrape the brownings from the bottom of the pan. Combine the flour and cream, and stir into the liquid in the pan to make a smooth gravy. Add salt and pepper to taste. Cook until the gravy is thickened. Pour over the meat rolls and serve hot. Serves about 4.

LEEK-CARROT-PORK CASSEROLE   Purjosipulipata

Authentically, this dish is made with leeks. If you do not have leeks, however, onions are an excellent substitute.

1 pound pork, cubed	water
4 cups carrots, peeled and cubed	1 teaspoon salt
4 leeks, washed and cut in 1-inch lengths (or 4 medium onions, quartered)	¼ teaspoon ground allspice

Brown the pork cubes in a frying pan until very brown on all sides (about 30 minutes over medium heat), stirring occasionally. Drain off any excess fat. Add the carrots, leeks (or onions), and just enough water to barely cover. Add the salt and allspice, and cover. Simmer for another 30 minutes or until the vegetables are tender and meat is cooked. Serve hot. Serves 4.

TENANT FARMER'S PORK POT Torpparin Pannu

The days of the tenant farmer in Finland are gone. However, this dish is an example of how common usage names a certain dish. The poor tenant probably could never afford anything but pork that he had raised himself.

1 pound pork chops	2 teaspoons salt
2 chopped onions	½ teaspoon allspice
4 large potatoes, peeled and sliced	green onions, chopped
1 cup water	

Brown the pork chops and onions well in a large frying pan. Lay the potatoes over the meat and onions into a thick layer. Mix the water with the salt and allspice and pour over the potatoes and meat. Cover tightly and simmer for 45 minutes to 1 hour or until the potatoes and meat are well done. In Finland, this dish may be garnished with chopped wild onions; however, chopped green onions sprinkled over the top are a suitable garnish. Serve hot. Serves 4.

PRESSED PORK Käärysyltty

You will have to buy lean side pork for this dish, but the end result is worth the extra trouble. Serve as you would any cold cuts, or on the *voileipäpöytä* (bread-and-butter table).

4 pounds leanest possible side pork	2 tablespoons salt
½ teaspoon pepper	½ teaspoon ground ginger
boiling water	6 whole allspice

Have the side pork split (or butterflied), so that it is half its original thickness, but be sure it is not cut all the way through. Sprinkle with pepper, roll up tightly, and tie securely. Place in a large pot that is deep enough to hold water to cover the meat roll and pour in boiling water to cover. Add the salt, ginger, and allspice. Bring to simmering and cook at that temperature for 3 hours. Remove from the heat. Let the meat cool in the broth for 30 minutes, then take it out of the broth, place under a weight, and refrigerate overnight. Makes about 40 thin slices.

REINDEER OR VENISON WITH BACON

Poronpaisti

Although this recipe originally called for reindeer meat, its flavor is so similar to venison that venison makes a good substitute. Some Finnish cooks soak the reindeer meat in beer to kill the wild flavor, some soak it in buttermilk. Others like the gamey flavor and do not soak the meat at all. Serve with fluffy mashed potatoes.

1 pound bacon
2 pounds reindeer meat or venison
   cut in paper-thin slices

1 teaspoon salt

Brown the bacon in a large frying pan and add the reindeer or venison slices. Be sure to keep the heat high and sear the meat quickly. When all the pieces are browned, sprinkle with the salt and lower the heat. Add enough water to cover the meat. Put the lid on the pan and simmer slowly for 20 minutes. Serve hot. Serves 6 to 8.

LAPP MEAT PLATTER

Lapin Keitos

If you can get reindeer meat, use it in this dish to be most authentic; however, venison makes an excellent substitute. The traditional delicacy of the Lapp Meat Platter is the cooked shinbones, for the marrow is not only very good but very nutritious. Serve this platter with very thin Rieska (see index).

4 reindeer or venison shinbones,
   cut in 6- to 8-inch lengths
salt
1 reindeer or venison tongue
1 pound reindeer, beef, or venison
   liver

water
pepper
6 whole allspice
1 recipe Finnish-style Mustard (see
   index)

Cook the bones in a large pot for 20 minutes in salted water (add 1 teaspoon salt for each quart of water needed to cover the bones); keep the liquid simmering. When the bones are cooked, remove from the pot and put in the tongue, liver, and allspice. Simmer for 1 hour. Remove the liver and the tongue; skin the latter and return to the liquid, cooking until tender (test the root end with a fork); the tongue will take 30 minutes to 1 hour longer to cook, depending on its size).

Serve the cooked shinbones piled on a platter. Chop the liver fine and season with salt and pepper to taste. Arrange on a serving plate. Slice the tongue and place it around the chopped liver. Serve with melted butter and the mustard. Serves 3 to 4 per pound of meat, discounting the shin bones.

SALTED TONGUE   Suolakieli

Salted tongue is served cold in sandwiches or on the bread-and-butter table, especially at Christmastime. Sometimes it is masked with a sour cream aspic and decorated fancifully.

1 beef tongue, 2½–3½ pounds   1 tablespoon salt
2 tablespoons sugar

Cooking broth
2 whole allspice   1 medium bay leaf   ⎫
5 whole black peppercorns   1 medium carrot, peeled ⎬ for each quart of water
1 whole clove   ½ small onion   ⎭

Salting water
3 tablespoons salt   ⎫
1 tablespoon sugar   ⎭ *for each quart of water*

Clean the tongue and rub evenly with the sugar-salt mixture. Cover and refrigerate until the next day. Put the tongue into a large pot and add the water to cover along with the allspice, peppercorns, clove, bay leaf, carrot, and onion. Bring to boiling, skim off the foam, and cook 2 to 3 hours, simmering gently, until the tongue is tender (test with a fork at the root end). Skin the tongue while hot and let it cool in the cooking broth. When the tongue has cooled, discard the cooking broth.

Bring the salting water to a boil and then cool. Add the cooled tongue to it and refrigerate overnight. Slice the tongue thinly to serve. This should make sandwiches for about 10 to 12 people.

TONGUE WITH CUCUMBER SAUCE
Keitetty Kieli Kurkkukastikkeessä

1 whole beef tongue   1 medium onion, cut in chunks
1 quart water   1 small carrot, peeled and cut in
1 tablespoon salt   chunks
6 whole allspice   1 bay leaf
6 whole cloves   1 recipe Cucumber Sauce *(see index)*

This is a very elegant meat dish to serve on the *voileipäpöypä* (bread-and-butter table) for a buffet, or with sandwiches.

Put the tongue into a pot and pour water over it. Add the salt, allspice, cloves, onion, carrot, and bay leaf. Bring to a boil, cover, and simmer for 1½ to 2 hours or until the tongue, tested at the root end with a fork, is tender. Remove from the pot, skin, and let cool. Cut into very thin slices and serve with the Cucumber Sauce. Serves 6 to 8.

■᠗᠗■᠗᠗■᠗᠗■᠗᠗■᠗᠗■᠗᠗■᠗᠗■᠗᠗■᠗᠗■᠗᠗■᠗᠗■᠗᠗■᠗᠗■

ROLLED VEAL ROAST WITH WHITE SAUCE
Vasikanpaisti Valkokastikkeessa

This is excellent for a fine company meal.

4–4½ pounds boned leg of veal
½ pound thinly sliced bacon
1½ teaspoons salt
½ teaspoon white pepper or allspice
butter
boiling water

2 cups White Sauce *(see index)*
2 eggs, separated
2 teaspoons prepared mustard
  (optional)
1 cup shredded Cheddar cheese
bread crumbs

Pound the meat as flat as possible. Spread the bacon evenly over the meat and sprinkle with the salt and pepper. Roll up as tightly as possible, and tie securely. (If you wish, ask your butcher to pound and roll the roast for you.) Brown the roll well in butter on all sides. Add enough boiling water to come halfway up the roll, cover, and let simmer, turning the meat occasionally, until it is tender when tested with a long-prongd fork (this should take about 1½ hours). Remove the meat from the liquid and cool. Cut into thin slices (discard the string), and arrange on an ovenproof serving platter.

Make the White Sauce. Stir in the egg yolks, and cook 1 minute. Beat the egg whites until stiff and fold into the sauce, then stir in the mustard. Pour the sauce over the meat slices and sprinkle with the cheese and bread crumbs. Bake in a hot oven (400°) for 10 minutes or until the cheese has melted and browned. If you wish, you may simply serve the sliced meat warm and pass the sauce separately to pour over it; or you may serve the meat cold, without the sauce.

MOLDED VEAL LOAF   Vasikansyltty

This is a very elegant meat dish to serve on the *voileipäpöytä* (bread-and-butter table) with sour cream and cooked sliced beets. In hot weather it makes an excellent cold-meat entrée. Serve it with a hot vegetable, salad, and perhaps a hot bread.

3 pounds veal (shoulder, breast,
  or neck)
8 whole allspice
4 teaspoons salt

1 bay leaf
2 tablespoons vinegar
boiling water
3 egg whites

Garnish
hard-cooked, sliced egg
carrot curls

parsley

Cut the meat into pieces and place in a large pot with the allspice, salt, bay leaf, and vinegar. Add boiling water just to cover. Simmer slowly until tender (about 1½ hours). Remove any scum that collects. Let the meat cool in the broth.

Remove the meat from the bones and cut into half-inch pieces, or put through a food chopper, using the coarse blade. Strain the broth through several thicknesses of cheesecloth. (If the broth is cloudy, pour it back into the pot and bring to a boil, whip in 3 slightly beaten egg whites, and strain again.) Pour half of the broth into a 1½- to 2-quart mold; chill until syrupy. Add the diced meat and remaining broth. Place in the refrigerator again until set (at least 24 hours). Before serving, unmold on a platter, and garnish with the parsley, egg slices, and carrot curls. Serves 12.

PAN-BROILED VEAL ROLLS Pariloituvasikankääryleet

Veal is one of the most popular and plentiful meats in Finland. This is just one of the interesting ways in which the Finns serve veal cutlets.

8 veal cutlets (about 4 inches square and ½ inch thick)	salt
	pepper
flour	¼–½ cup butter

Garnish
parsley sprigs   lemon wedges

Gravy
1 cup heavy cream   pepper
salt   lemon juice

Put the veal cutlets between two sheets of waxed paper and pound with a mallet until very thin. Roll each up. Dredge each roll in flour, and sprinkle with salt and pepper. Melt the butter in a frying pan and fry the rolls quickly until they are golden brown on all sides. Remove to a hot serving platter.

To make the gravy, stir about 2 tablespoons of the cream into the pan in which the rolls were cooked. Mix well with a fork to scrape up all the pan drippings and smooth out all the lumps, then add the remaining cream. Cook, stirring constantly, until the gravy is thickened. Add the salt, pepper, and lemon juice (a squeeze at a time) to taste.

Garnish the veal rolls with the parsley and lemon wedges and serve at once. Pass the gravy in a separate bowl. Serves 4 to 6.

■⊕✦■⊕✦■⊕✦■⊕✦■⊕✦■⊕✦■⊕✦■⊕✦■⊕✦■⊕✦■⊕✦■⊕✦■

RING BOLOGNA BAKE   Käyrämakkaraherkku

Ring bologna is as popular in Finland as wienies are in the United States. The Finns have many ways to cook it. They cut it into pieces and roast them over a campfire, as we cook wienies. A crowning touch to a sauna party in Finland is to roast bologna pieces over the hot sauna stove and eat the pieces with hot mustard. With these, one drinks *kalja* or *olut* (beer). Finns do not put the meat into bread as we do wienies.

Serve this dish for brunch, lunch, or supper with scrambled eggs or boiled potatoes.

1 whole ring high-quality bologna   ½ pound Swiss, Tybo, or Edam cheese

Place the bologna in a well-buttered casserole and slash it crosswise in eight or nine places, at about 2-inches intervals (cut almost to the bottom of the ring, but not all the way through). Cut the cheese into as many wedges as you have slashes in the bologna and fit the cheese pieces into the bologna slashes. Bake in a moderately hot oven (375°) for about 15 minutes or until the cheese has browned and meat is heated through. Serve hot. Serves about 4.

BREAKFAST FRANKFURTERS   Aamiaispaistos

Frankfurters made in Finland are of very high quality, well seasoned, always fresh. Finns use them in many ways. This dish is typical of those served for their 11:00 a.m. breakfast. We might well use this as a brunch dish, serving it with scrambled eggs instead of mashed potatoes.

1 pound high-quality frankfurters   4 tablespoons catsup (or 1 large
   or bratwurst   tomato, diced)
¼ cup finely minced sweet onion   ¾ cup cream
                                        1 tablespoon flour

Slit each frankfurter to about ½ inch of each end. Fill the frankfurters with minced onion and place in a casserole, close together, with the slit side up. Sprinkle with the catsup or tomato cubes. Mix together the cream and flour and pour over all. Bake in a moderately hot oven (375°) for 20 minutes or until the sauce bubbles. Serve hot. Serves 4 to 6.

SAUSAGE OVEN PANCAKE   Makkarapannukakku

This is ideal for a brunch or luncheon dish. You can make the pancake to serve a crowd because it is so easy to prepare. Serve with butter and syrup or lingonberry preserves.

2 eggs
1½ cups milk
1½ cups white flour
1 teaspoon baking powder
1 teaspoon salt

½ pound smoked link sausage, summer sausage, or salami, thinly sliced
1 small onion, sliced thinly crosswise
½ cup shredded sharp Cheddar cheese

Beat the eggs and add the milk, flour, baking powder, and salt. Mix until blended. Butter two 8- or 9-inch round cake pans very well. Arrange the slices of sausages and onion in the pans and pour the pancake batter over them, dividing it evenly between the two pans. Sprinkle the cheese evenly over the batter. Bake in a hot oven (400°) for about 20 minutes or until golden brown. Serve hot. Serves 6 to 8.

HOMEMADE SAUSAGES

You have a real feeling of accomplishment when you make your own sausages. Although the art of sausage-making is not widely practiced in modern-day Finland, there is a value in preserving a few of the outstanding sausage recipes.

Your local meat market may have to order the sausage casings especially for you. The casings come either salted or unsalted. Salted casings keep indefinitely in the refrigerator. To use them, soak in water for 5 to 10 minutes, then run warm water through them by fitting one end of the casing onto the water faucet. Cut the casings into 4-foot lengths to make them easier to handle.

To fill the sausages, you can use a sausage press made especially for this purpose. However, an ordinary pastry bag or metal cooky press fitted with the nozzle tip about a half-inch in diameter also works well. Simply fit one end of the casing onto the nozzle of the pastry bag or press and press the filling into the casing, working the mixture down toward the end of the casing. To separate the sausages, tie the filled casing at intervals with cotton string or twist casing.

MEAT SAUSAGE   Kestomakkara

This makes a sausage that is excellent for sandwiches.

sausage casings (see index)
2 pounds lean ground beef
¾ pound lean ground pork
3 teaspoons salt
1 teaspoon black pepper
1 teaspoon allspice
¼ teaspoon cloves
1 teaspoon sugar

¼ cup beer, cognac, or brandy
1 pound side pork, unsalted, cut in
   ¼-inch cubes
1½ tablespoons salt
1 tablespoon sugar
1 teaspoon saltpeter (optional, available in pharmacies)

Prepare the sausage casings as directed.

Combine the beef, pork, salt, pepper, allspice, cloves, sugar, and beer or cognac until thoroughly mixed. Knead the mixture until very smooth. Then add the side pork, kneading it in very well. If the mixture seems dry, add water until it is the consistency of a meat-loaf mixture.

Put the mixture into a sausage press, pastry bag, or large cooky press, and press into the sausage casings, packing it in well so there are no air bubbles. Tie the sausages in 4-inch lengths with string.

Rub the sausages with a mixture of the 1½ tablespoons salt, 1 tablespoon sugar, and 1 teaspoon saltpeter (the latter helps preserve the sausages). Cover and refrigerate for 2 days, turning the sausages as a brine collects in the pan. Remove from the brine, rinse, and smoke in a meat smokehouse or over very low coals on a covered barbecue for 3 to 4 hours, adding dampened hickory chips to the fire, which should be low so that the sausages neither break nor burn. Refrigerate or freeze or serve immediately. Slice to serve. Makes about 4 pounds of sausage.

RICE AND LIVER SAUSAGE   Riisimakkara

This was one of our favorite sausages while in Finland. We purchased it from the corner meat market. The flavor is similar to that of the Liver-Rice Casserole (see index).

sausage casings (see index)
¾ pound liver, sliced
1 medium onion, minced
¼ cup butter
2 cups cooked and chilled rice
2 eggs, slightly beaten

½ cup milk
1 cup raisins (optional)
¼ cup dark corn syrup
¼ teaspoon ground ginger
½ teaspoon white pepper
3 teaspoons salt

Prepare the sausage casings as directed in the instructions.

Put the liver through a meat chopper, using the finest blade (this is easiest to do when the liver is partially frozen). Brown the liver and onion in the butter until the redness disappears from the meat and the onion is cooked. Turn into a mixing bowl and add the rice, eggs, milk, raisins, syrup, ginger, pepper, and salt. The mixture will be very thin.

Put the mixture into a sausage press, pastry bag, or cooky press and press into the prepared sausage casings. Fill the casings very loosely, for they shrink quickly when cooked and if filled too full they will burst. Tie the sausages into 6-inch lengths, leaving plenty of room for the casings to shrink. Put into a large pot in one layer and add boiling water to cover them. With a needle, prick the sausages to let the air escape. Simmer (do not boil) for 30 minutes, pricking the sausages occasionally with a pin or needle. Drain and cool. Store in the refrigerator or freeze them. To serve, cook the sausages in the oven or brown them in butter in a frying pan until evenly browned and heated through. Makes about 1½ pounds sausage.

POTATO SAUSAGE   Perunamakkara

This is the most popular of the homemade sausages. It has a mildly spicy flavor and soft texture. Be sure to pack it loosely into the sausage casings because the casings shrink quickly when the boiling water is poured over them, and if they are filled too full they will burst.

sausage casings (see index)	4 cups milk
2 pounds ground lean pork	1 teaspoon ginger
1 pound ground lean beef	3 teaspoons salt
2 large potatoes, peeled, cooked,	¼ teaspoon ground nutmeg
and mashed	salt

Prepare the sausage casings as directed.

Combine the pork, beef, and potatoes thoroughly. Mix in the milk, ginger, 3 teaspoons salt, and nutmeg. Beat very well until the mixture is thick and smooth. Press through a large pastry bag, cooky press, or sausage press into the casings. Fill the casings loosely so the meat has room to expand while cooking. Tie in 6-inch lengths with string. Sprinkle the sausages lightly with salt and let stand in the refrigerator until the next day. Store in a salt-water brine (3 tablespoons salt to each quart water), or freeze.

Cook before serving by simmering in water to cover, or cook in a soup or bake in the oven until browned. Prick with a needle in several places while cooking to allow air bubbles to escape and keep the sausages from bursting. Serve hot. Makes about 5 pounds of sausages.

SMOKED SAUSAGES   Käristysmakkara

To smoke these sausages, have them treated in a commercial smokehouse, your own smokehouse if you have one, or in a covered barbecue with a very low fire. Serve them thinly sliced as an open sandwich topping, or brown them in butter and serve as a meat course.

sausage casings (see index)
1 pound veal, ground 4 times with
   fine blade
1 pound pork, ground 4 times with
   fine blade
1 pound ground suet
4 medium potatoes, peeled, cooked,
   and mashed
3 teaspoons salt

1½ teaspoons sugar
¾ teaspoon pepper
¾ teaspoon allspice
¾ teaspoon ginger, ground
¾ cup milk, scalded and cooled
water
2 tablespoons salt
2 tablespoons brown sugar

Prepare the sausage casings as directed.

Combine the veal, pork, suet, potatoes, 3 teaspoons salt, sugar, pepper, allspice, ginger, and milk into a smooth mixture. Add enough water (about 2 cups) so the mixture is soft enough to press into the sausage casings. (It will be somewhat softer than a meat-loaf mixture.)

Cut the sausage casings in 7-inch strips and knot an end of each. Press the mixture through a cooky press, sausage press, or pastry bag into the prepared casings, making individual sausages. Pack very well in the casings and knot the open end closed. Rub the sausages with the 2 tablespoons salt mixed with the brown sugar and put into a bowl or pan. Cover with cold water and let stand overnight in the refrigerator. The next day, smoke the sausages in a covered barbecue about 4 to 6 hours over very low coals (but in a smokehouse, this takes 2 to 3 days). Serve with Finnish-style Mustard (see index). Makes about 4 pounds sausages.

Poultry

FINNISH BRAISED CHICKEN   Kanavatkuli

Chicken is not a plentiful item in Finland, and the chickens that are available for cooking are usually not as tender as the specially bred broiler-fryers so common in the United States. This recipe has been adapted for the broiler-fryer; if you use a hen, you will need to increase the cooking time in the oven. This is oven-cooked chicken served on rice with a cream sauce.

1 broiler-fryer (about 3 pounds)
  cut in pieces
2¼ teaspoons salt
¼ teaspoon white pepper
4 tablespoons butter
3 tablespoons flour

dash pepper
1 cup cream
½ cup tomato sauce
3 cups hot cooked rice
fresh chopped parsley or chives

Sprinkle the chicken pieces with 2 teaspoons of the salt and the pepper. In a frying pan, brown the chicken in the butter over medium-high heat until golden on all sides. Remove from the pan and arrange in a casserole. Pour the pan drippings over the chicken. Cover, and cook in a moderately hot oven (375°) for 45 minutes to 1 hour or until the chicken is tender but not overcooked. Remove from the oven, drain the juices into the pan the chicken was browned in. Stir in the flour, ¼ teaspoon salt, and the pepper. Slowly add the cream and tomato sauce, and cook, stirring constantly, until the sauce is thick and smooth. Taste, and correct the seasonings. Arrange the chicken pieces on a hot platter over the rice. Pour the sauce over the chicken and garnish with the parsley or chives. Serve immediately. Serves about 4.

BRAISED GAME BIRDS   Paistettu Metsälintu

Use any small game birds (squab, quail, grouse, pheasant, partridge, chukars, and the like) or domestic Rock Cornish hens in this recipe. Most small birds are quite dry, but cooked like this they are juicy and tender.

4 small birds
2 tablespoons butter
1½ teaspoons salt

3 tablespoons flour
2 cups water
¼ cup black currant jelly

Clean the birds well. Dry them thoroughly. Heat the butter in a frying pan and add the birds, browning them well on all sides. Combine the salt and flour and rub the mixture well onto the outside of each of the birds. Arrange the browned birds, breast side up, in the pan, and add ½ cup of the water. Heat to boiling, cover, and turn the heat down to low so that the water barely simmers.

Add the remaining water at 15-minute intervals or when water has evaporated away, keeping the pan moist at all times. Cook for 45 minutes to 1 hour or until the birds are tender. Remove to a serving platter and garnish with the parsley. Stir the black current jelly into the drippings in the pan and serve this sauce separately at the table (strain, if necessary). Allow 1 bird per person if the birds are small, or 1 for two persons if they are large.

VII. Vegetables and Salads

One of the greatest challenges to Finnish home economists today lies in thinking of ways to make vegetables more appealing to the public. They have succeeded in producing some interesting dishes and in making some progress with the modern generation, but there still is a segment of the older population that considers vegetables to be only "cows' food."

Potatoes, however, are universally used. They are especially filling as an evening snack, on camping trips or during the long summer nights, when it is easy to forget that it is really nighttime—and you are hungry. We often ate potatoes with relatives by the light of the midnight sun. Campers would not think of leaving home without a boxful of potatoes included in their gear. At the campgrounds, while the men set up the tent, the women get the potatoes scrubbed and onto the campfire.

When the new potatoes are finally big enough to eat, it is not uncommon for a Finnish family to make a whole meal of them. Cooked with the skins on and with lots of melted butter, I agree they are delicious.

Mushrooms are another abundant vegetable. They grow wild in more than one hundred varieties. The first mushrooms are picked soon after the snow has melted in April or May, and the last are picked in the autumn. They are preserved in a salt brine to use during the winter.

One of our group of Fulbright scholars thought cauliflower should be named the national flower of Finland, it is served so often and in so many different ways!

BEETS IN ORANGE SAUCE
Punajuuret Appelsiinikastikkeessa

These are good to serve with pork.

2 cups orange juice	2 teaspoons cornstarch
1 tablespoon brown sugar	1 tablespoon butter
dash salt	2 cups cooked and sliced beets
⅛ teaspoon pepper	

In a saucepan, combine all the ingredients except the beets. Bring to a boil, stirring constantly to keep the sauce smooth. Add the beets (these can be either freshly cooked or canned), and continue to cook over medium heat until they are heated through. Serves 4.

■෨෨■෨෨■෨෨■෨෨■෨෨■෨෨■෨෨■෨෨■෨෨■෨෨■෨෨■෨෨■෨෨■෨෨■

CARAWAY CABBAGE   Kuminakaali

Serve this cabbage dish with baked or fried sausages, bologna, or frankfurters.

¼ cup butter
1 small head cabbage, shredded
1 small onion, sliced
½ cup water
3 fresh tomatoes, chopped

1 teaspoon salt
1½ tablespoons caraway seed
2 tablespoons sugar
finely chopped parsley

Melt the butter in a large pan and add the cabbage and onion. Cook, turning with a fork, until the vegetables are limp but not browned. Add the water, tomatoes, salt, caraway seed, and sugar. Cover and simmer for 30 minutes. Serve hot, garnished with the parsley. Serves about 6.

CARROT CASSEROLE   Porkkanalaatikko

1 cup cooked rice
2 cups milk
5 medium carrots, shredded
1 teaspoon salt

1 tablespoon dark brown sugar
2 eggs
3 tablespoons butter
⅓ cup fine bread or cracker crumbs

Combine the rice, milk, carrots, salt, sugar, and eggs. Pour into a well-buttered 1½-quart casserole. Melt the butter in a separate pan and stir the crumbs into it. Sprinkle over the top of casserole. Bake in a moderately hot oven (375°) about 40 minutes or until the top is lightly browned. Serves 6.

CARROT CREPES   Porkkanaohukaiset

Serve these for brunch or supper with spicy sausages, butter, and lingonberries.

4 medium carrots, peeled, cooked,
   and mashed
2 eggs
1 teaspoon salt

1 cup white flour
2 teaspoons sugar
2 cups milk
butter

Combine all the ingredients, and beat until smooth. Let stand for 30 minutes. Bake the pancakes in a small amount of butter making them about 3 inches in diameter until golden on both sides. (If you have one, use a Scandinavian pancake pan for these.) Makes about 40 pancakes.

CRUSTED CARROTS   Kuorretetut Porkkanat

These carrots have a crispy outer crust—delicious served with baked ham.

6 medium carrots, peeled   1 teaspoon salt
¼ cup milk   ½ cup white flour
1 egg, beaten   1 tablespoon butter

Quarter the carrots lengthwise. Combine the milk and egg in a bowl. In another bowl combine the salt and flour. Dip the carrots first into the milk mixture, then into the flour-salt mixture. Arrange in a well-buttered baking dish in a single layer. Dot with the butter. Bake in a moderate oven (350°) until the carrots are tender (about 45 minutes). Serve hot. Serves 4 to 6.

CAULIFLOWER CUSTARD
Kukkakaalia Ja Munakokkeli

This is good to serve with Ring Bologna Bake (*see index*).

1 medium cauliflower, separated   1 tablespoon minced parsley
  into flowerets   2 cups milk
2 tablespoons butter   3 eggs
3 tablespoons flour   ¼ teaspoon white pepper
1 teaspoon salt

Cook the cauliflower until tender-crisp in salted water to cover. Drain. Arrange in a buttered 1½-quart casserole. Melt the butter in a pan, add the flour, ½ teaspoon of the salt, and the parsley, stirring until smooth. Slowly add 1 cup of the milk and cook until thickened, then pour over the cauliflower.

Beat the eggs in a bowl, add the remaining ½ teaspoon salt, the pepper, and the rest of the milk. Pour over the creamed cauliflower in the casserole and bake in a moderate oven (350°) for 30 to 35 minutes or until the custard is set. Serve hot. Serves 4 to 6.

CAULIFLOWER WITH HAM SAUCE
Kukkakaali Kinkkukastikkeen Kera

This makes an attractive vegetable dish that is easy to do yet interesting enough to serve to guests.

1 head cauliflower (about 2½
    pounds)
½ pound cooked ham, finely diced
2 tablespoons minced onion
3 tablespoons flour

1 cup half-and-half cream
salt
sliced tomatoes
parsley

Cook the cauliflower in enough salted water to cover until tender-crisp (about 25 to 30 minutes). Drain, and arrange on a serving platter. Meantime heat the ham and onion in a pan and sprinkle with the flour, stirring until all the pieces are evenly coated. Add the cream, stirring vigorously, and cook until thickened. Taste, and add salt. Pour enough of the sauce over the cauliflower head to coat it evenly. Garnish the platter with the tomatoes and parsley. Serve the remaining sauce in a bowl to spoon over the individual servings. Serve immediately. Serves about 6.

CAULIFLOWER-RICE CASSEROLE
Kukkakaali Ja Riisi

1 small head cauliflower
½ cup cooked rice
3 eggs, beaten
1 cup milk

½ teaspoon salt
dash allspice
fresh chopped parsley

Cook the cauliflower in salted water to cover until tender-crisp (25 to 30 minutes). Separate the flowerets and arrange in a greased casserole. Combine the rice with the eggs, milk, salt, and allspice, and pour over the cauliflower. Bake in a moderate oven (350°) for 30 to 35 minutes or until the custard has set. Garnish with the parsley. Serve hot. Serves about 6.

CREAMED MUSHROOMS   Sienimuhennos

Serve this with boiled new potatoes, and spoon over a meat loaf or slices of a roast.

4 tablespoons butter
4 cups sliced fresh mushrooms
1 medium onion, finely chopped

4 tablespoons flour
1½ cups cream
salt to taste

Melt the butter in a frying pan, add the mushrooms and onion, and cook over medium heat, stirring constantly, until the mushrooms and onions are browned. Stir in the flour and the cream. Taste, and add salt. Simmer slowly for 30 minutes. Makes about 2½ cups.

POTATO CASSEROLE   Imellettyperunasoselaatikko

Potato Casserole is such an old familiar dish, that when we visited relatives during Christmas, it was not even put on the table until we begged to taste it. The lady of the house had made it, and at the last minute had decided it was not fancy enough to be served. We thought it was wonderful and went back for more. The uniqueness of this potato dish is that it undergoes what the Finns call a "malting" process wherein the starch of the potatoes breaks down to form a simpler sugar. The Finnish farm wife lets the mixture stand on the side of her large wood stove for several hours during the "malting." In Western Finland this dish may be baked in a large pan to make a flatter casserole. It is then called *kropsu*.

4 cups fluffy (not dry) mashed   4 tablespoons dark corn syrup
    potatoes   (optional)
¼ cup flour

Beat the mashed potatoes with a rotary beater or a whip (if too stiff, add a little milk). Mix in the flour until well blended, then add the syrup (some Finns add the syrup, some do not). Turn the mixture into a heavy buttered casserole, cover tightly, and let cook in a warm oven (turn oven to the very lowest heat possible) for 5 hours. Check it occasionally to be sure that it does not get dry. Add milk if necessary. During this time the potatoes should become soft and sweet, and they will have a flavor similar to sweet potatoes. When they are yellowish in color, add a pinch of salt and stir to make smooth again. Leave uncovered, but dot the top with butter, and continue to bake in a moderate oven (350°) for 15 minutes or until browned on top. Serve hot. Serves 6 to 8.

MUSHROOM-MACARONI CASSEROLE
                              Makaronisienilaatikko

This is a version of the old Finnish favorite, Macaroni Casserole. To make the latter, you do not include the mushrooms and onions. Serve as a side dish.

1 medium onion, finely chopped   2 eggs, slightly beaten
3 cups fresh mushrooms, chopped   1½ teaspoons salt
2 tablespoons butter   ½ teaspoon pepper
2 cups cooked macaroni   ⅓ cup fine dry bread crumbs
2 cups milk

■҈■҈■҈■҈■҈■҈■҈■҈■҈■҈■҈■҈■҈■҈■

Brown the onion and mushrooms in butter in a frying pan over medium heat, stirring constantly. Butter a 2-quart casserole and place half the macaroni on the bottom. Spread the onions and mushrooms over it, and distribute the remaining macaroni evenly over all. Combine the milk, eggs, salt, and pepper and pour over the ingredients in the casserole. Top with the bread crumbs. Bake in a moderate oven (350°) for 30 minutes or until the casserole is set and the top slightly browned. Serve hot. Serves about 6.

GRATED POTATO CASSEROLE   Riivinkropsu

From the province of Satakunta in Western Finland comes this traditional dish. This is a "Sunday" potato dish.

2 eggs
1 cup milk
2 tablespoons flour
1 teaspoon salt

2 medium potatoes, grated
2 tablespoons butter
parsley

Beat the eggs and add the milk, flour, salt, and potatoes. Melt the butter in the bottom of a 1- to 1½-quart baking dish, and spread evenly over the bottom and sides. Pour in the egg-potato mixture and bake in a moderately hot oven (375°) for 45 to 50 minutes or until the potatoes are tender and the casserole is set. Serve hot, garnished with chopped parsley. Serves 4 to 6.

MASHED-POTATO CASSEROLE   Perunasoselaatikko

6 medium potatoes, peeled
2 eggs, beaten
1 cup cream or milk

salt
butter
6 tablespoons fine dry bread crumbs

Cook, then mash, the potatoes. Whip in the eggs, cream or milk, salt to taste, and 4 tablespoons butter; beat until very fluffy. Turn into a buttered 1-quart casserole and sprinkle with the bread crumbs. Dot with more butter. Bake in a moderately hot oven (375°) for 20 to 25 minutes or until the top is nicely browned. Serve hot. Serves 6.

BAKED POTATO CAKES   Perunakakkuja

Make these like Filled Potato Dumplings (see index) but omit the flour. Place the filled cakes in a well-buttered casserole, dot with butter, and bake in a hot oven (400°) for 15 minutes. Serve immediately with meat, a vegetable, and salad. Makes 8.

AALAND ISLAND POTATO PATTIES
Oolanin Kakut

The Aaland Islands belong to Finland but the people lack the traditions of the Finns and speak only Swedish. The islands are situated off the south-west coast of Finland and usually are the first sight of Finland the traveler approaching by boat has.

There are various versions of these potato patties: some of them have the onion and bacon added as a filling in much the same style as the recipe for Filled Potato Dumplings (see *index*). Serve with meat, vegetable, and salad.

¼ pound bacon, cooked until crisp and crumbled (reserve drippings)	1 tablespoon milk
	1 egg, slightly beaten
	½ teaspoon allspice
4 large potatoes, peeled, cooked, and mashed	½ teaspoon salt
	1 small onion, finely minced

Cook the bacon until crisp, reserving the drippings. Crumble it and combine with the potatoes, milk, egg, allspice, salt, and onion, into a smooth mixture. Shape into patties and fry in the bacon drippings. Serve hot. Serves 4.

CREAMED POTATOES AND CELERY ROOT
Sellerisose

Serve this with hot cooked meats.

1 large celery root	1 teaspoon salt
5 medium potatoes	2 teaspoons sugar
2 tablespoons butter	½ teaspoon pepper

Pare, cut up, and cook the celery root in enough salted water to cover. Peel, cut up, and cook the potatoes until tender. Force both vegetables through a potato ricer, or mash until smooth. Stir in the butter, and season with the salt, sugar, and pepper. Serve hot. Serves 6 to 8.

HASSELBACK POTATOES   Hasselbackan Perunat

These potatoes spread out slightly (somewhat like a fan) during the baking and have an interesting appearance and texture.

Choose potatoes as uniform in size as possible to serve them attractively, and allow about 1 potato per person. Peel the potatoes and make cross-wise slashes in each, about ⅛ inch apart (be sure to cut only three quarters of the way through the potato). Arrange the potatoes, uncut side down, in a well-buttered casserole, and brush them well with melted butter. Sprinkle with salt, pepper, and fine dry bread crumbs, and dust lightly with Parmesan cheese. Dot with butter. Bake in a hot oven (400°) for 35 to 40 minutes or until the potatoes are tender, basting them occasionally with water if their edges seem to be browning too much. Or put them into the same pan as a meat roast and baste them with the roast drippings during the cooking.

FILLED POTATO DUMPLINGS   Perunakakut

This recipe requires very dry cold mashed potatoes. If you use instant mashed potatoes, use only three-fourths of the liquid called for on the package. Serve these with melted butter or hot gravy.

Dumplings

2 cups cold dry mashed potatoes	1 tablespoon plus ½ teaspoon salt
1 egg yolk	1 quart water
¼ cup flour	

Filling

1 cup finely diced cooked ham	¼ teaspoon ground allspice
2 tablespoons minced fresh onion	

Combine the potatoes, egg yolk, flour, and the ½ teaspoon salt in a bowl, mixing well with a fork. In another bowl, combine the ham, onion, and allspice until well mixed. To make the dumplings, use a tablespoon to scoop up enough of the potato mixture into a piece about the size of an egg. Press 2 teaspoons of the ham mixture into the center of the dumpling, en-closing it completely within the potato. Moisten the top and seal (use your fingers or the teaspoon to do this). Refrigerate or freeze the dumplings before cooking them.

To cook the dumplings, bring to a boil the quart of water with the table-spoon salt. Reduce the heat so the water just simmers and drop in 2 or 3 of the filled dumplings. Simmer (do not boil or the dumplings will break) for 10 minutes. Remove from the broth with a slotted spoon onto a hot serving platter. Repeat until all are cooked. Makes 8 dumplings.

BAKED POTATO CAKES
Uunissa Paistettu Perunakakkuja

Make these like Filled Potato Dumplings (*above*) but omit the flour. Fry them in butter in a hot frying pan until golden on both sides. Serve hot. Makes 8.

RADISHES IN PEPPER SAUCE   Retiisimuhennos

Serve these over Carrot Crepes or Spinach Pancakes (*see index*), with broiled, barbecued, or roasted meat.

large radishes	¼ teaspoon pepper
2 tablespoons butter	2 teaspoons sugar
2 tablespoons flour	½ teaspoon salt
1 cup cream	chopped parsley

Choose radishes that are too large to serve as a relish. Clean them well and place in a saucepan in enough water to cover, adding about ½ to 1 teaspoon salt to the water, and cook until tender. Drain (but reserve the liquid), and chop them, then put aside. You should have 2 cups. In another pan, melt the butter, and to it add the flour, mixing until smooth. Slowly add the hot liquid from the radishes, stirring constantly to keep the mixture smooth, then blend in the cream. Add the radishes, pepper, sugar, and ½ teaspoon salt. Just before serving, heat almost to boiling and garnish with the parsley. Serves 4.

RUTABAGA CASSEROLE   Lanttulaatikko

You may use either turnips or rutabagas in this dish. This is an old, traditional dish which is (or was) always part of the Christmas dinner menu. Serve it with a meat dish.

2 medium rutabagas, peeled and diced (about 6 cups)	½ teaspoon nutmeg
¼ cup fine dry bread crumbs	1 teaspoon salt
¼ cup cream	2 eggs, beaten
	3 tablespoons butter

Cook the rutabagas until soft (about 20 minutes) in salted water to cover. Drain and mash. Soak the bread crumbs in the cream and stir in the nutmeg, salt, and beaten eggs. Combine with the mashed rutabagas. Turn into a buttered 2½-quart casserole, dot the top with butter, and bake in a moderate oven (350°) for 1 hour or until lightly browned on top. Serves 6 to 8.

BROWNED RUTABAGA CUBES   Ruskitetut Lantut

¼ cup butter
4 cups raw rutabaga

1 teaspoon salt
2 tablespoons dark brown sugar

Melt the butter in a frying pan. Add the rutabaga cubes and cover. Cook over low heat, stirring frequently until all sides are browned. Add salt and sugar, stirring well so they are evenly distributed. Continue to cook over low heat (covered) until the rutabaga is fork-tender (about 20 minutes). Serve hot. Makes 4 to 6 servings.

SPINACH PANCAKE   Pinattipannukakku

This is the basic oven pancake that is baked in an oblong pan, filled, and rolled up like a jelly roll. Serve with a bowl of grated cheese to sprinkle over individual servings.

2 eggs
2 cups milk
1 cup sifted white flour
1½ teaspoons salt (approximately)
1 teaspoon baking powder

4 tablespoons butter
1 pound fresh spinach
¼ teaspoon nutmeg
pepper

Beat the eggs with the milk. Sift the flour with 1 teaspoon of the salt and the baking powder into a mixing bowl. Stir in the egg-milk mixture all at once and mix until smooth. Let stand for 30 minutes before baking. Melt 1 tablespoon of the butter in a 10- by 14-inch jelly-roll pan and spread it evenly over the bottom. Pour in the pancake batter. Bake in a moderate oven (350°) for 20 minutes or until set (do not overcook). Meanwhile, cook spinach in a small amount of water until tender; drain thoroughly; add the butter, nutmeg, salt, and pepper to taste.

Spread the prepared spinach over the baked pancake and roll up like a jelly roll. Slice and serve hot. Serves 6 to 8.

SPINACH MASHED POTATOES Pinaatti Perunasose

Fluffy mashed potatoes with chopped spinach whipped in are a favorite with children, served hot with an "eye" of butter or with gravy.

6 medium potatoes, peeled   ½ to 1 cup hot milk
1 teaspoon salt   butter
1 10-ounce package frozen
chopped spinach

Cook the potatoes until tender with the salt in just enough water to cover. Drain and mash them. Meanwhile put the spinach into another saucepan, pour the milk over it, and cook over low heat until it is done. Add the spinach-milk mixture to the mashed potatoes and whip until fluffy. Serve immediately. Serves about 6.

VEGETABLE POT   Kasvispata

Serve this vegetable-bologna dish for lunch with crisp bread, rye bread, and cheese.

3 leeks, cut in 1-inch lengths, or 3   1 small head cauliflower separated
  white onions, quartered   into flowerets
2 medium carrots, peeled and cut   1 pound ring bologna or all-meat
  in 1-inch lengths   frankfurters cut in 1-inch lengths
2 cups peas, fresh or frozen   2 cups beef broth

Combine the leeks, carrots, peas, cauliflower, and bologna or franks in a 2-quart casserole. Pour the beef broth over all. Cover, and bake in a moderate oven (350°) for 30 to 45 minutes or until the vegetables are tender. Serve hot. Serves about 4.

VEGETABLE-RICE PLATTER   Vihannekset

This is an ideal accompaniment for a roast or pot roast.

1 cup hot cooked brown rice   2 cups hot cooked cauliflower,
1 cup hot cooked carrots, cubed   separated into flowerets
¼ cup melted butter   1 cup cooked grean peas
¼ cup finely chopped parsley   2 sliced, peeled tomatoes
1 tablespoon finely chopped chives   recipe Mushroom Sauce (see
                                            index)

Spread the rice in an even layer on a hot platter. Brown the carrots in the butter and stir in the parsley and chives. Arrange in a ring over the cooked rice. Arrange the cauliflower attractively over the carrots, and then arrange a ring of green peas next to the cauliflower. Garnish with the tomatoes and serve hot with the Mushroom Sauce. Serves about 6.

VEGETABLES AU NATUREL   Vihannekset au Naturel

Arrange several cooked vegetables attractively on a tray to accompany a meat dish. By doubling proportions, you can serve a large group of people.

1 head cauliflower
1 pound young carrots
1 pound fresh peas

1 pound whole green beans
½ cup butter
¼ cup finely chopped parsley

Cook the whole head of cauliflower in salted water to cover until tender-crisp. Meanwhile, cook the carrots, peas, and green beans in separate sauce-pans. Place the cauliflower in the center of a large serving platter, arrange the carrots on either side of it, then mound the green beans and peas around it. Pour the butter over all and sprinkle with the parsley. Serve at once. Serves 10 to 12.

AUTUMN SALAD   Syyssalaatti

½ head fresh cauliflower, chopped
¼ pound fresh mushrooms, chopped
2 medium carrots, peeled and
   shredded

1 small onion, minced
½ teaspoon salt
½ teaspoon sugar
French dressing

In a bowl, toss together the raw cauliflower, mushrooms, carrots, onion, salt, and sugar until mixed. Chill. Serve on lettuce, adding French dressing to taste. Serves 4 to 6.

BEET-HERRING SALAD   Rosolli or Punajuurisalaatti

This salad has two Finnish names. *Rosolli* is the version that usually has the herring and *punajuurisalaatti* is the one without the herring. This salad is food even without the fish!

2 medium potatoes, cooked, peeled, and diced
2 tart apples, peeled and diced
2 carrots, peeled, cooked, and diced
1 small onion, minced
2 medium dill pickles, diced

¾ cup diced pickled or salted herring, or minced sardines, or anchovies (optional)
⅛ teaspoon white pepper
2 cups cooked beets, peeled and diced
1 recipe Whipped Cream Dressing or Sour Cream Dressing (see index)

Combine the potatoes, apples, carrots, onion, pickles, herring, and pepper. Just before serving, carefully add the beets. (If the beets are added too long before serving, the salad will be a deep pink, whereas it should be tinted only mildly pink.) Turn into a salad bowl lined with crisp lettuce and serve chilled with either the Whipped Cream Dressing or Sour Cream Dressing. Serves 8 to 10.

GOLDEN CARROT SALAD   Kultasalaatti

Serve this with broiled chicken, roast duck, or game.

6 medium carrots, peeled and finely shredded
2 oranges, peeled and cut in segments (or 1 11-ounce can mandarin oranges, drained)

2 tablespoons finely chopped parsley
½ cup orange juice
2 teaspoons honey
lettuce

In a serving bowl, toss together the carrots, orange segments, and parsley. Combine the orange juice and honey and pour over the salad. Serve in lettuce-lined salad bowls. Serves 4 to 6.

CUCUMBER SALAD   Kurkkusalaatti

Make this salad 2 hours before you plan to serve it to allow the flavors to blend.

4 medium cucumbers, peeled and thinly sliced
1 tablespoon chopped fresh or dried dill
½ cup white wine vinegar

½ cup water
3 tablespoons sugar
1 teaspoon salt
2 tablespoons salad oil

Arrange the cucumber slices in a chilled glass bowl and sprinkle with the dill. Combine the vinegar, water, sugar, salt, and salad oil, and pour over the cucumber slices. Serves about 6.

LEMON-LEAF-LETTUCE SALAD   Sitruunasalaattii

1 quart salad greens
2 tablespoons lemon juice
1½ teaspoons sugar

¼–½ teaspoon salt
dash freshly ground pepper
2 tablespoons heavy cream
   (optional)

Wash, dry, and crisp the greens. Tear into bite-sized pieces and put in a salad bowl. Sprinkle with the lemon juice and toss well, then sprinkle with the sugar, salt, and pepper, and toss again until well mixed. Add the cream if you wish, and toss until evenly blended. Serves 3 to 4.

FRESH MUSHROOM SALAD   Sienisalaatti

1 pound small mushrooms, well
   shaped
2 quarts salad greens
   (approximately)
2 tablespoons grated fresh onion

1 teaspoon sugar
2 tablespoons cream
dash white pepper
salt

Parboil the mushrooms for 2 minutes in enough salted water to cover. Drain and dry thoroughly. Slice very thin and arrange in a salad bowl over the washed and crisped greens. Combine the onion, sugar, cream, and white pepper, and sprinkle over the salad. Toss. Add salt to taste, if needed, toss again, and serve at once. Serves 4 to 6.

ORANGE AND CARROT SALAD
Appelsini Porkkanasalaatti

4 cups finely shredded carrots
1 orange, juice only

lettuce
seedless raisins
chopped nuts

Mix the carrots with orange juice and arrange on lettuce leaves, either on individual plates or in a salad bowl. Serve immediately. If you wish, you may add the raisins or nuts to the salad. Serves 4 to 6.

SPRINGTIME SALAD   Kevatsalaatti

This is a light salad that you can enjoy almost any time of year. Serve it on a bed of early leaf lettuce.

3 red apples, unpeeled but diced
1 cup finely sliced celery
½ cup finely diced cucumber
3 tablespoons lemon juice
3 teaspoons sugar

½ teaspoon salt
½ cup sour cream or mayonnaise (optional)
crisp salad greens

Put the apples, celery, and cucumber into a bowl and sprinkle with the lemon juice, distributing it evenly over all the pieces to prevent browning. Sprinkle with the sugar and salt. Mix well. Cover and chill until serving time. Fold in the sour cream or mayonnaise, if you wish, or serve in a separate bowl at the table. Line a salad bowl with the crisp greens and arrange the salad over it. Serve chilled. Serves 4 to 6.

HOT SQUASH SALAD   Kurpitsasalaatti

I received this recipe when attending a cooking school session in Helsinki sponsored by the Home Economics organization.

4 cups yellow squash cubes (firm winter squash is best)
1 cup sugar

½ cup white wine vinegar
1 cup water
3 whole cloves

Put the squash into a large kettle that has a lid. Combine the sugar, vinegar, and water, and pour over the squash. Add the cloves, cover, and simmer over medium heat until the squash is tender (about 30 minutes). Drain, and serve hot. Serves 6 to 8.

VIII. Desserts

Fruit soups, whipped berry puddings, and porridges comprise most of the everyday desserts in Finland. They are light, yet refreshing after a meal. Desserts as we think of them usually appear on the coffee table in Finland.

The fruit soups called *kiisseli* toppled with mounds of whipped cream, the whipped desserts, the summertime fresh wild berries are among the favorites. The most common everyday dessert is a hot cooked cereal such as farina or creamed rice topped with butter and milk or cream, at other times with fruit soup.

Viili piimä, a special clabbered milk set in bowls and eaten with a spoon, is so delicious it makes the best yoghurt seem ordinary. A special culture called a "seed" or a "start" is necessary to make it.

Wild berries available in Finland are eaten in abundance when they are in season. The remainder are preserved either in the form of whole fruit or as a fruit syrup to be used later in making clear fruit soups. Lingonberries, called *puolukka* and similar to our cranberries, are used as a meat accompaniment as well as in desserts. There are two varieties of wild berries which grow only in arctic or near-arctic climates and that are a real delicacy. One is the *lakka*, a yellow-orange berry that resembles a raspberry in appearance, and the other is *mesimarja*, which grows in swampy areas on a very low bush. Special liqueurs are made of these two berries.

CLEAR FRUIT SOUP   Marjakiisseli

Pour this berry soup, warm, over hot cooked and Creamed Rice (see *index*) to serve a Finnish-style dessert. Or serve as suggested, with whipped cream.

2 cups fruit juice (currant, blueberry, strawberry, or cranberry)
2¼ cups cold water
1 cup sugar (or more if needed)

4 tablespoons cornstarch or potato starch
1 cup heavy cream, whipped

Pour the fruit juice, 2 cups of the water, and the sugar into saucepan. Bring to a boil. Dissolve the cornstarch in the remaining water and add slowly to the boiling liquid. Cook until thickened and clear. Remove from the heat, cool, and pour onto a large shallow platter to serve. Garnish with mounds of whipped cream (one mound per serving). Serves 6 to 8.

■໐໐■໐໐■໐໐■໐໐■໐໐■໐໐■໐໐■໐໐■໐໐■໐໐■໐໐■໐໐■໐໐■

MIXED FRUIT SOUP   Sekahedelmäkeitto

1 pound mixed dried fruits (apricots,
   prunes, pears, and apples)
2½ quarts (10 cups) water
1 stick cinnamon
1 cup sugar

2 tablespoons cornstarch or potato
   starch
2 tablespoons cold water
whipped cream (optional)
1 recipe Creamed Rice (see index)

Simmer the dried fruits in the water with the cinnamon and sugar until
the fruits are tender (about 1 hour). Dissolve the cornstarch or potato starch
in the 2 tablespoons of cold water, bring the soup to boiling, and stir in the
starch mixture. Cook, covered, until the soup has thickened and is clear.
Cool with the cover on to prevent a skin from forming on top. To serve,
pour over Creamed Rice or top with whipped cream. Serves 8 to 10.

GOOSEBERRY SOUP   Karviaismarjakiisseli

2 cups water
2 cups fresh gooseberries
3 tablespoons sugar
1 stick cinnamon

3 tablespoons corn starch or
   potato starch
3 tablespoons cold water
whipped cream

Bring the 2 cups of water to a boil in a saucepan and add the gooseberries, sugar, and cinnamon. Add the cornstarch to the 3 tablespoons cold
water and mix into a smooth paste. When the berries have cooked about
10 minutes, slowly stir the starch mixture into the boiling soup. Cook 2
minutes more, or until clear and thickened. Pour into a wide-topped serving
bowl or a platter with a rim. Cool quickly. Serve chilled, topped with fluffs
of whipped cream. Serves 6.

BLUEBERRY SOUP   Mustikkakiisseli

Use blueberries in place of gooseberries in the above recipe. Add lemon
juice to taste.

RASPBERRY SOUP   Vadelmakiisseli

Use fresh raspberries in place of gooseberries in the recipe for Gooseberry Soup. Add a drop of almond flavoring.

CREAMY LEMON SOUP   Sitruunakeitto

4 cups water	2 tablespoons cornstarch or potato
1 stick cinnamon	starch
¼ cup farina (regular, quick, or	2 tablespoons cold water
instant)	1 cup sugar
¼ cup currants	¼ cup lemon juice
2 tablespoons grated lemon peel	dash salt
	light cream

Pour the 4 cups of water into a 2-quart saucepan and add the cinnamon, farina, currants, and grated lemon peel. Bring to a boil and cook over medium heat, stirring constantly, until thickened and smooth (about 10 minutes at a low boil). Dissolve the starch in the 2 tablespoons cold water and stir into the hot soup. Bring to a boil again, stirring all the while, and cook for 3 or 4 minutes or until the soup is smooth and thick. Remove from the heat and stir in the sugar, lemon juice, and salt. Serve the soup hot, or set it to cool in a pan of water and whip, using a wire whip or electric mixer, until it has turned light and creamy. (The longer you whip it the creamier it gets.) Pour into a serving dish, and serve it chilled with light cream to pour over it. Serves 6 to 8 generously.

RHUBARB SOUP   Rapaperikiisseli

Use rhubarb, cut into 1-inch pieces, in place of gooseberries in the recipe for Gooseberry Soup, and increase the sugar to ½ cup (or more, if the rhubarb is very tart).

STRAWBERRY SOUP   Mansikkakiisseli

Use fresh or frozen strawberries in place of gooseberries in the recipe for Gooseberry Soup. Omit the cinnamon and add a dash of nutmeg, if you wish.

ROSE HIP SOUP   Ruusunmarjakeitto

Rose hips are the "fruit of the rose." Certain roses develop swollen round buds after blooming which are picked and then dried. Dried rose hips are available in health food stores. Serve this warm or chilled.

½ cup dried rose hips
4 cups water
¾ cups sugar
3 tablespoons cornstarch

3 tablepoons cold water
½ cup chopped almonds (optional)
whipped cream (optional)
1 recipe Creamed Rice (see index; optional)

Soak the rose hips in the quart of water overnight. Cook in the same liquid for 5 minutes. Strain and discard the seeds and petals. Heat to boiling. Add the sugar and stir until dissolved. Dissolve the cornstarch in 3 tablespoons cold water and stir into the boiling liquid. Cook for about 3 minutes or until the soup is thickened and clear. Pour onto a large flat serving dish.

Sprinkle with the chopped almonds just before serving, and serve warm over Creamed Rice, or chilled, garnished with mounds of whipped cream. Serves 4.

PRUNE CREAM MOLD   Luumukermahyytelö

½ pound (1 cup) uncooked prunes
1 teaspoon unflavored gelatin
1 tablespoon cold water

2 cups heavy cream
¼ cup sugar
chopped nuts (optional)

Cook prunes according to the directions on the package. Pit them and force through a wire strainer or whirl in a blender until they are puréed. Soften the gelatin in the water and place over hot water until dissolved. Whip the cream and add the sugar to it. Slowly whip in the dissolved gelatin. Fold in the puréed prunes and turn into a dessert mold or ring mold that holds about 4 cups. Chill in the refrigerator for about 4 hours or until set. Turn out of the mold onto a serving dish and garnish with more whipped cream and chopped nuts, if desired. Serves 6.

APRICOT CREAM   Aprikoosipuuro

1 cup dried apricots
4 cups water
1 cup sugar

½ cup farina
light cream or slightly sweetened whipped cream (optional)

Cook the apricots in the water until they are tender and fall apart when touched with a spoon (30 to 40 minutes). Measure the fruit and liquid together, and add enough water so the total measure is 6 cups. Stir in the sugar and farina and cook until thickened. Pour into the large bowl of your electric mixer and whip at highest speed until the pudding is light and fluffy. Serve either hot, with light cream to pour over it, or chilled, topped with whipped cream. Serves about 6.

SAVO CRANBERRY PUDDING   Savolainen Tirri

This age-old recipe comes from the province of Savo. It is a pudding that is baked slowly, and it has a wonderful texture and flavor as a result. In Finland, lingonberries are used for this, but cranberries make an excellent substitute. Serve with cream and sugar.

2 cups whole cranberry sauce   ¼ cup white flour
2 cups cold water   ¼ cup rye flour
½ cup sugar

Combine the cranberry sauce, water, and sugar. Mix the two flours together and whip into the cranberry mixture. Pour into a 2-quart casserole. Cover and bake in a slow oven (300°) for 3 hours. After each hour of baking, stir the pudding. Uncover it during last hour. If the pudding gets too thick to stir, add hot water until it has the consistency of a thick porridge. If it is too thin at the second stirring, add more flour, a little at a time, mixing it in well. Beat, and return to the oven. Serves 6 to 8.

WHIPPED BERRY PUDDING OR "AIR PUDDING"   Ilmapuuro

It is amazing how this pudding whips up into two or three times its original volume. The favorite flavor in Finland is lingonberry, but you can use cranberry or any other tart fruit juices. This should be eaten the same day it is made.

3 cups fruit juice   ½ cup sugar
½ cup uncooked farina   lemon juice

Heat the juice to boiling and sprinkle in the farina. Stir quickly to prevent lumping and cook slowly for about 30 minutes or until the farina is done. Pour into the large bowl of your electric mixer and whip at highest speed until very light colored, creamy, and fluffy (this takes about 20 minutes). Sweeten to taste. If you are using a non-tart juice such as raspberry, strawberry, or apple, add lemon juice to taste. Serve with rich milk or cream. Serves 4 to 6.

■◎♣■◎♣■◎♣■◎♣■◎♣■◎♣■◎♣■◎♣■◎♣■◎♣■◎♣■◎♣■◎♣■◎♣■

RYE CRANBERRY PUDDING   Karpaloruispuuro

This old-time recipe is a favorite among the "oldest generation." Rye flour gives this pudding an interesting texture and wonderful flavor. Once you become accustomed to this pudding, your taste for it grows to the point where you sometimes "crave" it! Serve with cream to pour over it.

2 cups cranberry juice
2 cups plus 2 tablespoons water
½ cup sugar
dash salt

1 cup rye flour
2 tablespoons dark corn syrup
2 tablespoons cornstarch or potato starch

Combine the cranberry juice, 2 cups of water, the sugar, salt, and rye flour in a 2-quart saucepan. Bring to boil and cook, stirring constantly, for 10 minutes. Cover, turn heat to low and cook for 45 to 60 minutes or until the mixture is thickened and has a glossy appearance. Stir in the dark corn syrup. Dissolve the starch in the 2 tablespoons cold water and add to the pudding. Bring to boiling point again and cook for 5 minutes longer, stirring constantly. Pour into a serving dish and cover while cooling to keep a skin from forming on top. Sprinkle the surface with sugar before serving.

BUTTERMILK MOLD   Kirnupiimähyytelö

This dessert has a refreshing citrus flavor. Shape it in a ring mold and serve with fresh fruit in season.

2 cups buttermilk
2 tablespoons lemon juice
2 tablespoons grated orange peel
1 tablespoon grated lemon peel
¾ cup sugar

1 package (1 tablespoon) unflavored gelatin
2 tablespoons cold water
1 cup heavy cream, whipped until stiff
fresh fruit

In a large bowl, combine the buttermilk, lemon juice, grated peels, and sugar. Soften the gelatin in the cold water, then dissolve over hot water. Beat into the buttermilk slowly and carefully to prevent the gelatin from lumping. Fold in the whipped cream. Turn into a 1-quart mold (either tube or fancy), and chill until set (about 4 hours). Turn out onto a serving plate. Garnish with fresh berries or fruit and serve with extra fruit. Serves 6.

POOR KNIGHTS   Köyhät Ritarit

1 egg
2 teaspoons flour
2 cups milk
¼ teaspoon ground cardamom or
   cinnamon
dash salt

12 inch-thick slices stale French or
   Italian bread
butter
sugar
cinnamon

Beat the egg, add the flour, milk, cardamom, and salt. Dip the bread slices in the milk mixture but do not let them get soggy. Heat 2 tablespoons butter in a heavy frying pan until it begins to brown, and fry the bread slices for about 3 minutes on each side, adding more butter as needed. Serve hot from the pan with berries and cream, or jam.

Variation:

Slice the bread only ½-inch thick. Butter one slice and spread apple butter on another, and sandwich the two together. Dip the sandwich into the egg-milk mixture and proceed as above. Repeat for the rest of the slices. Serve sprinkled with sugar and cinnamon.

RICH KNIGHTS   Rikkaat Ritarit

2 egg yolks
¾ cup half-and-half or light cream
8–10 slices stale French or Italian
   bread

½ cup applesauce (or other fruit or
   berry sauce)
2 egg whites
4 tablespoons sugar

Beat the egg yolks and cream together. Dip the bread slices into the mixture and place on a well-greased baking sheet. Spread each evenly with the applesauce. Whip the egg whites until stiff, gradually adding the sugar. Spoon the meringue evenly onto the bread slices. Bake in a moderate oven (350°) for about 10 minutes or until the meringues are lightly browned. Serve immediately. Serves 6 to 8.

APRICOT RICE   Aprikoosiriisi

Prepare like Raspberry Rice *(see index)* but use 2 cups fresh ripe apricots or canned drained apricot halves in place of the raspberries.

■╰◢■╰◢■╰◢■╰◢■╰◢■╰◢■╰◢■╰◢■╰◢■╰◢■╰◢■╰◢■╰◢■╰◢■╰◢■

CREAMED RICE   Riisipuuro

This creamy rice is the base for various desserts when combined with fruit soup, fresh fruit, or cinnamon sugar. Spoon chilled fruit soup over still warm *Riisipuuro,* or serve fresh fruits, cubed, over it, or simply sprinkle servings with cinnamon sugar.

1 cup uncooked white rice
6 cups milk
½ teaspoon salt
2 teaspoons sugar

1 cup heavy cream, whipped
   (optional)
cinnamon sugar (½ cup sugar
   mixed with 3 teaspoons cinnamon;
   optional)

Combine the rice, milk, salt, and sugar in the top of a double boiler. Cook over boiling water for 2 hours, stirring occasionally, until the rice is creamy and the milk is absorbed. Cool for 30 minutes and fold in the whipped cream. Serves 6 to 8.

BAKED RICE PUDDING   Unni Riisipuuro

At Christmastime, a blanched almond is often pressed into this pudding before it is served, and it is said that the person who gets it will have good luck during the following year.

1 cup uncooked rice
3 cups milk
¼ cup melted butter
½ cup sugar
3 eggs, beaten

½ teaspoon salt
½ cup sliced unblanched almonds
1 teaspoon cinnamon
1 whole blanched almond
light cream

Cook the rice according to the directions on the package. Drain and rinse with cold water.

Combine the milk, melted butter, sugar, eggs, and salt. Stir in the rice and pour into a well-buttered 2-quart casserole. Combine the sliced almonds and cinnamon and sprinkle over the pudding. Bake in a moderate oven (350°) for about 1 hour or until the pudding has thickened sufficiently. Press the whole almond into the pudding and cover the mark left. Serve either hot or chilled with the light cream to pour over it. Serves 6 to 8.

EASTER MÄMMI   Mämmi

This is a baked rye pudding flavored with orange and raisins. There are so many stories connected with this traditional dessert that a whole book could be made just from them. (Many of them are unprintable in a cook-book.) In the old days, Mämmi was baked in birchbark baskets, but today it is against the law to use the latter, as removing the bark kills the trees. Today cardboard baskets are used instead.

The consistency of mämmi varies from one part of the country to another. In one region it is so thin that it has to be drunk from a cup, but the most common consistency is that of a baked pudding.

4 cups water	2 tablespoons grated orange peel
½ cup sorghum or dark molasses	¼ cup seedless raisins
½ teaspoon salt	sugar
1 cup rye flour	cream

Heat the water, molasses, and salt in a pan until just warm. Stir in about ¼ cup of the rye flour, bring to a slow boil, while beating constantly with a whisk. Turn the heat off and let mixture cool. (It can stand from 10 minutes to 2 hours, depending on your convenience.) Stir in the remaining rye flour, orange peel, and raisins, and bring to a boil again, stirring with the whisk. Remove from the heat and pour into a 1½-quart casserole. Do not fill the dish to the top because the mämmi will rise during baking, although it will fall afterward. Bake in a slow oven (275°) for 3 hours. Cool. Cover tightly to prevent drying. Store in a cool place. Serve with lots of sugar and cream, but make the servings small at first. Serves 6 to 10.

CHOCOLATE MOLD   Suklaahyytelö

You can either use one fancy mold for this chocolate pudding or individual serving dishes. Serve with a fluff of whipped cream.

1 package (1 tablespoon) unflavored gelatin	2½ cups rich milk, cream, or half-and-half
2 tablespoons cornstarch	1 teaspoon vanilla
½ cup sugar	whipped cream
3 tablespoons cocoa	
dash salt	
dash cinnamon	

In a saucepan, combine the gelatin, cornstarch, sugar, cocoa, salt, cinnamon, and milk, stirring until thoroughly blended. Let stand for 5 minutes, then bring to a boil over medium-high heat, stirring constantly, and cook until slightly thickened. Remove from the heat, stir in the vanilla, and cool. Pour into a mold or individual dessert dishes and chill. Unmold and serve with whipped cream. Serves 4 to 6.

STRAWBERRY SNOW   Mansikkalumi

The "snows" are quick desserts to make, and they are relatively low in calories. Serve them immediately after making them, or freeze them to make a very nice sherbet.

1 package (1 tablespoon) unflavored   4 egg whites
  gelatin   ½ cup sugar
¼ cup water   1 cup heavy cream, whipped
2 cups crushed strawberries   whole strawberries for garnish

Soften the gelatin in the water. Heat 1 cup of the crushed strawberries to the boiling point, and stir in the gelatin. Chill until syrupy. Beat the egg whites until stiff, adding the sugar to them gradually. Fold the egg-white mixture into the cooled strawberry-gelatin mixture. Fold in the remaining cup crushed strawberries. Fold in the whipped cream and serve immediately, garnished with the whole strawberries. Or, turn into ice-cream tray and freeze. Serves 6 to 8.

RASPBERRY SNOW   Vadelmalumi

Make like Strawberry Snow, (above) but use crushed raspberries in place of strawberries and increase the sugar to 1 cup. Garnish with whole raspberries.

SNOW BALLS   Lumipallot

This is a nice family or company dessert.

4 egg whites (½ cup)   2 tablespoons cornstarch
¾ cup sugar (approximately)   1 teaspoon vanilla
2 cups milk   nutmeg
2 egg yolks

Beat the egg whites until foamy, add ½ cup sugar gradually, then beat until stiff. Bring the milk to a boil in a large saucepan and drop large spoonfuls of the meringue mixture into the milk. When the milk boils again, lift the meringues out with a slotted spoon onto a serving dish.

Beat the egg yolk, 2 to 4 tablespoons sugar (according to taste), cornstarch, and vanilla together and stir a small portion of the hot milk into it. Stir until smooth, then pour into the remainder of the hot milk. Cook, stirring constantly, until thickened. Pour this custard over the meringues in the serving dish. Serve hot or chilled with a dash of nutmeg. Serves 4 to 6.

APPLE SNOW   Omenalumi

Although the Finns serve Apple Snow immediately after it is made, I find it is too filling that way, and prefer it frozen. This is a dessert low in calories.

½ cup egg whites   2 cups tart applesauce
½ cup sugar   dash cinnamon
dash salt

Beat the egg whites until foamy, slowly add the sugar and salt, and beat until very stiff. Carefully fold in the applesauce until it is thoroughly combined. Turn into serving dish and top with cinnamon; serve immediately. Or, turn into ice-cube tray and freeze. Serves 4.

EASTER PASHA   Pääsiäispasha

This dessert is traditional in Karelian homes at Easter. It is a molded cheeselike dessert served with whipped cream and fruit.

2 pints cottage cheese   ½ cup finely chopped almonds
½ cup sour cream   1 cup sugar
2 tablespoons soft butter   1 cup seedless raisins
2 egg yolks   whipped cream
1 tablespoon grated lemon peel   fruit

Force the cottage cheese through a strainer or whirl in a blender until smooth. Add the sour cream, butter, and egg yolks, mixing well. Stir in the lemon peel, almonds, sugar, and raisins. Mix until all the ingredients are evenly blended. Wash a crockery flower pot (the type with a hole in the bottom), about 6 to 8 inches deep, and line with several layers of cheesecloth. Press the pasha mixture into the lined pot, and place a weight on top. Set on a rack in a pan to catch the liquid that will drain off. Place in the refrigerator, and let set at least 1 day but preferably 2 or 3 days. (If dry spots appear, simply remove them.) Unmold on a serving plate and remove the cheesecloth carefully. Garnish with whipped cream and fruit. Serve with more whipped cream and fruit to spoon over individual servings. Serves 6 to 8.

LEMON DESSERT DUMPLINGS   Mykyjä

These are dumplings that you cook in any of the fruit soups (see index).
Cook them under a tight-fitting cover—and do not peek until they are done!

1 cup white flour
1½ teaspoons baking powder
½ teaspoon salt
2 tablespoons sugar
2 tablespoons butter

1 tablespoon grated lemon peel
⅓ cup milk
1 egg, beaten
2 tablespoons chopped almonds

Sift together the flour, baking powder, salt, and sugar into a mixing bowl.
Cut in the butter until the mixture resembles fine crumbs, then stir in the
grated lemon peel. Combine the milk and egg and add the dry ingredients,
stirring lightly until they are evenly moistened. Add the almonds. Drop by
teaspoonfuls into boiling fruit soup, cover tightly, and cook over medium
to low heat for 10 to 15 minutes.

PARSONAGE EMERGENCY DESSERT

Pappilan Hätävara

This dessert resembles the English trifle. It is quick to make, as its name
suggests.

2 cups fine butter-cooky or graham-
cracker crumbs
1 cup milk
1½ cups whipping cream

1 tablespoon sugar
1 teaspoon vanilla
1½ cups fruit or berry preserves

Soak the crumbs in the milk. Whip the cream, and to it add the sugar
and vanilla. In a glass dessert serving-dish, layer the crumbs, preserves, and
whipped cream in that order. Decorate the top with a dab of the preserves
and a sprinkling of the crumbs. Serves 4 to 6.

PRUNE RICE DELIGHT   Luumuriisi

Rice, prunes, and whipped cream are the main constituents of this dessert.
It is one that children like.

1 cup cooked fluffy rice
1 cup prunes, pitted
1 cup water
¼ cup sugar
1 cup heavy cream

1 teaspoon vanilla
3 tablespoons sugar
¼ cup toasted, sliced almonds
1 teaspoon grated lemon peel

Chill the rice thoroughly. Cook the prunes in the water with ¼ cup sugar until tender (about 15 minutes). Drain and chill.

Whip the cream until stiff, flavor with the vanilla and 3 tablespoons sugar; fold in the almonds and lemon peel. Fold the whipped cream mixture into the rice, and layer this in a serving bowl with the cooked prunes. Reserve enough of the cooked prunes to garnish the top. Serves 4 to 6.

RASPBERRY RICE   Valdemariisi

Rice, whipped cream, and raspberries folded together make a favorite summertime dessert. You can use frozen raspberries when the fresh are out of season, but then decrease the sugar.

1 cup cooked fluffy rice, chilled   ¼ cup sugar
dash salt   2 cups fresh raspberries
1 cup heavy cream

Add the salt to rice. Whip the cream until stiff and add the sugar to it. Fold the whipped cream into the rice and turn into a serving dish. Top with the raspberries and serve. Serves 4.

STRAWBERRY RICE   Mansikkariisi

Prepare like Raspberry Rice (above), but use strawberries in place of the raspberries.

RASPBERRY WHIP   Vadelmavaahto

This meringue-berry dessert may be served immediately after it is made, but it is also very good frozen and served as a sherbet. Serve with cookies or vanilla wafers.

3 egg whites   1 cup crushed raspberries
4 tablespoons sugar   whole raspberries for garnish

Beat the egg whites and sugar together until stiff, then beat in ½ cup of the crushed raspberries. Continue beating until very stiff. Fold in the remaining crushed raspberries. Turn into serving dishes and garnish with the whole raspberries. Or, turn into an ice-cube tray and freeze. Serves 4.

■❦■❦■❦■❦■❦■❦■❦■❦■❦■❦■❦■❦■❦■❦■❦■

RHUBARB CRISP Raparperipaistos

Sliced fresh rhubarb tops a rich, buttery, cookylike batter. Serve it with whipped cream or ice cream.

¼ cup butter
¾ cup sugar
1 egg
1 cup sifted white flour
1 teaspoon baking powder

¼ teaspoon salt
2½ cups thinly sliced fresh rhubarb
½ cup sugar
2 teaspoons cinnamon
whipped cream or ice cream

Cream the butter and sugar until light and add the egg, beating until thick and lemon colored. Sift the flour with the baking powder and salt into the creamed mixture. Stir until smooth and well combined. Turn into a buttered 9- by 12-inch pan, spreading the batter evenly over the bottom. Top with the rhubarb and sprinkle with the cinnamon sugar. Bake in a moderate oven (350°) for 45 minutes or until the edges are browned and pulled away from the sides of the pan. Cut into 3-inch squares, and serve warm, topped with whipped cream or ice cream. Serves 12.

APPLE CUSTARD Omenamunakas

Bake whole apples in a custard for a spiced dessert that can be served hot or chilled.

6 small apples, peeled and cored
sugar
1½ cups milk
3 eggs

3 tablespoons flour
dash salt
3 tablespoons sugar
cream

Roll the apples in sugar until they are evenly coated. Place them close together in a well-buttered baking dish. Beat the milk, eggs, flour, salt, and sugar together and pour over the apples. Bake in a moderate oven (350°) for 30 to 40 minutes or until the apples are tender. Serve with cream to pour over it. Serves about 6.

KARELIAN OAT KIISSELI Karjalainen Kaurakiisseli

This is one of the oldest of Karelian desserts. It may seem to be a strange dessert; however, it should be included in a collection of traditional Finnish recipes. It tastes like smooth cooked oatmeal with a yeasty tang, and is traditionally served hot with lots of butter and cream. The most authentic version calls for a slice of sour rye bread or sour-dough start instead of the yeast.

2 cups quick-cooking oatmeal	¾ teaspoon salt
½ teaspoon active dry yeast	butter
4 cups lukewarm water	hot milk

Put the oatmeal into a 2-quart pot, add the yeast, and pour in the water. Stir until well mixed. Cover and let stand at room temperature overnight. Press the mixture through a strainer, then return to the pot and bring to a boil, stirring constantly. Cook over medium to low heat until thick and smooth. Stir in the salt and serve hot with plenty of butter and hot milk. Serves 6 to 8.

APPLE MERINGUE   Omenamarenki

Serve this dessert—apple slices topped with a meringue, then baked— either hot or cold.

2 tablespoons butter	½ cup egg whites
½ cup granulated or brown sugar	¾ cup granulated sugar
2 teaspoons cinnamon	dash salt
8 large tart apples, peeled, cored, and sliced	

Melt the butter in the bottom of a large flat baking dish (about 9 by 12 inches) and sprinkle ¼ cup of the granulated or brown sugar and 1 teaspoon cinnamon over it. Arrange the apples over the sugar layer and top with another ¼ cup sugar and teaspoon cinnamon.

Beat the egg whites until foamy, then slowly beat in the ¾ cup granulated sugar and the salt until the mixture is very stiff. Drop by spoonfuls or press through a pastry bag over the apples into a pretty design. Bake in a moderately slow oven (325°) for 35 to 40 minutes, or until the apples are tender and the meringue is golden. Serves 8.

HONEY STEWED PRUNES   Hunajaluumut

1 pound prunes	1 cup honey
2 cups water	cream

Soak the prunes in the water overnight. Bring to a boil and add the honey. Cook, simmering, until the prunes are tender (about 30 minutes). Cool, then chill. Serve the prunes and liquid with plain or whipped cream. Serves about 6.

■ 🍂 ■ 🍂 ■ 🍂 ■ 🍂 ■ 🍂 ■ 🍂 ■ 🍂 ■ 🍂 ■ 🍂 ■ 🍂 ■ 🍂 ■ 🍂 ■ 🍂 ■ 🍂 ■

APPLESAUCE MERINGUE   Omenasosemarenki

Make like Apple Meringue (*above*), but use 4 cups applesauce in place of the apples and reduce the first amount of sugar to ¼ cup. Bake in a moderate oven (350°) for 15 or 20 minutes or until the meringue is golden. Serves 8.

RYE PORRIDGE   Ruisjauhopuuro

This porridge dates back to the days of the *Kalevala* (Finland's national epic). Traditionally, it is served as a dessert or as a supper main dish, but it is delicious as a variation on the breakfast menu, too.

1½ cups water	butter
dash salt	milk
½ cup rye flour	

Bring the water to a boil and add the salt and rye flour, beating with a whisk until all flour lumps are dissolved. Turn the heat down very low, and cook very slowly until thickened (about 30 minutes). Serve hot with butter and milk. Serves 3 to 4.

WHOLE BARLEY PUDDING   Ohraryynipuuro

This is the traditional dessert or supper main dish in the province of Satakunta in Western Finland, but you may prefer to serve it as a breakfast dish or in place of a starch dish in any menu. Serve with butter.

½ cup whole pearl barley	2 tablespoons butter
1½ cups water	½ teaspoon salt
2⅔ cups milk	

Cook the barley and water slowly for 30 minutes or until the barley begins to expand. Stir in the milk, bring to a boil, and pour into a casserole. Dot with the butter, add the salt, and bake in a slow oven (250°) for 4 hours or until all the liquid is absorbed. Stir occasionally as the casserole bakes. Makes about 6 servings.

FINNISH CHOCOLATE PUDDING   Suklaapuuro

In Finland this is a dessert, but our children enjoy it for breakfast. Serve it hot with milk or cream.

2 cups milk
1 tablespoon powdered cocoa
⅓ cup farina

dash salt
2 tablespoons sugar

Bring the milk to a boil. Combine the cocoa and farina with the salt and sugar and stir into the milk. Continue cooking, stirring constantly, until thickened. Serves 4.

IX. Dairy Foods

The commercial cheeses of Finland are of very high quality. Particularly, the Emmenthal (Swiss) cheese made in Finland is the highest possible quality. One Finnish tourist in Sweden said that he had seen a Swedish advertisement saying, "Original Finnish Swiss cheese made in Sweden sold here."

We were told by the Finns to be selective when buying Swiss cheese and to accept a piece only from the round that "weeps" (that is, one that has drops of liquid in the eyes of the cheese).

There are many other Finnish cheeses of highest renown, such as Tilsitter, Kreivi, Kesti, and Aura, which are now being imported into the United States.

Besides commercial cheese, Finns make their own local fresh-milk cheeses (we would classify them as "breakfast" cheeses). Two of these are *Pohjalainen Leipäjuusto* and *Hämeläinen Pääsiäisjuusto,* and the recipes for making them are included in this chapter; they are surprisingly easy to make, and they are delicious.

EGG BUTTER   Munavoi

Egg Butter is spread over piirakka (*see index*) or any other pastry having a savory filling. It is also served with cold sliced meats and hot cooked vegetables.

1 cup soft butter
3 hard-cooked eggs, finely chopped

salt

Cream the butter, blend in the eggs, and add salt to taste. Heap in a bowl, provide a spoon, and let the guests help themselves.

BAKED FLAT CHEESE   Pohjalainen Leipäjuusto

This is sometimes called "squeaky cheese" because, properly made, it should squeak as you chew it. This cheese comes from Pohjanmaa (Bothnia) in Northwestern Finland. The farther north you go, the flatter the cheese of the region becomes. In areas near Lapland, the cheese is baked in a large flat round and cut into wedges. These are eaten rolled up. In areas near Vaasa the cheese is thicker, and it is sometimes cut into thin slices that are fried in butter.

This recipe makes just a very small amount of cheese, but you can double or triple the recipe very easily to make more.

1 quart skim milk   1 tablespoon water
1 rennet tablet   salt

Heat the milk to just 100° (use a candy thermometer to check it). Crush the rennet tablet in the water, dissolve, and add to the warmed milk. Pour the mass that forms onto the center of a large dish towel that you have draped over a colander, and bring the corners of the towel together to make a bag. Let drain until the mass is fairly dry. Discard the whey. Line an 8-inch round cake pan with foil. Pat the curd into a cake about 5 inches in diameter and center it in the pan. Bake in a very hot oven (550°) for 10 minutes. Remove from the oven and press the cheese into a firmer mass, again draining off the whey, and let it cool. Sprinkle with salt, cut into wedges, and serve. Makes about ¼ pound of cheese.

EASTER CHEESE OF HÄME
Hämeläinen Pääsiäisjuusto

In the country just north of Helsinki, this cheese is made abundantly around Eastertime. I used to buy it from the bread and milk shop. It is delicious and mild—quite unlike any cheese we know in the United States. It makes an excellent breakfast cheese or dessert cheese to serve with fresh fruits.

This recipe makes a very small amount. Once you master the recipe, you can easily double or triple it. The cheese is best made with unpasteurized raw milk, but skim milk is a quite acceptable substitute.

1 quart skim milk   1 rennet tablet
1 egg   1 tablespoon water
1½ cups buttermilk   salt

Heat the milk to 175° (use a candy thermometer to check the temperature, or check it by the old Finnish method: it should be so hot that when you put your finger into the milk in the pot, you will be able to twirl it around only once). Remove from the heat.

In a small bowl, beat together the egg and buttermilk, and stir into the hot milk. Dissolve the rennet tablet in the water, and stir this into the milk mixture. Cover, and let stand until cold.

Drape a dish towel over a colander and pour the mixture into it. Let it drain until the curd no longer drips whey. Discard the whey. Line a very small (3- by 5-inch) bread pan with foil and press the curd into it. Bake in a very hot oven (550°) for 10 minutes. Remove from the oven and cool. Drain. Sprinkle with salt, and refrigerate until serving. Makes about ¼ pound of cheese.

POT CHEESE   Ruukujuusto

To make this cheese, you can use up dried pieces of leftover chee:e that you have on hand. Swiss, Cheddar, Gruyère, Edam, Tybo, Tilsitter, and Fontina, for instance, are all suitable. Serve this cheese on the *voileipäpöytä* (the bread-and-butter table), or with a bread-and-butter tray.

3 cups grated leftover cheese   3 tablespoons brandy or cognac
1 cup beer

Combine the cheese with the beer, and beat at low speed with an electric mixer for about 30 minutes or until the mixture is creamy (or whirl in a blender until smooth and creamy). Let the mixture stand in a cool place (not in the refrigerator) for 3 days; stir it once each day. Then add the brandy or cognac, mixing it in well. Turn the mixture into a glass jar, cover, and store in the refrigerator for 3 or 4 days or until you are ready to use it.

EGGS AND MACARONI   Munat Ja Makarooni

Children especially like this.

Follow the recipe for Eggs in a Rice Nest, but substitute 2 cups cooked elbow macaroni for the rice.

■◎■◎■◎■◎■◎■◎■◎■◎■◎■◎■◎■◎■◎■◎■◎■

BAKED CUSTARD OVER TOMATOES
Muna Ja Tomatti

3 medium tomatoes, sliced   4 eggs
salt   2 cups milk
3 tablespoons melted butter

Arrange the tomatoes in a buttered casserole. Sprinkle with salt and brush
with the butter. With a fork, beat together the eggs, milk, and ½ teaspoon
salt. Pour this mixture over the tomatoes and bake in a moderate oven (350°)
for 15 minutes or until the eggs have set. Serve immediately. Serves 3 to 4.

CARAWAY CREAM CHEESE   Kermajuusto

2 cups sour cream   ¼ cup shredded sharp Cheddar
½ teaspoon salt   cheese
caraway seed   ¼ cup shredded blue cheese

Line a large wire strainer with 4 thicknesses of cheesecloth. Turn the sour
cream into it and let drain for several hours, preferably overnight, in a
warm place. Turn the curd that is left in the cheesecloth into a mixing
bowl and stir in the salt, 2 teaspoons caraway seed, and the Cheddar and
blue cheeses.

Turn the cheese mixture into a dampened cheese mold or bowl, pressing
it in firmly. Turn out onto a serving tray and garnish with a sprinkling of
caraway seed. If you wish, you may refrigerate the cheese in the mold or
bowl until serving time.

Serve on the *voileipäpöytä* (bread-and-butter table) or as an accompaniment to a buffet meal, luncheon, or supper. Spread on dark bread or rye
crispbread.

BAKED CHEESE   Uunijuusto

This is a dessert cheese made from beestings (the first milk given by cows
that have newly calved). The milk is supposedly very high in nutritional value
and is considered a delicacy. Finns serve it hot with cinnamon and sugar.

6 cups beestings (2nd- or 3rd-day's   sugar
   milk after calving)   cinnamon
1 teaspoon salt

Combine the milk and salt and pour into a 2-quart casserole. Bake in a moderately slow oven (325°) for 30 minutes, then sprinkle with sugar and cinnamon and return to the oven. Bake for another 30 minutes or until the milk has set. Test by inserting a table knife into the center of the cheese; if it comes out clean, the cheese is done. Serve hot or cold.

MILK TOAST   Maito Korpuu or Leiparessu

In the province of Pohjanmaa (Bothnia), this dish was considered festival fare in the past. It is simply Finnish toast or *korppu* broken into hot milk. In the past, it was also made on "churning days" with whey.

Break korpuu (*see index*) or rusks in pieces, place in a small pan, and pour in enough buttermilk, whey, or fresh whole milk to cover the toast entirely. Let stand for about 15 minutes, then heat slowly, stirring, until mixture comes just to the simmering point. Pour immediately into bowls, sprinkle with cinnamon and sugar and serve. Break 1 korppu into about 1 cup of hot milk to make 1 serving.

BREAKFAST EGGS IN CASSEROLES
Aamiaisherkku

This dish is the answer for weekend breakfasts when everyone does not eat at the same time.

mild cheese (jack, Cheddar, or Swiss)	eggs
	cream
boiled ham slices	

Butter individual casseroles or large custard cups well and place in each a slice of cheese. Top the cheese with a slice of boiled ham. Carefully crack 1 egg onto the ham in each casserole. Pour 1 tablespoon cream over the yolk of each egg, and bake in a moderately hot oven (375°) for 7 to 12 minutes, depending on how you like your eggs. Remove from oven when eggs are just underdone, or the heat of the casserole will continue to cook the eggs beyond the degree of doneness you prefer.

FARMER'S EGGS
Talonpoikais Munat

¼ pound bacon or bologna, thinly
    sliced
2 large uncooked potatoes, peeled
    and diced

2 eggs
1 cup milk
salt
pepper

Sauté bacon or bologna in a frying pan until browned. Add the potatoes, and cook over low heat until tender (about 15 minutes). Drain off the excess fat. Beat together the eggs and milk and pour over the meat and potatoes. Cover the pan and cook over low heat until the eggs are set. Add salt and pepper to taste. Serve immediately. Serves 2.

EGGS IN A RICE NEST
Riisimuna

Serve this dish as a main course for breakfast or lunch.

1 large onion, chopped fine
2 cups cooked fluffy rice
4 tablespoons butter or shortening

1 teaspoon salt
¼ cup catsup
4 eggs

Combine the onion and rice. Melt the butter or shortening in a frying pan, add the onion-rice mixture, and stir in the salt. Cook, stirring constantly, until the onion is limp. Stir in the catsup. Turn the mixture into a shallow casserole and make a hole in the center. Crack the eggs carefully and slip into the hole. Bake in a moderate oven (350°) until the eggs are set (about 10 to 15 minutes). Serve immediately. Serves 4.

EGG CASSEROLE
Munalaatikko

This is like custard without sugar and vanilla. It is served as everyday fare in the countryside, and is considered healthful children's food. It is also an excellent breakfast dish, served with crisp bacon and sausages.

4 eggs
2 cups rich milk or half-and-half

dash salt

Beat the eggs slightly and whip in the milk and salt. Pour into a buttered casserole and set in a pan of water. Bake in a moderate oven (350°) for 30 minutes, or until the custard is set (check by inserting a knife into the center of the casserole; it will come out clean). Do not overcook.

HAM AND EGG CASSEROLE   Munakinkkulaatikko

Prepare like Egg Casserole (*above*), but add 2 cups finely diced cooked ham to the egg-milk mixture. Bake as directed.

EGGS WITH MUSHROOMS   Munat Herkkusienessä

Serve this as a luncheon, supper, or first-course dish. Use individual casseroles, or use scallop shells, if you have them.

8 large eggs	salt
2 tablespoons butter	1 cup heavy cream
2 cups sliced fresh mushrooms	parsley sprigs

Use eggs that are at room temperature. Lower the eggs into boiling salted water and cook for 6 minutes; drain, and run cold water over them for 1 minute. Cool, then peel. The whites will be set but the yolks will still be soft.

Melt the butter in a frying pan and add the mushrooms and ⅛ teaspoon salt. Cook, stirring constantly, until the mushrooms darken and are limp. Butter 4 individual casseroles or serving dishes and divide the mushrooms evenly among them. Place 2 eggs on the mushrooms in each casserole.

Pour the cream into the pan in which the mushrooms were cooked and stir to deglaze the pan. Add ½ teaspoon salt, and continue to stir until the cream comes to a boil. Let it boil rapidly, and stir it all the while, for about 4 minutes (until the cream is reduced and thick). Spoon the cream over the eggs, dividing it evenly among the casseroles. If you wish, put a mushroom slice on each egg. Bake the casseroles in a hot oven (400°) for 5 minutes, garnish with a sprig of parsley, and serve immediately. Serves 4.

X. Beverages

The most revered of all beverages in Finland is coffee. The Finns appreciate good coffee, and drink lots of it. During the war, when coffee was not available, the Finns tried to make it out of substitutes. They ground and roasted almost every imaginable available root or grain, and even the bark of trees. It was amazing how good some of the "coffee" turned out. At first the substitute was mixed with a small portion of real coffee. Later, when no real coffee was available to anybody, whenever a root, bark, or herb was discovered that tasted like coffee, the word spread through the country like wildfire. Some people eventually gave up the search for a suitable coffee substitute and made tea substitutes out of different leaves, saying that mock tea tasted more like real tea than mock coffee tasted like coffee.

One of our relatives was very skilled at making "real"-tasting coffee. A traveler stopped in her house one day, and she served him her "coffee." The guest tasted it and, ecstatic over it, insisted that there was some real coffee in the blend. Though she declared the coffee was not a bit real, he was so insistent and elated that she finally gave in and said, "Yes, there's just a bit." When she said this her face turned red—she had been forced to tell a lie.

Other beverages popular with Finns in the summertime are various types made with yeast, a flavoring, sugar, and water. The best known are non-alcoholic, but the yeast makes them bubbly. *Kalja,* a bubbly drink tasting almost like beer, is popular because it characteristically is not sweet. Even the little old ladies in Finland like to have kalja with their meals in the summertime.

Milk is still the nationwide everyday drink. It is so universally drunk that in most cafés and restaurants you have a choice of having an *iso* (big) or a *pieni* (little) glass of milk or buttermilk with your food.

One cannot mention beverages without answering a few questions about the drinking habits of the Finns. Perhaps this old Finnish proverb portrays the idea: "It is hard to know the right measure when one is too few and two are too many." And there are the defenders of the Finnish habits who say: "The Finns don't drink any more than anybody else—they just drink it all at once." The Finns take a two-fisted approach to drinking that is somewhat offset by a temperance campaign which is largely supported by the government alcohol monopoly called Alkoholiliike Oy. The punishment for driving after having even one drink is severe. Regardless of a man's position in life, he might end up on a government work project somewhere for a couple of weeks. . . . The favorite alcoholic drinks are a domestic gin, *jaloviina,* a domestic brandy, and *paloviina,* a domestic schnapps which is served only with food in restaurants. It is found on the market under two brand names; one of them is jokingly said to be a by-product of the forest industry— made by moonshiners from sawdust!—and the other is made from grain and potatoes.

■◌◌◌■◌◌◌■◌◌◌■◌◌◌■◌◌◌■◌◌◌■◌◌◌■◌◌◌■◌◌◌■◌◌◌■◌◌◌■◌◌◌■

FINNISH EGG-CLEARED COFFEE   Kahvi

Coffee is the Finnish national drink, and it is drunk many times during the day. It is authentically served in pot-bellied copper coffee pots. This is the favorite method for making it.

The secret to making really good coffee is *never, never* to boil it. The coffee should be brought to the boiling point and taken off the heat immediately. The egg settles and clears the coffee. Finnish coffee is not as strong as that preferred by many Americans.

8 cups cold water
1 egg, well washed

16 slightly rounded teaspoons coffee
   plus 1 for the pot

Bring the cold water to a boil in a coffeepot or saucepan. Meanwhile, in a small bowl, crush the egg (shell and all) into the dry coffee grounds and mix thoroughly. When the water has come to a rolling boil, add the egg-coffee mixture and stir quickly. Let it come to the boiling point, and remove from the heat. Repeat this twice more. Then cover and let stand about 5 minutes so the grounds can settle. Makes 8 cups.

CRANBERRY SPARKLE   Karpalojuoma

This is a clear, yeast-sparkled drink that Finns love to serve in the summertime.

2 cups cranberry juice
8 cups water

1–2 cups sugar (depending on
   whether juice is sweetened)
⅛ teaspoon active dry yeast

Heat the juice and water to boiling. Dissolve the sugar in it and let stand until lukewarm. Add the yeast (according to the directions for Sima, *above*) and pour into a non-metallic container. Let stand overnight or until little bubbles appear around the edge of the liquid. Pour into sterilized bottles with an airtight cap. Close tightly. Let stand at room temperature about 3 days, or until the liquid has bubbles in it. Chill and store in the refrigerator or a cool place. Makes about 2½ quarts.

■௸■௸■௸■௸■௸■௸■௸■௸■௸■௸■௸■௸■௸■

SIMA   Sima

Sima is the May Day drink of Finland. Serve it with Tippaleipä (see *index*). Finns serve this refreshing drink throughout the summer. Its tangy characteristic taste comes from the yeast that is added in the beginning.

4 quarts water
1 cup brown sugar
1⅛ cups (approximately) granulated sugar

2 lemons, washed and thinly sliced
⅛ teaspoon active dry yeast
1 tablespoon raisins

Heat the water to boiling and stir in the brown sugar and 1 cup of the granulated sugar. Add the lemon slices. Cool to lukewarm and transfer the liquid to a non-metallic container. Add the yeast and stir (but do not add the yeast until the liquid has cooled, or it will not work. To test for the correct temperature, place a few drops of the liquid on your wrist; if it feels neither warm nor cold, it is the right temperature). Let this water-sugar-lemon-yeast mixture stand overnight or at least 8 to 10 hours in a warm place. There should be tiny bubbles around the edge of the liquid after this length of time.

Sterilize 8 pint bottles, 4 quart bottles, or 1 gallon jug, and place 1 or 2 teaspoons granulated sugar per quart of liquid into each container, as well as 3 or 4 raisins. Strain the liquid and pour into the containers. Cork tightly. Let stand at room temperature until the raisins have risen to the top of the bottle (this indicates that the Sima has fermented enough and is ready to drink). In the winter, this may take 2 days or more; in warm weather, only 8 hours. Chill and store in the refrigerator or a cool place. Makes 1 gallon.

QUICK HOME BREW   Pikakalja

This non-alcoholic drink is popular in the summertime for its refreshing and nonsweet flavor. It is commonly called *talouskalja*, meaning "home beer." Serve it chilled with meals or with sandwiches. It is ready the day after you make it. (Another homemade beer called *sahti* is similar to this one, and in the past was served at country weddings and celebrations.)

1 cup sugar
1 tablespoon malt extract

4 quarts (16 cups) water
1 teaspoon active dry yeast

Mix the sugar, malt, and water and bring to boiling point. Cool, and when lukewarm, add the yeast. Stir until it is dissolved. Let stand in a non-metallic container overnight to ferment. Pour into a gallon jug or into 4 1-quart bottles to store. Cap tightly. Chill and store in the refrigerator or a cool place. Makes 1 gallon.

> "If into the casks you pour it,
> And should store it in the cellar,
> Store it in the casks of oakwood,
> And within the hoops of copper.
> Thus was ale at first created,
> Beer of Kaleva concocted . . ."

> from *Kalevala, the Land of Heroes,* Finnish national epic

BERRY PUNCH   Mehu

This is a light-flavored, red-colored punch that is ideally refreshing on a hot summer's day.

1 cup raspberry juice (or thawed, crushed, and strained frozen raspberries)

1 cup blackberry juice (or thawed, crushed, and strained frozen blackberries)

1 cup gooseberry juice (or 1 8-ounce can crushed and strained gooseberries)

1 quart sparkling water
1 quart lemon soda
ice

Combine the fruit juices, cover, and refrigerate for several hours. Just before serving, pour in the sparkling water and lemon soda. Serve over ice cubes in a punch bowl or individual glasses. Makes 11 to 12 cups punch.

MILK FRUIT DRINK   Maitojuoma

Whip together 1 cup ice-cold buttermilk and ½ cup ice-cold orange juice, pineapple juice, or applesauce, and a dash of lemon juice. Serve immediately. Serves 1 or 2.

ORANGE MILKSHAKE   Appelsiinimaito

Combine 2 cups ice-cold milk with 4 tablespoons frozen orange juice concentrate or 6 tablespoons ice-cold freshly squeezed orange juice and 3 tablespoons sugar. Serve immediately. Serves 2.

NEW YEAR'S PUNCH   Uuden Vuoden Malja

New Year's Eve is usually a family affair. Many families enjoy melting tin and from the strange shapes the tin takes after it is cooled in a bucket of water, determining what is in store for the new year. This is especially an activity of teenagers. Refreshments for the evening include the coffee table for adults; however, a fruit punch such as this is typical of one that the children would enjoy.

1 cup currant juice concentrate   lemon slices for garnish
  (available in specialty food stores)   ice
1 quart lemon soda

Combine the current juice with the lemon soda and pour into individual glasses containing a lemon slice and ice. If you wish, you may first "frost" the glasses by rubbing the rims with a slice of lemon and dipping them into granulated sugar. Fill with the punch and serve. Makes 5 cups.

ROSE HIP TEA   Ruusunmarjatee

You can buy dried rose hips in health food stores. The Finns grow roses that produce fruit, and either dry or preserve the "rose berries" for later use. The berries are very high in vitamin C and when freshly harvested, are often mashed and frozen and sold in little packages as a special baby food.

Try serving rose hip tea as an alternate to regular tea for a ladies' luncheon or afternoon gathering. Serve with sugar or honey and/or lemon.

1 quart water   sugar (optional)
4 teaspoons dried rose hips (more or
  less according to taste)

Bring the water to a boil and pour into a heated teapot; add the rose hips and steep for 5 to 10 minutes. Serves 4.

MOCHA MILKSHAKE   Mokkajuoma

Mix 2 teaspoons instant-coffee powder with 3 tablespoons sugar, and combine the mixture with ½ cup vanilla ice cream; whip into 2 cups ice-cold milk until smooth. Serve immediately. Serves 2 to 3.

BUTTERMILK WITH HONEY   Hunajapiimä

Combine 1 cup buttermilk with 1 tablespoon honey, stirring until well blended. Serve with a dash of nutmeg, if you wish. Serve immediately Serves 1.

XI. Sauces

A good sauce adds flavor and brings out flavor; it moistens food and adds color. A good sauce will also do much to improve and change the appearance of leftover meats, fish, and vegetables.

Perhaps the most traditional of the classic Finnish sauces is Finnish Pork Gravy (see index). It has various names, but the two most common are läskikastike and läskisoosia. According to some of our relatives in the Western Finnish province of Satakunta, läskisoosia and mashed potatoes are the greatest of herkkua (delicacies).

The selection of sauces in this chapter runs the gamut from the classic Finnish ones to those that are widely used but are almost international in popularity.

WHITE SAUCE   Peruskastike

This is a basic, medium-thick cream sauce. There are several variations following.

2 tablespoons butter   salt
2 tablespoons white flour   pepper
1 cup light cream, fish stock, chicken
   broth, or meat broth

Melt the butter in a saucepan and stir in the flour until smooth. Slowly stir in the cream or stock, and cook, stirring constantly, until smooth and thick. Add salt and pepper to taste. Makes 1 cup sauce.

DILL SAUCE   Tillikastike

Make White Sauce (above), but add 2 tablespoons finely chopped fresh or dried dill. Serve with fish, vegetables, or eggs.

LEMON SAUCE   Sitruunakastike

Make White Sauce (above), and add two tablespoons fresh lemon juice
to it after the sauce is thickened. Serve with fish, broccoli, eggs, or chicken.

CHIVE SAUCE   Ruohosipulikastike

Make White Sauce, as above, and add 2 tablespoons finely chopped
chives to it. Serve with fish, eggs, veal, or beef.

CAPER SAUCE   Kaapriskastike

Make White Sauce, as above, but use beef broth in place of the cream.
Add 2 tablespoons capers. Serve with cold sliced beef, veal, or eggs.

CURRY SAUCE   Cuurykastike

Make White Sauce, as above, using chicken broth as the liquid. Mix 1 teaspoon of curry into the sauce. Serve with veal, chicken, eggs, or fish.

FINNISH HOLLANDAISE SAUCE
Hollantilainen Kastike

Serve this sauce with vegetables or fish.

¼ cup soft butter
2 tablespoons flour
3 egg yolks
1½ cups vegetable broth or fish
   broth

½ teaspoon salt
dash sugar
⅛ teaspoon white pepper
2 tablespoons lemon juice

In the top of a double boiler, rub the butter and flour together until
smooth; mix in the egg yolks, 1 at a time. Put the pot over boiling water
and slowly whip in the vegetable or fish broth, keeping the sauce smooth.
Cook until thickened, and beat in the salt, sugar, pepper, and lemon juice.
Serve hot. Makes about 2 cups sauce.

EGG DILL SAUCE   Muna-Tillikastike

Serve this over poached or fried salmon steaks or other seafood, or over poached eggs on toast.

¼ cup butter
½ cup white flour
2 cups milk
½–¾ teaspoon salt
 dash pepper

4 eggs, hard-cooked and chopped
 fine
¼ cup fresh dill, finely chopped
lemon juice

Melt the butter in a pan and add the flour, stirring well. Slowly stir in the milk, salt, and pepper. Cook, stirring constantly, until thickened. Stir in the eggs and dill, add lemon juice to taste. Serve hot. Makes about 3 cups.

MUSTARD CREAM SAUCE FOR COLD MEATS
Kermakastike

Serve this sauce with Molded Veal Loaf *(see index)*.

1 cup heavy cream, whipped
1 tablespoon sugar
2 tablespoons white wine vinegar

1 tablespoon prepared mustard
½ teaspoon salt

Blend the sugar, vinegar, mustard, and salt, mix in the whipped cream, and serve immediately.

BASIC SAUCE FOR POACHED FISH   Kalakastike

3 tablespoons butter
4 tablespoons flour
2 cups fish stock (strained from
 poaching liquid)
salt to taste

2 teaspoons chopped fresh or dried
 dill
1 tablespoon chopped parsley
1 tablespoon chopped chives
2 hard-cooked eggs, chopped
 (optional)

In a saucepan, melt the butter and stir in the flour. Slowly stir in the fish stock and bring to a boil; cook until thickened. Season with salt, add the dill, parsley, chives, and eggs. Serve hot. Makes 2 cups.

HORSERADISH SAUCE   Piparjuurikastike

Make Basic Sauce for Poached Fish (above), but omit the dill, parsley, chives, and eggs. Add 3 to 5 tablespoons grated fresh horseradish.

■☙■☙■☙■☙■☙■☙■☙■☙■☙■☙■☙■☙■☙■☙■

CREAM CAPER SAUCE FOR FISH
Kermakapriskastiki

Make Basic Sauce for Poached Fish (*above*), but omit the dill, parsley, chives, and eggs. Add 2 tablespoons chopped capers, 2 teaspoons sugar, and 1 egg yolk mixed with ¼ cup thick cream, stirring into the hot boiling sauce quickly. Cook while stirring for 2 minutes or until thickened. Add lemon juice to taste.

FINNISH-STYLE MUSTARD   Sinappi

You can vary the hotness of this sauce by substituting cornstarch for part of the dry mustard, as you wish.

4 tablespoons powdered dry mustard   4 tablespoons boiling water
2–4 tablespoons sugar   1 tablespoon vinegar
½ teaspoon salt

In a custard cup, combine the mustard, sugar, and salt. Mix the water and vinegar together and stir into the dry ingredients. Place over hot water and stir slowly to make a smooth paste, but do not beat. Cook until smooth and thickened. The mustard will be slightly runny. Makes about 1/3 cup.

MUSHROOM SAUCE   Sienikastike

Serve this over cold sliced roasts or beef steaks, meat loaf, eggs, and hamburger.

2 tablespoons butter   2 tablespoons flour
2 cups finely chopped mushrooms   2 cups cream or milk
1 small onion, finely chopped   salt

Melt the butter in a pan and stir in the mushrooms. Cook over medium heat for 1 to 2 minutes; add the onion and cook until limp (about 2 minutes more). Stir in the flour, then the cream or milk. Add salt to taste. Simmer for 10 to 15 minutes or until smooth and thickened. Makes about 3 cups.

TOMATO SAUCE   Tomatti Kastike

This sauce is good with hard-cooked or poached eggs, beef patties, veal cutlets, or broiled chicken.

1 tablespoon minced onion
2 tablespoons butter or salad oil
2 tablespoons flour
1 cup fresh tomato pulp (made from red or yellow tomatoes pressed through strainer)

¼ cup chopped parsley
½ teaspoon sweet basil
salt

Cook the onion in the butter until limp, then stir in the flour. Add the tomato, parsley, and basil, and simmer for 15 to 20 minutes. Taste, and add salt. Makes about 1 cup sauce.

SWEET-SOUR SAUCE   Hapanimeläkastike

This sauce is nice for meat balls, especially if you are serving them as an appetizer. Or, serve with the Herring-Meat Balls *(see index).*

2 tablespoons butter
2 tablespoons flour
1 cup beef broth

1–2 tablespoons vinegar
1–2 tablespoons sugar

Melt the butter in a pan and stir in the flour until blended. Slowly add the beef broth, stirring over medium heat until the sauce is thickened and smooth. Season to taste with the vinegar and sugar. Makes about 1 cup sauce.

CUCUMBER SAUCE   Kurkkukastike

Serve this sauce with cold sliced meats.

1 cup freshly made mayonnaise
1 cup heavy cream, whipped
1–2 tablespoons lemon juice

¼ teaspoon salt
2 cups peeled, finely diced cucumber
2 teaspoons chopped fresh dill

Whip the mayonnaise until fluffy and fold in the whipped cream. Stir in the lemon juice and salt, and just before serving, fold in the cucumber and dill. Makes about 4 cups.

■🌀■🌀■🌀■🌀■🌀■🌀■🌀■🌀■🌀■🌀■🌀■🌀■🌀■

BUTTER SAUCE FOR POTATOES   Perunavoi

Use this sauce over mashed potatoes or boiled new potatoes. Some Finns use boiling water in the recipe, others use milk. Take your choice.

½ cup butter   salt (optional)
1 cup boiling water or milk

Stir the butter into the liquid until it is melted. Pour into a gravy boat and serve with hot cooked potatoes. Add salt to taste (but if the potatoes were cooked with salt, the sauce may not need it). Makes about 1¼ cups sauce.

COUNTRY-STYLE MILK GRAVY Talonpoikaiskastike

This is how to make gravy from roasting pan drippings, Finnish style.

pan drippings   salt
1 onion, chopped (optional)   pepper
3–4 tablespoons white flour   mustard
1 cup cream or milk

After cooking the roast, remove it to a platter. Brown the onion in the drippings. Remove all but 3 to 4 tablespoons of the fat, pour the juices into a measuring cup; reserve. Add the flour to the pan and stir with a fork over medium heat until it is well browned. Add about 1 cup of the reserved drippings and 1 cup cream or milk slowly to the pan, stirring constantly, until the gravy is thick. Strain. Taste, and add salt, pepper, and mustard. Serve hot. Makes about 1 cup.

FINNISH PORK GRAVY OR SAUCE
Läskikastiketta or Läskisoosia

This is as common in Finland as sour rye bread. It is a rich, thick, smooth pork gravy with pork slices in it that is served over mashed or boiled new potatoes.

1 pound pork loin or salt pork,   2 cups boiling water
   thinly sliced   salt
4 tablespoons flour

Cook the pork slices in a hot frying pan until very well browned on all sides (about 30 minutes). Remove from the heat; stir in the flour until it is well mixed. Slowly add the water, return to the heat, and stir until smooth. Add salt to taste, and cook until thick and smooth. Serve hot. Serves about 4.

WHIPPED CREAM DRESSING FOR SALADS
Punajuurikermakastike

This is one of the choices of dressings for Beet-Herring Salad *(see index)*. It is fluffy, and lightly pink in color.

1 cup heavy cream, whipped
2 tablespoons lemon juice
2 teaspoons beet juice

dash salt
dash sugar

Combine the whipped cream with the lemon juice, beet juice, and the salt and sugar. Blend thoroughly. Turn into a small serving bowl or arrange in a mound on top of beet salad or a red cabbage slaw. Makes 2 cups.

SOUR CREAM DRESSING FOR SALAD
Hapankermakastike

1 cup sour cream
1 tablespoon lemon juice
2 teaspoons beet juice

¼ teaspoon salt
dash sugar

Combine the sour cream with the lemon juice, beet juice, salt, and sugar until well blended. Serve in a bowl or arrange on top of the salad. Makes 1 cup.

BANANA MAYONNAISE   Banaanimajoneesi

Serve this over mixed fruit salads or berries.

2 medium ripe bananas
1–3 tablespoons lemon juice
3 tablespoons salad oil

½ cup heavy cream
1 tablespoon sugar or honey
dash salt

Mash the bananas until smooth or press them through a strainer or whirl in a blender. Add the lemon juice and oil, beating well (or whirl with the banana pulp in the blender). Whip the cream until stiff and fold into the bananas. Flavor with the sugar or honey, and add salt to taste. Makes 2 cups.

■❦■❦■❦■❦■❦■❦■❦■❦■❦■❦■❦■❦■❦■❦■❦■❦■❦■

VANILLA SAUCE   Vaniljakstike

This sauce is delicious spooned over a combination of chopped fresh apple, sliced banana, and orange segments, or any cold fresh-fruit combinations.

2 cups milk   1–4 tablespoons sugar
2 teaspoons cornstarch   1 teaspoon vanilla
1 egg, slightly beaten   dash salt

Put the milk, cornstarch, egg, and sugar into a pan and mix until blended. Cook over medium heat, stirring constantly, until thickened. Add the vanilla and salt. Chill, or serve hot. Makes 2 cups.

EGG CREAM SAUCE   Munakermaa

Finns pour this creamy sauce over fresh berries or other fruit or on servings of fruit soup.

2 cups milk   1 tablespoon sugar
2 egg yolks   ¼ teaspoon cinnamon, cardamom,
1 egg white   grated lemon peel, or vanilla

In a small saucepan, bring the milk to a boil. Whip together the egg yolks and egg white, add the sugar and your choice of flavoring. Using a wire whisk, beat the milk into the egg-sugar mixture, beating vigorously to keep it smooth. Pour back into the pan and cook over low heat, stirring constantly, until thickened and smooth.

XII. Sandwiches

Sandwiches are important in all the Scandinavian countries. You buy them in the kiosks, in cafeterias and coffee shops, from vendors on trains, and in the prepared-foods sections of grocery stores. They are often a part of the first course of a meal, but they may also compose the major part of breakfast or lunch for many Finns both at home and at work.

Sandwiches are a simplified version of the bread-and-butter table—the voileipäpöytä. You can serve two or three very small sandwiches as an appetizer before dinner—but make sure that they represent different categories of sandwiches: fish, meat, vegetable, or fruit.

■⊘◈■⊘◈■⊘◈■⊘◈■⊘◈■⊘◈■⊘◈■⊘◈■⊘◈■⊘◈■⊘◈■⊘◈■⊘◈■⊘◈■

The recipes that follow fall into three categories: Sandwich Spreads or Pastes, Cold Sandwiches, and Hot Sandwiches.

Sandwich Spreads or Pastes

In Finland, as in most of the Scandinavian countries, you can buy many kinds of food pastes in tubes ready to squeeze out onto breads to make sandwiches. In certain parts of the United States you can buy caviar paste as well as anchovy paste.

These recipes make small amounts of paste. With each is given a suggestion for its use.

SALMON AND EGG PASTE   Lohi Ja Munatahna

Use this paste as a filling for either open-faced or closed sadwiches that have been spread with mayonnaise. You can freeze the excess.

2 cups finely mashed fresh salmon
4 hard-cooked eggs, minced
2 teaspoons salt

2 tablespoons lemon juice
4 tablespoons minced onion
¼ cup sour cream or mayonnaise

Combine the salmon, eggs, salt, lemon juice, onion, and sour cream until smooth and well blended. Makes about 3 cups.

SMOKED FISH PASTE   Savukalatahna

This paste is wonderful for open-faced sandwiches, or mixed in salad dressings, in fish casseroles, as a spread on crackers, or as a garnish on halved, hard-cooked eggs. You can store it in the refrigerator for 1 to 2 weeks, or freeze to keep it longer.

½ pound smoked fish
1 hard-cooked egg, chopped

¼ cup soft butter
dash pepper

Clean the fish and remove the bones and skin. Place in a bowl and break into small pieces. Add the egg, butter, and pepper, and rub the mixture against the side of bowl, using a wooden spoon, until a smooth paste is formed, or force it through a wire strainer, or whirl it in a blender until smooth. Pack it into a container having a close-fitting lid. (Cover lightly with waxed paper before putting on the lid.) (To garnish hard-cooked eggs, force the paste through a cake decorator or cut a hole in a corner of plastic bag and use it in same manner as a force bag.) Makes about 1 cup.

PIQUANT ANCHOVY PASTE   Anjovistahna

Spread this strongly flavored paste on tiny open-faced sandwiches and broil them just before serving.

10–12 boneless anchovy fillets
2 teaspoons grated onion
1 teaspoon vinegar

3 tablespoons olive oil or salad oil
¼ tablespoon pepper

Mash the anchovy fillets until smooth, and blend with the onion, vinegar, olive or salad oil, and pepper until thoroughly combined. Store in a small covered container until ready to use. Makes about ½ cup.

CAVIAR CREAM SPREAD   Kaviaarikerma

Spread this on toasted rye bread, or use it to fill tiny cream puffs and serve as cocktail hors d'oeuvres.

½ cup sour cream
2 tablespoons caviar

1 tablespoon grated onion or 3
tablespoons finely chopped chives

Whip the sour cream until fluffy and mix the caviar into it (you may use lumpfish caviar, which is less expensive than sturgeon caviar for this). Add the onion or chives. Makes about ¾ cup.

CAVIAR AND CREAM CHEESE PASTE
Kaviaari-Juusto Tahna

Spread this on toasted bread or use it to fill celery stalks for hors d'oeuvres.

1 3-ounce package cream cheese
1 1-ounce jar caviar

1 teaspoon grated onion

Mix the cream cheese and caviar together until very well blended. Cream the onion into the mixture. Makes about 2/3 cup spread.

CHEESE AND CHIVE PASTE   Juustoruohosipulitahna

Spread this on tiny toasted canapé bread rounds, or on crisp salted crackers.

¼ pound Roquefort or blue cheese
1 tablespoon olive oil or salad oil
1 tablespoon white wine vinegar

3 tablespoons finely chopped chives
 dash pepper

Cream the cheese until smooth, and mix with the oil and vinegar. Press the mixture through a strainer to combine well and make it smooth. Add the chives and pepper, mixing well. Makes about 1/3 cup.

Cold Open-faced Sandwiches

A great variety of unusual sandwiches are offered in Finnish cafés. They are usually displayed in large glass cases and you point to the one you want. Following are a dozen examples, but the variety is as limitless as the cook's imagination.

ROAST BEEF SANDWICH   Paahtopaistivoileipä

Spread a thin slice of firm rye bread with soft butter. Cover with thin slices of rare roast beef. Top with a fried or poached egg (with yolk still soft), and garnish with fried onions.

ROAST PORK SANDWICH   Sianpaistivoileipä

Spread a thin slice of dark rye bread with soft butter. Cover with thin slices of lean roast pork. Top with sliced pickled beets and sliced dill pickles.

ROAST VEAL SANDWICH   Vasikanlihavoileipä

Spread a thin slice of light rye bread with soft butter. Cover with thin slices of cold roast veal. Top with chilled, finely chopped beef aspic (canned or fresh). Garnish with thinly sliced fresh cucumber.

TONGUE SANDWICH   Kielivoileipä

Spread a thin slice of dark rye bread with soft butter. Cover with thin slices of cooked tongue. Top with 2 tablespoons whipped mayonnaise and 1 to 2 tablespoons cooked tiny peas and diced carrots. Garnish with stalks of cooked white asparagus.

HERRING SANDWICH   Sillivoileipä

Spread a thin slice of white or whole wheat bread with soft butter. Cover with a leaf of lettuce on it. Arrange 3 or 4 pickled herring rolls over the lettuce. Top with 3 tablespoons sour cream, and garnish with sliced hard-cooked egg and chopped chives.

ANCHOVY SANDWICH   Anjovisvoileipä

Spread a thin slice of firm white bread with soft butter. Cover with thinly sliced tomato and thinly sliced hard-cooked egg. Arrange 2 anchovy fillets, crisscrossed, on top. Garnish with parsley.

SMOKED SALMON SANDWICH   Lohivoileipä

Spread a thin slice of rye bread with soft butter. Arrange a slice of smoked salted salmon (lox) over the bread. Top with sliced hard-cooked egg and a sprig of fresh dill.

SHRIMP AND VEGETABLE SALAD SANDWICH
Katkarapuvoileipä

Spread a thin slice of rye or white bread with soft butter. Cover with a crisp leaf of lettuce. Arrange rows of tiny cooked shrimp on half of the lettuce. Combine 3 tablespoons cooked tiny peas with 1 teaspoon minced onion and 1 tablespoon salad dressing or mayonnaise, and add salt to taste. Pile the salad onto the other half of the lettuce. Garnish with fresh dill and serve with lemon wedges.

CARROT-BEET SANDWICH
Porkkana Punajuuri Voileipä

Spread a slice of firm rye bread with butter and mayonnaise. Arrange grated raw carrots over half of the bread and spread the other half with grated raw beets. Center a raw egg yolk on the sandwich and serve with lemon wedges.

BANANA DESSERT SANDWICH   Banana Voileipä

If you have a specialty-foods store available, buy the imported, slightly sweet, round or oblong biscuits or crackers for this sandwich, or use graham-cracker squares. Spread the cracker with soft butter. Arrange thinly sliced bananas over it, and dot the center with red current jelly.

GRAPE DESSERT SANDWICH   Viinirypäle Voileipä

Spread a slice of white bread (sliced pulla is very good for this) with soft butter. Cover with thinly sliced blue cheese, Port Salut, Edam, or Swiss cheese. Arrange halved, seeded purple grapes, cut side down, on the cheese.

Hot Sandwiches

The variety of hot sandwiches available in Finland's cafés and restaurants is almost limitless. Here is a selection of some of our favorites.

HOT EGG-AND-ANCHOVY SANDWICHES
Lammin Muna-Anjovisvoileivät

These are excellent served as an appetizer or as an accompaniment to hot or cold soup.

3 hard-cooked eggs
10 anchovy fillets
1½ teaspoons anchovy juice (drained from a can of anchovies)

9 thin slices of French bread, halved

Mash together the eggs, anchovy fillets and anchovy juice to make a smooth paste. Butter the bread slices. Spread the anchovy mixture on half of them, and cover with the rest of the slices to make sandwiches. (You can do this well ahead of serving time, if you wish.) Cover over and refrigerate.

Just before serving, melt enough butter in a frying pan to cover the bottom evenly. Fry the sandwiches until they are piping hot, turning them once and browning both sides. Remove to a serving tray. Makes 9 small sandwiches halves. (Or you might wish to cut each of these into 3 finger-shaped sandwiches to serve as cocktail appetizers.)

SARDINE SANDWICH   Sardiinivoileipä

For this open-faced sandwich, spread a thin slice of toasted dark rye bread with soft butter. Cover with ½ cup scrambled eggs, sprinkle with salt, and top with a drained, canned sardine. Garnish with tomato catsup and chopped parsley.

HOT FILLET OF SOLE SANDWICH
Kalafileellä Paalystetty Voileipä

For each open-faced sandwich, spread 1 thin slice of dark rye bread, preferably crosswise slices from a round loaf of rye bread, with soft butter. Roll a small sole fillet, first in milk, then in seasoned flour, then in beaten egg, then in seasoned rye flour or bread crumbs. Fry quickly in butter over high heat until golden brown on both sides. Lay 1 fillet on each slice of buttered bread and garnish with a twist of lemon. Serve Finnish Hollandaise Sauce (see index) at the table to spoon over the sandwich, (allow 1 to 2 tablespoons per serving).

Note: If you use bread slices from an oblong loaf, halve the fillets and make two smaller open-faced sandwiches from each.

OPERA SANDWICH   Ooperavoileipä

A more descriptive name for this open-faced sandwich would be "Hamburger-with-Egg-on-Top." It is surprising what the soft egg does to a patty of ground lean beef; the resulting flavor is very rich. Serve with hot mustard or Finnish-Style Mustard (see index). This is eaten with a knife and fork.

1 ¼-pound ground beef patty	butter
1 egg	salt
1 thick slice of French, Italian, or homemade white bread	pepper

Fry the hamburger patty in the butter in a hot pan, remove from the pan and keep warm. Fry the egg (but only until the white is set; the yolk should still be soft) and place it on the meat. Brown the bread on both sides in the buttered pan, and place the meat and egg on top. Add salt and pepper to taste, and serve immediately. Makes 1 sandwich.

GROUND-BEEF SANDWICHES   Lihamurekevoileivät

Serve this open-faced sandwich with hot Tomato Sauce (see index).

½ pound ground lean beef
⅓ cup cream
1 tablespoon bread crumbs
1 egg
½ teaspoon salt

dash of white pepper
1 tablespoon grated onion
6 thick slices French bread
cooked parsnips
chopped parsley

Combine the meat, cream, bread crumbs, egg, salt, pepper, and onion and mix thoroughly. Spread this mixture on the bread slices, dividing it evenly. Melt enough butter in a frying pan to coat the bottom and fry the sandwiches, first on the meat-coated side for about 3 minutes; turn over, and brown the bread on the other side. Lift the sandwiches onto a serving platter and serve with hot Tomato Sauce (see index). Garnish with cooked parsnips and parsley. Serves 6.

HOT TOMATO SANDWICHES   Tomattivoileivät

Serve this open-faced sandwich with soup, or simply with a crispy green salad.

½ cup mayonnaise or Finnish Hollandaise sauce (see index)
1 raw egg yolk
¼ cup finely diced boiled ham
dash salt
1–2 tablespoons lemon juice

4 thick slices French bread or sour dark rye bread
4 large thin slices fresh tomato (8 slices if tomatoes are small)
grated Cheddar, Edam, or Gouda cheese

Combine the mayonnaise or Hollandaise sauce with the egg yolk and the boiled ham until thoroughly blended. Stir in the salt and add the lemon juice to taste. Spread half of this mixture on the bread slices and top with the tomato, then spread on the remaining mayonnaise mixture. Sprinkle with the cheese. Bake in a hot oven (400°) for about 10 minutes or until the cheese is melted and the sauce bubbles. Makes 4 sandwiches.

HOT MUSHROOM SANDWICHES   Sienivoileivät

Make like Hot Tomato Sandwiches (above), but substitute the following mushroom mixture for the tomato slices: Brown 2 cups sliced fresh mushrooms in 2 tablespoons butter over medium to high heat, stirring constantly and cooking until the mushrooms turn dark and limp. Divide into 4 parts and spread evenly on the prepared slices of bread.

■◎◈■◎◈■◎◈■◎◈■◎◈■◎◈■◎◈■◎◈■◎◈■◎◈■◎◈■◎◈■◎◈■

BAKED EGG-FILLED BUNS   Täytetyt Sämpylät

Serve these for lunch, supper, or a snack, and supply a knife and fork. For each serving, cut a lid off a hard dinner roll and pull out as much of the soft interior as you can (reserve this to use for bread crumbs, if you wish). Into the cavity, put finely minced ham or finely chopped bologna. Carefully crack open an egg and slip it on top of the ham. Bake in a very hot oven (400°) for 5 to 7 minutes (depending on the size of the bun and egg) or until the egg has begun to set. Remove from the oven and sprinkle with salt; sprinkle 2 tablespoons shredded Cheddar cheese over each egg. Return to oven and bake for 2 to 3 minutes more or until the cheese has melted. Do not overcook. Put the top back onto the bun before serving. Serve immediately.

HOT CHEESE AND EGG SANDWICH
Juusto-Muna Voileipä

For each sandwich, butter a slice of dark bread and spread thinly with prepared mustard. Top with a thin slice of Swiss, Edam, Gouda, or other semimild cheese. Separate an egg, being careful not to break the yolk. Whip the white with a dash of salt until stiff and spread evenly over the cheese, and place the egg yolk on the center of the sandwich. Bake in a hot oven (400°) for 3 to 4 minutes or until the egg white is slightly browned. Garnish with chopped parsley and serve immediately.

HOT CHEESE-BOLOGNA SANDWICH
Peitetty Makkaravoileipä

2 tablespoons milk
½ cup shredded mild Cheddar
  cheese
¼ teaspoon paprika
4 slices buttered toasted French
  bread

4 thick slices (about 3½ inches in
  diameter) high-quality bologna
4 cherry tomatoes
parsley sprigs

Heat the milk in a saucepan, add the cheese and paprika, and stir until the cheese has melted. Arrange the bread slices on a heatproof serving tray and top each with a slice of bologna. Slip under the broiler for 1 minute or until lightly browned. Garnish with a sprig of parsley and a cherry tomato. Serves 4.

CHAPEL SANDWICH   Kappelivoileipä

How this sandwich was named, I will never know, but it is delicious as a breakfast dish, luncheon or supper sandwich, or even for a midnight snack. Eat it with a knife and fork.

Brown thick slices of French bread on both sides in a frying pan with plenty of butter. Keep hot while you fry enough bacon and eggs to cover the slices of bread. Arrange the fried bacon on top of the hot French bread, and top with a fried egg, cooked just enough so the white is set but the yolk is still soft. (If you wish, you may prefer to fry the bacon first and then brown the bread in the bacon drippings.) Serve hot. Add salt and pepper to taste.

HOT APRICOT SANDWICH   Aprikoosivoileipä

Apricot and cheese are a surprisingly flavorful combination! Serve this open-faced sandwich for lunch or a snack.

For each serving, butter a slice of whole wheat, white, or French bread on one side. Cut the slice in half. Arrange 2 halved apricots (canned, drained, or fresh), cut side down, on each piece of bread. Top with a slice of mild Cheddar cheese, and bake in a moderately hot oven (375°) for 5 to 10 minutes or until the cheese melts and bubbles.

HOT CHEESE-FILLED PAN BREAD
Täytetty Vuokaleipä

Serve this cheese-filled loaf of bread with a meal in the same manner as garlic bread.

1 whole unsliced loaf of white, rye, or whole wheat bread butter 1 medium onion, finely chopped	¼ pound bacon, cooked until crisp, drained, and crumbled ½ pound (about 16 slices) sliced cheese finely chopped parsley

Slash the bread at 1½-inch intervals to about ½ inch of the bottom so the slices do not separate. Butter the slices, and sprinkle with the onion and bacon. Slide a slice of cheese between each 2 slices of bread. Arrange the filled loaf of bread on a baking sheet or on a sheet of foil and bake in a hot oven (400°) for about 15 minutes or until the cheese is melted and the loaf is heated through. Sprinkle with finely chopped parsley and serve. Serves 4 to 6.

QUICK TOASTED-CHEESE SANDWICH
Yksinkertaiset Juustovoileivät

Arrange bread slices (whole wheat, rye, or French) on a baking sheet and spread with butter and mustard. Top with a thin slice of Edam, Gouda, Cheddar, jack, or Swiss cheese. Sprinkle each sandwich with about 2 tablespoons chopped almonds, and bake in a hot oven (400°) for 8 to 10 minutes or until the cheese melts and bubbles.

FRENCH-TOASTED CHEESE SANDWICH
Juustovoileipä

Currant jelly is a good accompaniment for these sandwiches.

12 slices thinly sliced rye or French bread	1 egg
soft butter	½ cup milk
bacon-flavored cheese spread	dash of salt
	1 teaspoon flour

Butter 6 of the bread slices and cover the other 6 with the cheese spread. Press the buttered and cheese-spread surfaces together, making sandwiches.

In a small bowl, beat the egg, milk, salt, and flour to combine well. Dip the sandwiches on both sides in this mixture. Melt butter in a frying pan and brown the sandwiches on both sides. Serve immediately. Makes 6 sandwiches.

XIII. Special Menus
and Special Occasions

THE COFFEE TABLE

We have already discussed this (see *Chapter II*), the most popular Finnish way to entertain. It is usually a buffet-style service, and, as mentioned earlier, the menu is built around a definite framework and served in a particular order. For simple occasions the menu may have just one to three items, but for more elaborate occasions it may include five to seven items. If the menu has just one, it is usually pulla (see *index*). If it has three, it includes pulla, a cooky, and a cake. If it has five, it has pulla, a sweet yeast roll, an uniced cake, perhaps a fancy cake and cooky, and pepper cookies. The seven-item coffee table adds two different kinds of cookies to the five-item coffee table.

You may wish to plan coffee tables to celebrate special occasions (such as birthdays, anniversaries, welcome and farewell parties), or just casually to entertain any group of friends. With freezers, this is particularly easy to do, because most cookies, cakes, and coffee breads freeze very well, and you can always freeze unused portions, adding them to the menu of your next coffee-table party.

THE VOILEIPÄPÖYTÄ OR
BREAD-AND-BUTTER TABLE

In Sweden it is called the *smörgäsbord*, in Norway it is the *koltbord*, in Denmark it is *smørbrod*. The very name of this type of buffet table discloses its purpose and the starting point when planning the foods to be served.

As the name implies, you begin with bread and butter. To build the menu, you simply add foods that go well *on* bread. You expand the menu further by adding dishes that go well *with* bread, starting with cold fish dishes, pickled fish, cold cuts, and then going on to warm foods.

Proper etiquette for the bread-and-butter table is as follows: First help yourself to bread and butter and the pickled fishes. Then take a clean plate (or else the rest of the meal will taste like pickled fish) and sample the fish combinations and cold cuts. Take another clean plate for the *pikkulämpimiä* ("little hot bits") or main-course hot foods. After that, sample the salads and cheeses, and the pasties and vegetables. Take another clean plate for dessert, which may or may not be arranged on the bread-and-butter table. Dessert may be fresh fruit or a fruit salad and various cheeses. Coffee comes after dessert.

Serving a bread-and-butter table in your home can be a mountainous chore if it is done the old-fashioned way. But it works well as "planned potluck," with several friends planning the menu and sharing in its preparation. Simplified menus, however, such as the ones suggested below, look like much more work than they really are.

The following list of food categories is a guide when planning a menu for a bread-and-butter table. You may wish to include only the first two or three for the simplest menu, or all seven categories for the most elaborate menu, to serve a large crowd.

1. Butter and breads in variety: dark, light, soft, crisp.
2. Salted and pickled herring, anchovies, or salmon.
3. Warm fish dishes and/or cold meat such as liver pâté, sliced cooked ham, salami, bologna, tongue, cold roast beef.
4. Little hot bits such as Finnish Meat Balls, or meat or vegetable piirakka.
5. Main-course meat dishes and boiled potatoes.
6. Salads and egg dishes and/or cheeses, fruit pastries.
7. Fruits or fruit combinations.

Beverages for the bread-and-butter table usually include kalja or olut (*see index*) and milk or buttermilk. Coffee follows dessert.

SAMPLE (SNACK) MENU TO SERVE 4

Rye Hardtack	Oulu Pumpernickel	Rye and Barley Bread
Butter	Salted Herring	Spiced Herring
Finnish Swiss Cheese		Edam Cheese
Fresh Tomatoes	Pickles	Pickled Beets

SAMPLE (SNACK) MENU TO SERVE 10 TO 15

Assorted Breads   Butter

Pickled Herring   Pickled Fish Rolls   Sardines

Smoked Salmon (Lox) Slices   Finnish Meat Balls

Potato Casserole   Golden Carrot Salad

Fresh Tomatoes   Pickles   Baked Cheese

SAMPLE MENU TO SERVE 30 OR MORE

Assorted Breads   Butter

Pickled Herring   Pickled Fish Rolls   Glass Master's Herring

Assorted Cold Cuts   Assorted Cheeses

Stuffed Meat Rolls   Meat Cabbage Casserole

Sliced Pork Roast   Potato Casserole

Golden Carrot Salad   Karelian Rice Piirakkaa

Baked Cheese   Caraway Cream Cheese

Fresh Fruit Compote   Vanilla Sauce

Beverages

CHRISTMAS DINNER

This may be served Christmas Eve afternoon before the church service, or later in the evening, after church. This is a traditional menu as it was served to us in Kauhajoki, a small village in the Western Finnish province of Pohjanmaa.

Beef Broth

Tray of Pickled Fish, Cheeses, Breads, Cold Cuts

Potato Casserole

Rutabaga Casserole   Beet Salad

Holiday Lutefisk with White Sauce

Christmas Ham with Prunes

Creamed Rice

Stewed Prunes and Whipped Cream

CHRISTMAS EVE COFFEE

Served after the church service, before or after *Joulupukki* (Santa Claus) arrives.

Pulla

Finnish Gingersnaps   *Christmas Tarts*

Coffee   Cream   Sugar

EASTER DINNER

There is no really traditional meat that is universally served in Finland on Easter, but there are two traditional desserts. Easter Mämmi, which varies in consistency from one part of the country to another, is traditional in all parts but Karelia. The Karelian dessert is Easter Pasha, a molded cream cheese.

MAY DAY

May 1 is the day of celebration over the coming of summer, and everybody has stocked up on Sima, a yeast-sparkled, lemon-flavored beverage, and on Tippaleipä, a special fried cruller *(see index for both)*.

MIDSUMMER DAY

It is traditional in the country to eat various provincial homemade fresh-milk cheeses on this day—June 24. These are served as a midnight snack. (Two appear in the Dairy Foods Chapter.) The same cheeses are also served at Eastertime, when milk becomes so plentiful that the Finns make cheese from the excess.

CRAYFISH SEASON

Beginning in August, many restaurants feature crayfish as a special item on the menu. Since crayfish are such a bright red color, they need no other garnish, nor does the table require decoration. The crayfish are piled in a huge mound on a platter and serve as both the centerpiece and main course. Each person cracks his own. Provide bibs!

Breads in variety   Butter   Cold Cut Tray
Cooked Peas or Green Beans   Cauliflower with Ham Saurce
Hot Cooked Crayfish   Melted Butter
Beer or Kalja   Jaloviina (Finnish Schnapps)   or Aquavit
Fresh Berries   Cream   Sugar
Coffee

DINNER MENU   Karelian Ragout
Baked Mashed Potatoes
Lemon—Leaf-Lettuce Salad
Finnish Rye Bread
Butter
Fresh Berry Soup
Milk
Coffee

Selected Reading List and Bibliography

FROM THE SHORES OF LADOGA by Tauna Hammar; published by Meador Publishing Company, Boston. A historical novel depicting life in Karelia in the early 1900's; translated from the Finnish by Emilia Ritari. 1947.

GREEN GOLD AND GRANITE by Wendy Hall; published by Max Parrish, London. A background to Finland. Second Edition, 1957.

INTRODUCTION TO FINLAND 1960 by Urho Toivola; published by Werner Söderström Oy., Porvoo, Finland. This book is designed to introduce foreign readers to life and thought in Finland today. 1960.

KALEVALA, in two volumes, by Elias Lönnrot, translated by W. F. Kirby; published by J. M. Dent & Sons, Ltd., London, and E. P. Dutton & Co., Inc., New York. This is the Finnish national epic and it is written in poetic form.

SEVEN BROTHERS by Aleksis Kivi; published by Tammi Publishers, Helsinki, Finland. The story of seven brothers growing up wild on their farm in Southern Finland. It is a story mingled with humor and pathetic events that illustrate the plucky Finnish character often described as "*sisu.*" English translation 1959.

THE LAND AND PEOPLE OF FINLAND by Erick Berry; published by J. B. Lippincott Co., New York. A portrait of Finland simply written to tell of Finnish character and Finland's natural beauty. 1959.

THE UNKNOWN SOLDIER by Vaino Linna, translated from the Finnish; published by G. P. Putnam's Sons, New York. This is one of the outstanding contemporary war novels that has been described as "tough and realistic." 1957.

WHO ARE THE FINNS? by R. E. Burnham; published by Faber and Faber, Ltd., London. This describes well the history of the Finnish language and race.

THE WINTER WAR by V. Tanner; published by the Stanford University Press, Stanford, Calif. 1957.

SISU by Austin Goodrich; published by Bantam Books, New York. A short modern history of Finland. 1960.

INDEX

233

■௸■௸■௸■௸■௸■௸■௸■௸■௸■௸■௸■௸■

■❦■❦■❦■❦■❦■❦■❦■❦■❦■❦■❦■❦■❦■

■❧■❧■❧■❧■❧■❧■❧■❧■❧■❧■❧■❧■❧■

■۞■۞■۞■۞■۞■۞■۞■۞■۞■۞■۞■۞■۞■

■◎■◎■◎■◎■◎■◎■◎■◎■◎■◎■◎■◎■◎■◎■◎■